159 Mistakes
Couples Make
In The Bedroom

And How To Avoid Them

Dr. Bea M. Jaffrey

Disclaimer

This book is designed to provide helpful information on the subjects discussed. This book is not meant to be used, nor should it be used, to diagnose or treat any psychological or medical condition. For diagnosis or treatment of any psychological or medical issue, consult your own physician. The publisher and author are not responsible for any specific health needs that may require medical supervision and are not liable for any damages or negative consequences from any treatment, action, application or preparation, to any person reading or following the information in this book. The author and publisher disclaim any and all warranties, liabilities, losses, costs, claims, demands, suits and actions of any type or nature whatsoever, arising from or any way related to this book. References are provided for informational purposes only and do not constitute an endorsement of any books, websites or other sources. Readers should be aware that the websites listed in this book might change. Neither the publisher nor the author shall be liable for any physical, psychological, emotional, financial or commercial damages, including, but not limited to, special, incidental, consequential or other damages. The readers are responsible for their own choices, actions and results.

Copyright © 2016 Bea M. Jaffrey

ISBN: 1533412324
ISBN-13: 978-1533412324

Edition 1:17

Dr. Bea's web site: live-best-life.com

To my clients

thank you for letting me be a part of your journey.

Dr. Bea

CONTENTS

PREFACE

WHO THIS BOOK IS FOR AND WHY I WROTE IT

Fifty percent of couples are dissatisfied with their sex life. How do you keep the passion in a long-term relationship? In this book I write about common sex issues a couple may have, I give my advice and I offer solutions. When couples come to therapy, for whatever reason it may be, most of the time the subject of sex comes up. Sex is important in relationships; yet, many therapists don't know how to talk about it. There are sex therapists who know everything about sex but not so much about relationships. Then, there are conventional therapists who cringe when the client mentions sex. In this book, I try to explain some of the sexual issues that often come up in therapy and most importantly, how to deal with them. My book approaches sex as something natural, pleasurable and healthy. It will broaden people's perspectives, and contains accurate, practical information. It covers subject matter, topics or issues that are often not addressed or are tackled inadequately in other sex books.

In my private practice in Geneva, Switzerland, I counsel couples, families and individuals. My passion in life is to help people create fulfilling relationships and to achieve self-actualization. I want my couples to form a closer connection, to revitalize their sexual life, and to improve their communication skills. I believe that everyone is capable of having a great sex life regardless of how long they have been together. We need to be proactive and educate ourselves to create happy families.

Most of us did not learn about sex and relationships in school. We spent hours learning about topics that we rarely need a use for in our daily lives; yet, when it comes to sex, the subject was, and still is a taboo. You might come from a cultural or religious background that forbids talking about sex or considers it dirty or sinful; an environment that taught you that sex is only for procreation and only within marriage. The reality today is different. In 2010, 50% of American teens were sexually active by the age of 17. Taking into consideration that these teens will live long lives and engage in sexual activities until their 70s (more about sex and older adults in Chapter 14) we are talking about fifty plus years of activities that many of us feel insecure or confused about. In this book I include the majority of problems, preconceptions, myths or "mistakes" that couples bring to therapy. Some of them are explained briefly, and some have an in-depth discussion. Chapter 12 is about infidelity, Chapter 10 about sex addiction, Chapter 8 about accidents during sex, and Chapter 11 discusses kinky sex and odd fetishes, to mention a few.

This book is written for the general public, in straightforward and easy to understand language, so you don't need to be a psychologist or to have an academic degree to understand it. Any abstract words or terms are clearly explained. For the clinicians and practitioners, there is an index and a reference list at the back. When I did research for this book I came across many thought-provoking facts that I share with you and I believe this knowledge will be beneficial for other psychologists and therapists as well.

I need to clarify for those of you who are not familiar with academic writing and referencing of sources. On some pages you will see a name and a year in parenthesis, for example, Freud (1905) or (Freud, 1905). These are in-text citations according to the American Psychological Association (APA) publication style. This simply means that the statement you just read was from a book by Freud, written in 1905. At the back of this book you will find an alphabetical reference list with more detailed information. There, under the letter "F," you can read:

Freud, S. (1905). *Three essays on the theory of sexuality*. New York, NY: Basic Books Classics.

Some of the references are books, and some are research articles published in psychological journals. The point is to inform the reader of where the information originates. However, to make this book reader-friendly, only the most relevant references are included.

Finally, just a quick note to say that the names of clients mentioned in this book are fictitious; I would never disclose the real names, since therapy is confidential. The examples and statements are real as they did happen in therapy. However, to protect my clients, they might have been altered or some information might have been omitted. Thus, no one can identify the people involved. I hope you will enjoy reading this book as much as I enjoyed writing it.

So let's talk about love and sex....

MISTAKE # 1

"We waste time looking for the perfect lover,
instead of creating the perfect love."
~ *Tom Robbins*

CHAPTER 1

WHY DO WE FALL IN LOVE?
WHY DO WE HAVE SEX?

Have you ever been in love? How does it feel? How would you explain what love is to someone that just landed on planet Earth and knew nothing about it? How would you explain sex? Let's see what experts say about love and sex and how they define it.

Some people say that there is no love, that love is just an illusion, that we are tricked into feelings of love to have sex and to procreate. The human love bond that lovers create lasts only a couple of years, long enough to produce a baby and take care of it until it starts walking. Is this the reason why so many people fall out of love after couple of years together? Do you know anyone who can only sustain a relationship for that long and then moves on to the next partner? How about you? How long have you been in love?

Are we meant to be together with one partner for life? Is that even possible in today's fast-paced world? When the novelty of a new lover wears off, and sex becomes mundane, the problems start in relationships. Many people throw in the towel at this stage and move on to someone else. Some prevail and try to adapt, work things out, fix the problems and move on to the next stage in their relationship. Now, the real work starts because relationships are not planes; they can't be flying on autopilots as so many people assume. To be happily married takes hard work. To have great sex in long-term relationships takes knowledge and practice. This book is about what you need to know, what mistakes to avoid, and how to get there.

WHAT IS LOVE?

What is love to you? How do you define love? Is love important to you? Now, ask your partner the same questions. Were the answers what you expected? We express love in different ways. What is your way of expressing love? How would you like your partner to show his/her love for you?

Love has always been the greatest inspiration to artists, poets, writers and philosophers. Thousands of songs and books have been written about love. It exists in every culture. Is there any specific song or movie that you associate with love? If you are old enough to know who Elvis Presley was and remember some of his songs then "Always on My Mind" is a good example of a love song. Elvis recorded the song in 1972, shortly after his separation from Priscilla, his then wife. The song was later recorded by Willie Nelson in 1982. You can hear both versions on YouTube. Another great song is "I Will Always Love You" written and recorded by Dolly Parton in 1973. Whitney Houston recorded the song in 1992 for the movie *The Bodyguard*.

The movie of my generation was *Love Story* from 1970 with Ali MacGraw and Ryan O'Neal. I was too young to see it at the cinemas, but I finally saw it on TV a few years later. Which movie do you associate with love? And if you could make a movie about your love story, what would it look like?

Attachment styles

We become influenced by movies, songs and books, but our view of love starts already when we are born. The bond between the mother and her baby is the first love that we know. In psychology, we call this bond *attachment*. There are a few kinds of attachments as you can see on the next page. Why is that important? Because we bring the attachment style that we learned in childhood into our adult relationships. The two partners' styles can exist happily together or collide, creating conflicts in the relationship.

The attachment theory in babies originates from work by Mary Ainsworth and John Bowlby. Originally, there were three attachment styles: secure, insecure-anxious/ambivalent, and insecure-avoidant. A fourth one was added later on called disorganized/disoriented. Cindy

Hazan and Phillip Shaver (1987) expanded the theory to adult relationships. Without going too much into details the adult attachment styles can be explained as follows:

- **Secure** attachment - this is the best attachment style for happy relationships. Individuals with this attachment style feel secure in relationships, are confident, positive, give and take emotional support and don't fear abandonment. Obviously, the happiest couples are both secure attachment style individuals. Over half of the U.S. population has the secure attachment style.

- **Anxious/Ambivalent** attachment - Individuals with this attachment style feel insecure in relationships. They fear being abandoned, have low self-esteem, are self-critical, need approval and reassurance, are clingy and dependent on their partners. They are emotionally unstable. Twenty percent of U.S. adults have the anxious/ambivalent attachment style.

- **Avoidant** attachment - Individuals with this attachment style don't feel comfortable in relationships and don't want to get close to others. They have a fear of intimacy and want to be independent of others. When in a relationship they believe that they will be let down because their partners can't be trusted. Twenty-five percent of U.S. adults have the avoidant attachment style.

What is your attachment style? And your partner's? You can find several tests online to see where you fit in by typing "attachment style test or quiz." Research shows that people with secure attachment styles form secure and happy relationships (Kirkpatrick & Davis, 1994). Furthermore, the attachment style affects sexual desire and sexual functioning in relationships (Birnbaum, 2015). Could this be the reason why half of marriages end in divorce? If you belong to the 45% of people with a "wrong" attachment style, does it mean that you will spend the rest of your life in solitude or in dysfunctional relationships? It doesn't need to be like that at all. You can change your behavior and alter your thoughts. Individual cognitive therapy and emotionally focused therapy for couples is a good start. Attachment style is only one of the factors in relationships. There are many more important issues to take into consideration. Let's have a look at maladaptive schemas.

Maladaptive Schemas from childhood

Early Maladaptive Schemas (EMS) can be defined as broad and pervasive character traits, themes or patterns of expectations. They consist of thoughts, feelings, sensations and memories, in regards to oneself and one's relationships with others. Schemas usually develop during childhood or adolescence in reaction to toxic or traumatic early experiences. They elaborate throughout life and are dysfunctional because they lead to self-defeating behaviors (Young et al., 2006).

Schemas initiate in early childhood and repeat throughout life. They are made up of emotional memories and interpretations of past unmet safety needs, abandonment, neglect, hurt, abuse, fear, tragedy, or lack of normal human affection per se (Young et al., 2006). Schemas affect our relationships, often creating chronic interpersonal difficulties. They can cause psychological distress and affect one's choices in life, such as choosing a career or a spouse.

When people come together and form a couple, they bring two different sets of schemas into the relationship. Sometimes, these schemas can work in harmony, but very often, they collide as we trigger each other's schemas in our daily interactions. In schema therapy, we investigate which schemas each person has by answering a questionnaire that takes approximately 30 minutes to complete. Once we know the schemas we analyze them individually and then compare yours with your partner's schemas to see any possible conflicts. This is a thought-provoking process that many couples enjoy because they learn a lot, first about each individual, and then, of course, about the couple as a unit. Understanding the childhood issues of your partner and how they influenced his or her view of love and relationships is crucial for a happy and fulfilling life together.

The science of love

The science of love is complex and fascinating. For centuries, people have tried to understand the meaning of love. Is it only for procreation? If that is so, why do we still fall in love at an old age when it's not possible anymore to become pregnant? There must be more to love than reproduction. The same goes for sex. Older people have plenty of sex, sometimes more frequently than younger people (see Chapter 14). If we were programmed to have sex only to make babies, why can we still enjoy it after menopause? We will get back to this later, but first, let's see what the experts say about love and sex.

Sternberg's triangular theory of love

Psychologist Robert Sternberg's (1986) triangular theory of love is based on three components: **intimacy, passion**, and **commitment**. He postulated that more elements than one in a relationship make it stronger, the ultimate being all three at once, that he calls "Consummate Love."

- **Intimacy** is feelings of attachment, closeness, connectedness, trust, friendship and bondedness.
- **Passion** is the excitement, the intense emotional desire, physical and sexual attraction, arousal, the chemistry in a relationship.
- **Commitment** is the decision to stay with each other in the future, making plans together and investing long term in the relationship.

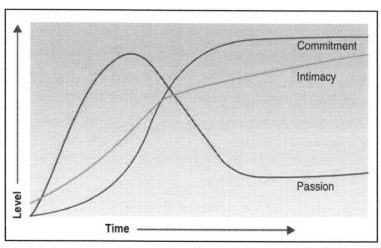

Source: Crooks and Baur (2011).

9

MISTAKE # 2
Our love will last forever

As you can see on the Sternberg's graph on the previous page, passionate love doesn't last forever. It peaks early in the relationship but quickly subsides. This is the period when we idealize our partner, but soon enough you will realize that your prince charming picks his nose, breaks wind in bed and his poop smells bad. The things about him that seemed endearing at first, like calling his mother every day or letting his dog lick his face, start to irritate you now. The euphoria of passionate love is short-lived; it usually lasts only a few months. For lovers who are separated by distance or see each other sporadically, it may last a little longer but at some point, the relationship will transform into the next phase.

"The madness of love is the greatest of heaven's blessings."
Plato (written 360 B.C.E)

The intense feeling of being in love, the high, the passion, being blinded by love, is desired so much by humans that if I could bottle up this feeling and sell it, I would be the richest person in the world.

Emily (19) says:
> *I think about him day and night. From the minute I wake up to my last thought before falling asleep. I count hours and minutes until I can see him again. This is crazy. I can't concentrate on anything else. My exams are next week, and I can only think of him. What shall I do? Is this normal?*

Daniel (21) says:
> *I can't live without her. She is the love of my life. We were meant to be together. Her parents don't like me and they told her not to see me again but we will run away together. My uncle lives in Australia. We will go there and stay with him, as soon as I have the money to buy airline tickets. My uncle doesn't know yet but I'm sure he will be fine with it.*

Going back to Sternberg's types and stages of love, they can be explained as different combinations of the three elements: intimacy, passion and commitment.

Non Love (the absence of all primary aspects)

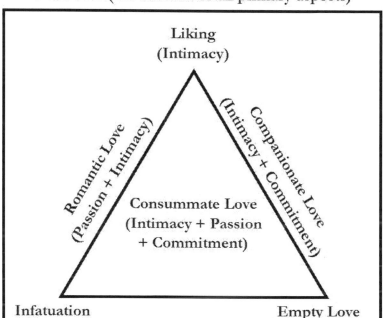

Non Love (the absence of all primary aspects)

The following are all of the combinations of Sternberg's (1988) love triangle: intimacy, passion and commitment:

- Non love – has none of the components. Usually refers to casual relationships or acquaintances.

- Empty love – commitment without passion or intimacy. May happen in long-time marriages or arranged marriages. The status may change with time though.

- Liking or friendship – has intimacy but not passion or commitment. True friendships are found here.

- Infatuated love – has passion but no intimacy or commitment. This is often the first stage of a relationship or "love at first sight."

- Romantic love – has intimacy and passion but no commitment. An example from the movie Titanic: Jack and Rose fall in love and have a passionate relationship onboard the Titanic. Unfortunately, Jack dies shortly after so there is no time for the relationship to develop into commitment.

- Companionate love – has no passion but has intimacy and commitment. Usually found in long-term marriages, family members or platonic friendships. The movie *Hope Springs* describes such love between the characters played by Meryl Streep and Tommy Lee Jones. Married for more than 30 years, they emotionally drifted apart. The couple seeks therapy to reignite their passion.

- Fatuous love – has passion and commitment but no intimacy. This happens when people fall in love and get married quickly. The union is based on passion without the necessary intimacy to deepen the bond between them. An example from the celebrity world would be Kim Kardashian and Chris Humphries, who were married only 72 days.

- Consummate love – has all three components present. This is the complete or ideal form of love. This is also the most difficult one to achieve and to maintain. One example from the movies would be *The Notebook* – a romantic drama about two people who fall in love and stay in love "until death do us part" more than 50 years later.

"You are my best friend as well as my lover, and I do not know which side of you I enjoy the most. I treasure each side, just as I have treasured our life together."

Nicholas Sparks, *The Notebook*

"When you fall in love, it is a temporary madness. It erupts like an earthquake, and then it subsides. And when it subsides, you have to make a decision. You have to work out whether your roots are to become so entwined together that it is inconceivable that you should ever part. Because this is what love is. Love is not breathlessness, it is not excitement, it is not the desire to mate every second of the day. It is not lying awake at night imagining that he is kissing every part of your body. No...don't blush. I am telling you some truths. For that is just being in love, which any of us can convince ourselves we are. Love itself is what is left over when being in love has burned away. Doesn't sound very exciting, does it? But it is!"

Louis de Bernières, *Captain Corelli's Mandolin*

There are so many words of wisdom when it comes to love. Ask anyone and they will have a love story to tell. Some skeptics will say that there is no romantic love, only lust. That passionate love is indeed lust and nothing else. But love and lust can exist simultaneously, don't you think? Enough about love for now, let's talk about sex. Sexology is the scientific study of sexuality. Human sexual behavior is difficult to research because it is a private matter that we don't share easily. Nevertheless, scientists want to understand what happens when we have sex.

INFLUENTIAL PEOPLE IN SEX RESEARCH

Sigmund Freud

Sigmund Freud (1856-1939) believed that the basis of every human action is sexuality. He postulated that children must go through several stages of psychosexual development – oral (0-1 year), anal (1-3 years), phallic (3 to 5 or 6 years), latent (5 or 6 to puberty) and genital (puberty to adult). If something went wrong during one of these stages, the child would be stuck in that stage or as Freud said, "fixated." This fixation could cause personality and behavioral disorders.

Freud's model of psychosexual development theorized that males and females are anatomically different, therefore, always struggle with diverse issues. His "penis envy" and "Oedipal complex" theories may be old-fashioned; yet, there is evidence that they are still recognized and used today by many professionals, thus, affecting today's gender relations (Cohler & Galatzer-Levy, 2008). His male-centered work popularized the belief that women are inferior to men and that manhood equals aggressive sexual impulses. He was wrong when he said that vaginal orgasms are superior to clitoral orgasms (more about that in Chapter 5). Furthermore, Freud stated that only men could have fully developed superegos (Schultz & Schultz, 2009). Though he passed away over 75 years ago, his gender-based theories, as well as those of many of his followers, are still here with us today.

Alfred Kinsey

Alfred Kinsey (1894-1956), a professor at Indiana University, was interested in sexual behavior. In 1947, he founded the Institute for Sex Research where he interviewed voluntary participants - both men and women - about their sexual practices (Gebhard & Johnson, 1979). Over the years, he gathered almost 20,000 records that were based on personal interviews (Robinson, 1976). He asked taboo questions about first sexual encounters, masturbation, infidelity, homosexuality, oral sex and more.

His findings showed that women could enjoy sex as much as men did. His interviews concluded that 64% of women achieved orgasm before marriage and 50% by the age of 20. Among married women, 75% experienced orgasm within one year of marriage. Ninety percent of men and 60% of women masturbated. Ten percent of men were homosexual and sexual orientation could change during the course of life (Bullough, 1998).

Another issue that he focused on was the social class differences in sexual activities. Upper-class women would engage in homosexual and extramarital relations more often than lower-class women would. In other areas such as masturbation, sex dreams and premarital sex, he found no differences between the social classes (Robinson, 1976).

Kinsey wrote several books that were published during the 1940s and early to mid-1950s. At this time, very little research had been done on human sexuality so his books became highly popular but also controversial (Brown & Fee, 2003). The critics said that Kinsey was homosexual, thus, conducted the research driven by his own sexual needs. They said that he would film his subjects during sexual acts at his home in Bloomington, Indiana. There were also rumors about pedophilia, incest and about using children for his research. Furthermore, that he used homosexuals, prisoners and prostitutes, and presented them as "normal" married people, thus, skewing the research data (Jones, 1997). Kinsey said: "The only unnatural sex act is that which you cannot perform." He encountered political and religious opposition that still exist today in the anti-Kinsey movement.

Regardless of the criticism mentioned above, Kinsey contributed to the sexual revolution in the United States and worldwide. He demystified sexual behavior and changed people's sexual attitudes, paving the road toward sexual liberation, especially for women.

Masters and Johnson

William Masters (1915-2001) and Virginia Johnson (1925-2013) were a research team at Washington University in St. Louis. From 1957 until the 1990s, they investigated human sexual behavior. In 1964, they opened the Reproductive Biology Research Foundation in St. Louis. In 1978, they renamed it to the Masters and Johnson Institute.

In the first years of their work, they observed 382 women and 312 men resulting in approximately 10,000 complete cycles of sexual response. The work was conducted in a laboratory setting where they let people masturbate or have intercourse while taking notes and filming. Many of the volunteers were married heterosexual couples. Masters and Johnson measured female and male sexual arousal and orgasmic response, vaginal lubrication and clitoral stimulation, among others. They discovered that some women could have multiple orgasms. They also debunked Freud's notion that vaginal orgasms were more mature and superior, stating that most women do need direct clitoral stimulation to achieve an orgasm.

Their clinical work also included sexual dysfunctions such as impotence, premature ejaculation, painful intercourse and lack of sexual desire. These problems took a long time to treat with psychoanalysis or psychotherapy, sometimes many years. Masters and Johnson developed sex therapy for couples based on their clinical approach. They treated sexual problems in a short time with great success. These couples did not have sex in the lab. They were treated by talk therapy only, just as it is done today.

The Masters and Johnson Institute was heavily criticized for their homosexual to heterosexual conversion program that they ran from 1968 to 1977. During this time, homosexuality was regarded as a disorder. William Masters might have lied when he stated that his program had a 72% success rate (Maier, 2009).

Masters and Johnson published their research in 1966. The book *Human Sexual Response* quickly became a bestseller. In 1970, they published their second book called *Human Sexual Inadequacy*. The books were translated into over 30 languages. Masters and Johnson were married from 1971 to 1992.

In 2013, a television series on Masters and Johnson, called *Masters of Sex*, aired in the U.S. It was based on a book of the same name written by Thomas Maier.

Shere Hite

Feminist and sexologist Shere Hite, born Shirley Diana Gregory (1942-), is an American born, (now German), sex educator and researcher.   In 1976, Hite published her book *The Hite Report on Female Sexuality* that shocked the U.S. nation, mostly the male population. The book sold over 50 million copies worldwide. It was based on interviews with over 3,000 women. The majority of these women proclaimed that they could easily achieve an orgasm by direct clitoral self-stimulation. And they could do this within minutes. This was a huge blow to the men and their egos. Since Freud's sexual theories, then Kinsey, and Masters and Johnson, no one challenged the male virility or the need for a penis for female satisfaction. Freud had said that if a woman could not climax through penetrative sex she was frigid, or she could be mentally ill.   To Freud, vaginal orgasms were superior to clitoral ones. Hite proved him wrong. She also criticized Masters and Johnson for stating that thrusting during intercourse should provide enough clitoral stimulation for a woman to achieve an orgasm and if she failed to do so, she could be diagnosed with female "sexual dysfunction."

Due to Shere Hite's report, for the first time in history, women understood that they were not alone in faking orgasms and that there was nothing wrong with them physiologically, as they could achieve one rather quickly by masturbating. Her research put focus on the clitoris, which was a significant step toward female sexual satisfaction. Unfortunately, Hite's work was largely attacked and criticized in the U.S.   In 1995, she renounced her U.S. citizenship to become a German citizen. She currently lives in London, England.

Magnetic Resonance Imaging (MRI)

Brain scans and body MRIs are common in today's sex research. MRI machines are large tubes with magnets. The human body slides inside the tube, and the magnetic field and radio waves produce detailed images of the organs inside the body. A Dutch team led by Dr. Van Andel put copulating couples inside the tube to see what happens during sex. They discovered that contrary to the previous belief that the uterus increases 50% to 100% in size during female sexual arousal due to engorgement with blood, it is actually the female bladder that fills with urine during intercourse. The reason for this could be that the woman needs to urinate after sex to clean the urethra, thus, reducing the risk of urinary tract (UTI) and bladder infections. This is not the case in men, maybe because they have longer urethras so they are less prone to infections. These compelling images can be seen on YouTube. You can also see what happens when a baby is born inside a MRI machine.

How compatible are you as a couple – Tests

At the end of this book (Annex page 213) you can find two tests: **Know Your Partner** by John Gottman and **Index of Sexual Satisfaction** by Crooks and Baur. There are two sets of the tests; one for you and one for your partner.

CHAPTER 2

**COMMUNICATION SKILLS – LET'S TALK ABOUT IT
WHY ARE FRENCH MEN GOOD IN BED?
WHAT DO WOMEN REALLY WANT?**

How much should we talk about the relationship and sex? Good communication about concerns and sexual desires is valuable to maintain a satisfying sexual relationship. We come from different cultural and religious backgrounds where often talking about sex was a taboo and where sex education was non-existent. We may have different sexual histories, norms and expectations. And why are French men good in bed? Okay, not all French men but many. Why are they different?

"Adam and Eve had an ideal marriage. He didn't have to hear
about all the men she could have married...
and she didn't have to hear about how well his mother cooked."

The power of "I love you"

A recent study published in the *Journal of Sex Research* concluded that saying "I love you" during sex is crucial for a happy sex life and high relationship satisfaction (Frederick et al., 2016). The study analyzed answers from longtime married or cohabited (minimum three years) heterosexual men and women. The average age of the men was 46 and 40 for women. The study measured current sexual satisfaction and sexual satisfaction in the first six months of the relationship. A total of 39,000 people participated in the survey.

Compared to the first six months of the relationship when 83% were sexually satisfied, the current situation was different, as only 43% of men and 55% of women were currently satisfied.

MISTAKE # 3
Not saying "I love you" during sex

In the happy group of people in the survey above, 75% of men and 74% of women said "I love you" during sex compared to the dissatisfied group where only 49% of men and 44% of women said "I love you" during sex (Frederick et al., 2016). Remember that this was for the long-term relationships so if you just met or are having a one-night stand, refrain from declaring your love or you will be considered crazy. And in a long-term relationship, only say it if you really mean it. If you are not in love with your sex partner, try to find something positive to say about them or about the experience.

MISTAKE # 4
Not praising each other

The happy couples in the survey praised each other for something they did and made fun of their mistakes during sex (Frederick et al., 2016). Keep it light and funny. Don't be afraid to ask your partner for something you want because this increased the sexual satisfaction. Communication before having sex was important as well. Texting, emailing and calling each other during the day was beneficial to having good sex at night.

MISTAKE # 5
Too little sex

One of the reasons for dissatisfaction in the marriage in the study mentioned above was the frequency of sex. In the happy relationships, couples had sex at least once per week. They concluded that the more sex the couple had, the more marital satisfaction there was (Frederick et al., 2016). In the beginning of a relationship, it is common to have sex every day, but the frequency subsides with time. After the initial honeymoon period that can last up to a year, things will finally settle down. Making sex a priority is a must in long-term relationships. More about this in Chapter 3 and 4.

MISTAKE # 6
Not planning to have sex

Robert and Anette say:
> *After not having sex for several months, we finally made a decision to put sex on our priority list. Each week we schedule private time together. Sometimes, we only have time for 30 minutes, but most often, we get an hour or so. Sex brings us together. By planning it in advance, we have something to look forward to.*

Are you headed for divorce?

Dr. John Gottman says that it only takes five minutes to know which couple will divorce and which one will stay together. How does he know that? By watching them argue. Clinical psychologist Gottman and his wife Julie Schwartz have over 40 years of experience with more than 3,000 couples. They ran a study at the University of Washington where they analyzed interactions and behavior of couples. They monitored their stress levels, tone of voice, facial expressions, body language, emotions and gestures, even their blood pressure. When it comes to divorce prediction and marital stability, Gottman's study is the most extensive to date.

MISTAKE # 7
Fighting dirty

The results showed that the number one predictor of divorce is contempt. Couples that use disrespectful words, condescending facial expressions (even for a second), sneering, or mockery, are doomed. Usually, contempt comes from long-standing negative thoughts. Words such as "you are stupid" or "you are useless" or "you never…" are deeply damaging to the relationship. Cynicism and sarcasm kill love.

Gottman says that there are "four horsemen of the apocalypse" for relationships: criticism, defensiveness, stonewalling (shutting down, no eye contact, avoiding communication) and contempt. Men are prone to stonewalling; meanwhile, women attack their partners with criticism. Defensiveness is equally common for both sexes, and it seems to be unproductive, as it quickly results in counterattack.

Lara says:

We fight all the time, mostly about stupid things like the dishes or laundry. It gets nasty at times.

MISTAKE # 8
Not being best friends

John Gottman says that there are only two things that discriminate couples with great sex lives from couples with awful sex lives. Happy couples that have great sex, romance and passion:

1. Stay friends. They laugh together.
2. They make sex a priority.

MISTAKE # 9
Not making sex a priority

Gottman says that you need to make sex a priority. Sex shouldn't be the last thing to do on a long priority list. It's special; happy couples know that.

MISTAKE # 10
Not talking about sex

Gottman says that most couples don't know how to talk about sex; they feel uncomfortable to bring it up. They might come from a cultural background where sex was never discussed. It is important to have intimate conversations to find out more about your partner's dreams, wishes and hopes, about their feelings, who they are. Women are better at discussing this; many men struggle to express their feelings and wishes. They are not good communicators. Guys can be loners.

MISTAKE # 11
Lack of respect

The basis of a good relationship is mutual respect and affection for one another, says Gottman. You should ask yourself if you feel respected in this relationship and if your partner is really fond of you.

MISTAKE # 12
Too shy to talk about sex

Why are we shy to talk about sex? Sex should be natural to us, just like eating, sleeping or going to the toilet. We can talk about these activities (Okay, not the toilet so much); yet, sex is different. When you go to a restaurant, you order what you want to eat. You discuss your food choice with the waiter; you ask for advice. Why is it so difficult to discuss sex with your partner? To ask for what you want? Lovers should listen to each other's sexual desires and fantasies. It doesn't mean they should act out on these fantasies; it's more about sharing, discussing and understanding your partner.

MISTAKE # 13
Sex is dirty

Most religions consider sex outside of marriage a sin. We were raised in families where sex was taboo. Our parents failed to explain why sex is "bad" or "dirty." They just used these words together with sex. The religious dogma taught us that sex is only for procreation, within marriage, so no babies should be born out of wedlock. We rarely talk about the health benefits of sex, the pleasure sex brings to us, the meaningful connection it makes in relationships. Having sex is an important part of human physiology; without it we are incomplete.

Violet says:
> *My mom always said that sex is bad, that men only want to have sex, and once they got it, they will leave you. She said that only men enjoy sex, and it's more like a chore for women.*

MISTAKE # 14
Men only want to have sex

The truth is that men are not so different from women when it comes to intimacy. They also need closeness and connection, to feel the soft embrace of a partner who gives them warmth and tenderness. Many men (just like women) are starved for affection. They pursue sex to get these feelings of intimacy and approval. It's not only about sex.

WHY FRENCH MEN ARE GOOD IN BED

- ✓ He is a good kisser.
- ✓ He listens.
- ✓ He is honest and loyal.
- ✓ He respects your integrity.
- ✓ He is romantic.
- ✓ He remembers your birthday and anniversaries.
- ✓ He buys you flowers and small gifts.
- ✓ He pays for dinner, coffee, drinks etc.
- ✓ He calls and texts you often.
- ✓ He doesn't check his phone 10 times during dinner.
- ✓ He likes good food.
- ✓ He knows all about wine and champagne.
- ✓ He takes you on a date, even after 10 years of marriage.
- ✓ He tells you he loves you.
- ✓ He asks you if you need anything.
- ✓ He likes going shopping with you.
- ✓ He feels secure in his masculinity.
- ✓ He is in touch with his feminine side.
- ✓ He knows how to clean up.
- ✓ He takes out the garbage without you reminding him.
- ✓ He doesn't watch sports all day long.
- ✓ He is clean and he smells good.
- ✓ He dresses well.
- ✓ He is a gentleman.
- ✓ He thinks about you when he is away.
- ✓ He is always happy to see you.
- ✓ He takes care of you.
- ✓ He makes sure you are safe.
- ✓ He makes you his first priority.
- ✓ He loves his mother but you always come first.
- ✓ He likes culture and art.
- ✓ He enjoys spending time with you.
- ✓ He makes you feel beautiful.
- ✓ He kisses you good morning and good night.
- ✓ He holds you when you are sad
- ✓ He takes time when he makes love.

What can you learn from this? Only the last statement was about making love; yet, all of the above is connected to sex. Good sex is much more than intercourse. It is about being in tune with each other, about caring for each other, because if he delivers all of the above, then good sex will follow. You might say that such a man doesn't exist, but I know he does because he is sitting next to me while I am writing these words. I suggest that you make your own wish list for a perfect partner and if your guy scores at least 80% of your list then hold onto him. The remaining 20% might be possible to fix if you tell him what you want. Men like to please their women, but they can't read your mind. Communication is crucial in healthy relationships.

Does the list apply to all French men? Certainly not; however, the French culture puts emphasis on love and relationships. French children are groomed to think about love in a positive way. Sex is not dirty or sinful in France; it is a natural necessity for a happy life. Compared to American men who rate their masculinity by engaging in violent sports such as American football, French men practice the art of seduction. Flirting and seduction are the national sports of France. It is a dance between two people who make contact and engage in a conversation. They show interest in each other. They share what they know on a particular subject. It doesn't need to be about sex. It could be anything from food or fashion to politics. The French like to talk but they would never admit that they talk too much. Growing up in Sweden, I learned that you don't speak unless you have something important to say. This rule doesn't apply in France, as everyone thinks they are intellectual. Thus they must talk to prove it to you. The great French philosopher René Descartes (1596-1650) wrote in 1637:

> Je pense, donc je suis; I think, therefore I am,
> Cogito ergo sum (in Latin),

which sums up the French mentality pretty well. Unfortunately, he succumbed to the Swedish winter when visiting Queen Christina in Stockholm. René Descartes died of pneumonia in February 1650, at only 53 years of age. Most of philosophies that developed after Descartes were reactions to his thinking and writings. He has been called the father of modern philosophy.

WHAT DO WOMEN WANT?

"The great question that has never been answered, and which I have not yet been able to answer, despite my thirty years of research into the feminine soul, is 'What does a woman want?'"
Sigmund Freud (Jones, 1953)

Poor Freud. Couples counseling was yet to be invented when he said this. If Freud were alive today, I would invite him to lie down on my couch, but instead of sitting behind him as he used to do so the client wouldn't see him, I would face him, look into his eyes and tell him what women really want. It is not that complicated at all. The list two pages back is a good start.

No, Dr. Freud, we don't envy your penis. We like penises when they come attached to a nice man. As for the single women out there, still waiting to find the perfect man, buy a substitute (aka dildo, rabbit, vibrator) and enjoy yourself. It is your human right. Don't have sex with a random guy just because you are longing for love. Fall in love first and then have sex. Women should be more assertive when it comes to sexual pleasure. Sexual liberation is one aspect of personal liberation. Taking control of our sexuality, at the most intimate, personal and fundamental level, leads to extending control over other areas of life. We need to learn to take responsibility for our own sexual fulfillment, with men, or without them.

MISTAKE # 15
Accepting booty calls and one-night stands

Say no to friends with benefits, booty calls, hook-ups and one-night stands. You deserve better.

More advice to men from real women:

- Cigars smell bad (take note, Dr. Freud).
- Smoking is not sexy.
- Facial hair is definitely not sexy.
- Listen to what we say, even if you think it's boring.
- You don't need to fix our problems, just listen to them.
- Do not lie.

- Your ex is never prettier than I am.
- Changing your underwear every day is a no-brainer.
- Changing your bedsheets once a week is a must.
- Clean towels are a necessity, not a luxury.
- Towels and bedsheets should be white, not black.
- Take your socks off.
- Keep your condoms close by; running after them makes you look stupid.
- Don't fart in bed. Even better, never fart or belch in front of us.
- Sometimes we snore, but you don't need to tell us.
- Kissing doesn't always lead to sex. Sometimes, it's just kissing.
- A threesome might be your fantasy but it will never be mine so never ask, or it will be the last time we will speak. The same goes for anal sex.
- When I tell you what I like in bed, I expect you to do it.
- Bad kisser equals bad in bed. So do something about it. Learn.
- Sometimes we fake it, no offense.
- Sometimes it helps to switch off the TV in the middle of the match to get laid.
- We like hugs and spooning.
- Kissing my hand makes you look sexy.
- We wax for you. You should groom your parts as well.
- Never be late.
- It's not our PMS that makes us angry. It's you.
- Let me know where you are so I know that you are alive.
- Call when you're supposed to call.
- If you text me, and I call you right back, do answer the phone.
- We don't want to see your phone cover during dinner.
- Checking your phone on a date is rude.
- Don't ask if we want a dessert; just order it.
- Never comment on how much food we eat.
- Always pay for dinner. Splitting the bill is not sexy.
- We spend a lot of time to prepare for the date so why don't you put in some effort as well?
- Wearing sneakers/trainers to dinner is not okay.
- Iron your shirt; it shows that you care.
- We see what you are wearing, from head to toe.
- A hat will not make your balding head go away. Accept it and

move on. We do.

- We need all the shoes we have. They have their own history, all 125 pairs of them.
- If you need to comment on how we dress, just saying "You look nice" is sufficient. Keep the constructive criticism to yourself.
- We know we have too many clothes; you don't have to say it.
- If we ask you "Do I look fat in this dress?" never say yes. If you think we look fat, just say, "You look uncomfortable. Maybe the other dress is better."
- Don't use my make-up.
- Notice my perfume; I spent a fortune on it.
- We notice when you are kind; we keep score.
- You can tease your little brother. Teasing us will get you nowhere.
- Cleaning up the dishes is hot; try it more often.
- Keeping down the toilet seat means that you are smart.
- We never forget any details, ever.
- Always make sure we get home safely.
- Sometimes, a NO means that we didn't shave our legs or we are wearing frumpy underwear. Try again another day.
- Call us back after the date even if you didn't score. We might like you. And don't wait three days; we don't like that. The next day is fine.
- Why are you still on Tinder?
- Apologize when you screw up. At least three times. And mean it.
- Read this list at least three times.

Make your own list here below for him to read:

What do men want? Advice from real men:

- No drama.
- Calm down. Relax.
- Be on time.
- Get ready faster.
- Don't nag.
- Don't sulk.
- Don't play games.
- Don't talk about your ex.
- Be honest.
- Be authentic.
- Be emotionally mature.
- Be confident.
- Be laid-back.
- Don't be a gold digger.
- Don't be jealous.
- Be sensual. Be sexy.
- Be feminine.
- Be intelligent.
- Don't baby talk to me.
- Don't be a pain in the ass.
- Don't tell me what to do.
- Don't control me; I'm a grown man.
- I already have a mother; don't mother me.
- Let me know what is bothering you; I'm not a mind reader.
- If you don't tell me your problem, I can't fix it.
- The bathroom is for me as well.
- I need more space in the closet.
- You have too many shoes.
- You have too many clothes.
- You have too much make-up.
- Be humble.
- Take care of yourself. Dress well and look sexy but not cheap.
- Don't drink too much.
- Be a lady. Have good manners.
- Don't call me 20 times when I'm at work or out with friends.
- Don't criticize me.

- I need your support. Have my back.
- Men do have feelings. Respect mine.
- Be independent and self-sufficient.
- Be playful.
- Have a good sense of humor.
- Know how to cook.
- Try new things in bed.
- Be adventurous.
- Have more sex.
- Have a threesome.
- Anal sex?
- Blowjob?
- Have more sex again.
- Be happy.
- Have your own friends.
- I need time alone with my friends.
- Don't be clingy.
- Don't be needy.
- Don't emasculate me.
- Validate me.
- Appreciate me.
- Praise me.
- Respect me.
- Inspire me.
- Love me. Inside I'm just a boy who needs love.

Make your own list here below for her to read:

CHAPTER 3

WE USED TO BE SO HAPPY!
WHAT HAPPENED?

How long is love suppose to last? Can we stay together forever? Here, I explain the different stages of romantic relationships and what to expect at each stage. How do you keep the passion in a long-term relationship? Is it even possible? Why does sexual satisfaction diminish when we have children? Are we meant to live alone or in pairs? What is spiritual partnership? These and many other existential questions are answered here, with several examples of common mistakes that we make.

MISTAKE # 16
No desire

Mating in Captivity

Esther Perel is a family therapist practicing in New York City. Her book *Mating in Captivity: Reconciling the Erotic and the Domestic*, published in 2006, has been translated into 25 languages. In the field of sex therapy today, she is recognized as the most provocative and original theorist. She says to couples that complain of loss of desire that love is about having and desire is about wanting. We need to improve the sex first and then look into the relationship, not the other way around (Perel, 2006). Too much closeness, she continues, is not good for passion and desire. Love seeks closeness but desire needs space just like fire needs air. To heighten the passion, we need to cultivate the mystery, to tolerate separation, to become unfamiliar and unpredictable. Absence, longing for the other, anticipation and fantasy can revive desire. Responsibility and security, often found in loving relationships, will clash with desire. With time, we become closer, more secure and comfortable in the relationship, losing the animalistic sexual passion that we had at the beginning. Perel says, "Fire needs air, and many couples don't leave enough air."

Popular perception is that in committed relationships the frequency of sex decreases, just as Perel writes in her book, but research shows that many people consider sexual desire the main ingredient of romantic love. Research conducted by Sarah Murray and Robin Milhausen (2012), of the University of Guelph, Ontario, who investigated couples that were together an average of two years, found that the length of relationship affected sexual desire for women but not for men. Another research study shows that men's sexual desire remained high while women's decreased as early as one year into the relationship (Klusmann, 2002).

Parenthood

Perel says that parents usually have low libidos because they are too stressed and too tired for sex. However, the very same people were also stressed when single, yet, they had more sex then. The reason is that parents transfer their erotic needs to the needs of the child. Kissing, hugging, playing around and touching, make a sensual connection with the child, so the need to connect with the spouse diminishes. We center our lives on the child and put our needs second. For the adult couple, intimacy, sexuality and communication are crucial. They need to set boundaries, to take their time, to lock the bedroom door, to keep the spark alive (Perel, 2006).

Dan says:
> *Our three-year-old sleeps with us and the baby sleeps in the cot in our bedroom. We have zero privacy and a nonexistent sex life. Married life sucks!*

Boundaries in relationships

Perel says that desire needs tension, insecurity, breaks and repairs to generate erotic energy in relationships. On the contrary, love needs intimacy, closeness and familiarity. Desire needs novelty, distance and surprise. Fights are good because they bring new energy into relationships, new aliveness. Some couples in healthy relationships never fight but their sex life is quiet as well and somehow flat because desire needs fights, she says. It needs an edge.

Sexual threat is not good for love, but it is good for desire. Knowing that your partner is sexually attractive to other people increases your desire. It makes a void between two people, a sexual edge that is good for the relationship. Perel worked with couples who had a good relationship but no sex. She helped other couples in bad relationships to make them better; still, the sex did not improve. So finally, she came to the conclusion that if sex is wrong, the relationship is wrong. Therefore, the sex needs to be fixed first.

Too much honesty, or in American terms, transparency, is not good for the relationship either. We all have secrets, and we can never know our partner completely, she says. We cannot heal the relationship with absolute honesty.

She calls infidelity the "shadow of the third." We never own our partner sexually. They have choices to be with other people. Sometimes, an affair can strengthen a relationship and sometimes destroy it, Perel says. We have a romantic ideal that monogamy is a "sacred cow." We think that marriage should fulfill every need we might have, that our spouses should be our best friend, confidant, companion and ally. When this model does not work, we want a divorce, to dissolve an entire family instead of renegotiating the boundaries (Perel, 2006).

Modern intimacy

Perel says that modern love has the romantic ideal that erotic life should be dominant in a relationship. Not so long ago, love had little to do with a marriage. Since then we brought love into the marriage and sexualized it. Then, women became liberated by contraception and sex became separated from its reproductive role. As Anthony Giddens (1991, 1992) says "it became a reflexive project of the self, an ongoing process of self-definition." Today, sexuality is not about having many children or about marital duties, it is about desire. Sexual satisfaction equals marital happiness today. Therefore, sexuality is so important in modern marriages.

Intimacy can sabotage sexual desire, Perel says. We assume that trust and intimacy must precede sexual enjoyment, but security and stability desexualize us instead (Perel, 2006).

Erotic blueprints

Perel states that our erotic blueprint is shaped by our emotional history from childhood. "Tell me how you were loved, and I'll tell you how you make love," she says. Were your parents responsive to your needs? Did they hold you, soothe you, rock you? Did you feel safe to trust, and were you protected? Or were you rejected, humiliated, abandoned and afraid? She sees a strong connection between childhood attachment and our sexual behavior and refers to "separation individuation" and "love maps," our psychological need for adventure and the opposing need for safety. We learned then about gender and our sexuality, consciously or unconsciously. Our family members modeled sexual behavior to us that we carry on in our adult erotic lives (Perel, 2006).

Perel makes several valid points in her book. I already mentioned the importance of childhood attachment in Chapter 1. Locking the bedroom door to have sex when you have children is another piece of advice that I advocate. Thinking that an affair can strengthen a marriage is like playing Russian roulette with your relationship so I would by no means advise it to my clients. More about infidelity and affairs in Chapter 12. Creating mystery is an interesting concept that I will explain next.

MISTAKE # 17
Lack of mystery

Though flatulence is a normal bodily function, breaking wind burping or picking your nose in the presence of your lover is not sexy. Too much familiarity kills sexual desire. If you can afford it, have separate bathrooms. Mystery is good in romantic relationships.

Otherwise, you become roommates or even worse, like brother and sister.

MISTAKE # 18
No date nights

In the beginning of the relationship, we make an effort to go on dates. We plan ahead, we dress up, we anticipate the romantic get together. We make it special. A few months down the road, or after a few years of marriage, we settle into a familiar routine that runs on autopilot. Driving kids to activities or food shopping comes first on any parent's priority list. We put dating and sex on the back burner. This is wrong. Once a week or once a fortnight, you need to go on a date, just the two of you, sans kids.

You need to rekindle the connection that you had in the beginning of the relationship. Because men are visual, he needs to see you dressed up and pretty, not the usual way you greet him when he comes home, wearing sweats. The same goes for the men. Your Prince Charming may be dressing up for work, but when he is around you, he wears shorts. This is not romantic. So plan a date night and stick to it. A recent study shows that 65% of happily married men and 55% of happily married women make sure to go on dates together (Frederick et al., 2016).

MISTAKE # 19
No sex

After a date, there is a potential for sex. You need to plan this in advance when you have kids. Some people say that planned sex is not fun because there is no spontaneity involved. Would you rather have planned sex or no sex at all? As I mentioned before, sex is important in the relationship because it strengthens the bond between the spouses. Sex is the glue that holds it together. Couples that have good sex don't rate it as a very important factor in the relationship. Alternatively, those who don't have a regular or satisfying sex life, rate sex as a very important factor for a happy relationship. If this is not convincing enough, I need to mention that frequent ejaculations in men lower the risk of prostate cancer by 22% (Rider et al., 2015). More about prostate cancer in Chapter 14.

MISTAKE # 20
Not enough sex

One of the most mentioned complaints in couples therapy is the frequency of sex. It used to be the man who brought it up but now even women want to have more sex. Research shows that in happy relationships couples have sex at least once per week. The more sex the couple has, the more marital satisfaction there is (Frederick et al., 2016). Making sex a priority is a must in long-term relationships. Some of my couples didn't have sex for several months. My recommendation is once a week if possible. Make it a planned activity so you have something to look forward to. The prostate cancer research mentioned above concluded that those men who ejaculated 21 or more times per month had the lowest risk of developing prostate cancer (Rider et al., 2015).

MISTAKE # 21
A new baby will save our marriage

Can a child save the marriage? The short answer to this question is no. However, let's look for the evidence. According to several research studies, most divorces happen within three years of a child being born. Why is that? Many couples are unprepared for the challenges a new baby brings into the relationship. Sleepless nights, breastfeeding, diaper changes, stress, and lack of sex contribute to conflict and emotional distance. Suddenly, life centers around the baby; thus individual needs of the parents come second. Many new parents are not prepared for this radical change. They spend more time planning and decorating the nursery than learning about how to cope with a new baby.

Another controversial issue is how to raise the child. Many parents disagree on fundamental issues such as religion or corporal punishment. You should be on the same page when it comes to discipline. In many countries, parents still have the right to smack, hit, slap, whip, kick or beat misbehaving children. This behavior is regarded as child abuse in Sweden, the first country in the world to introduce the anti-spanking law in 1979. Research indicates that corporal punishment of children has the opposite effect. It leads to aggressive behavior in children, less obedience, anxiety, depression and antisocial behavior. Young children don't understand the punishment and older children become hostile.

I have seen many couples that continually argue about this issue and some even split up because of it. Kids are smart, so they know when the parents disagree and might use it to create problems between the parents, thus, escaping the discipline in the first place by diverting the issue. Parents must follow the same disciplinary guidelines so children receive consistent treatment from both of them. Corporal punishment should never happen to a child. It only leads to more aggression and a lifetime of psychological damage to the child. You might think that you were spanked as a child and you turned out fine, so what is the big deal? It is a big deal to the child so stop now. Get help if you need to address your own anger management but most importantly, break the cycle! Your child doesn't need to suffer just because you did.

"Loving people live in a loving world.
Hostile people live in a hostile world.
Same world." ~ *Wayne Dyer*

MISTAKE # 22
Children in your bed

As a mother of six children, I could write another book on this subject. As a rule, a child should sleep in his or her own bed. However, sometimes, depending on the circumstances, it is more convenient for the parent to let the child sleep in the parents' bed, especially when the child arrives in the middle of the night. Because this book is about love and sex, having a child in your bed at night automatically eliminates intimacy and sex. As I mentioned before, locking the bedroom door is necessary for some private time together. Try to make time for sex at least once per week. Teaching your child to sleep in his or her own bed is important, but as a parent, you should decide what works best for your family.

Alicia says:
My five-year old daughter comes to our bed every night. Like a Swiss clock at 3:00 AM, she arrives with her teddy bear. At first, we walked her back to her own bed, but now we don't bother anymore.

MISTAKE # 23
Pets in your bed

I often hear complaints about pets sleeping in the bed or in the bedroom. Usually, one spouse is okay with it and the other one against. Having sex while your dog is watching you is not advisable. I will leave it at that.

Keith says:

> *I can't have sex while my girlfriend's dog is watching us. When we put him in the living room and close the door to the bedroom, he scratches the door and wants to come in. This puts me off altogether. It's either the dog or me.*

Samantha says:

> *I love my dog. He was a gift from my father. I got him ten years ago when he was only eight weeks old. We have been together for so many years and he always sleeps with me.*

THE BEDROOM

Though making love on the kitchen table or in the car might be fun once or twice, most couples prefer the comfort of their own bedroom, followed by the living room sofa or couch. The setup of the bedroom is important for happy liaisons.

MISTAKE # 24
TV in the bedroom

Having a TV in the bedroom can be good sometimes, but mostly it isn't a good idea. Let me tell you why. Unless you are sick and need to stay in bed all day, thus, having a TV to keep you company may be useful, consider the following reasons:

- Many people watch the late night news before falling asleep. Most of the time news is bad news. It affects our brains negatively. We are literary brainwashed by the TV. We are passive recipients of information that is manipulated by the media. It's much better to read and watch the news on the Internet. There, you have control over what you select to watch/read and it doesn't need to be just before you go to bed.

- Research shows that watching TV before falling asleep disturbs sleep cycles and lowers the number of nightly sleep hours, causing sleep deprivation. The same research shows that Americans watch television more than 35 hours per week.

- Couples that have a TV in their bedroom have less sex than couples who don't. Though some couples like watching porn before or during sex, most of the time, they watch something else.

- Couples without a television in the bedroom have more intimate conversations and cuddle time before falling asleep.

- TV advertisements are influencing us at the most susceptible moments, when we are tired. Use your time for something better, such as reading a book or talking to your partner.

- Before falling asleep is a good time for reflection and meditation, for assessing your day. Don't let other people influence your thoughts and feelings.

- Make your bedroom a sanctuary for sleep and sex. Make it calm, peaceful and relaxing. Surround yourself with positive items and colors that give you good vibes. Positive energy is important so check out some Feng Shui guidelines for bedrooms.

- Be a role model for your kids. Children who watch TV every day are more prone to obesity, have lower reading levels and lack of social development.

Hazel says:
> *We fall asleep with the TV on but whoever wakes up first, usually around 2:00 or 3:00 AM, turns it off and goes back to sleep. We are used to it now. When did we have sex last time? I don't remember. We are too tired to have sex.*

MISTAKE # 25
Electronic devices

Remove electronic devices from the bedroom. Many people charge their phones on their nightstands, close to their heads. Some even sleep with their phones. We are used to having them on all the time, to check the emails and messages. This is not a good idea; some reports state that there could be a connection between cell phone radiation and cancer. Research done by the World Health Organization (WHO) concluded in 2011: "After reviewing essentially all the evidence that is relevant... the working group classified radiofrequency electromagnetic fields as possibly carcinogenic to humans." The report stated that there is "some evidence" for an increased risk of brain cancer from mobile phone use.

Aside from the cancer risk, having phones, laptops, iPads and other devices in the bedroom while making love (or sleeping) is not a good idea. They are disturbing with their constant notifications and turning screens on and off.

MISTAKE # 26
Old bed or mattress

We have millions of mites in our beds. The older the mattress, the bigger the colony. Many people are allergic to mites. They can trigger allergy and asthma attacks in people. Researchers from Ohio State University have been studying mites for over 40 years. These small eight-legged creatures can't be seen by the human eye but pull out a microscope and you will see them for sure. They feed on our dead skin cells that we shed every night. We are actually allergic to their droppings because they excrete proteins. Since we sleep up to eight hours per night, there are plenty of skin cells to keep them alive. Mites are not the same as bedbug; these feed on human blood and can live up to a year without food.

MISTAKE # 27
Cold wash

Wash your bedsheets, pillows and blankets in minimum 60° C (140° F) water. That should be sufficient to kill the mites and their eggs. Bedsheets should be made of natural fibers and changed once a week. Pillows and blankets should be washed every few months, also in hot water. The bed, mattress and surrounding carpeting should be vacuumed once a week as well.

MISTAKE # 28
Not changing the mattress

Your bed should be inviting not only to good sleep but to great sex as well. Many people (especially women) have a psychological issue with sleeping or making love on a bed that was used by your ex. Try to understand this and invest in a new mattress. Make her come with you to the store and chose it; this way, she will know that you care.

Amanda says:
> *Sleeping in the same bed that he shared with his ex-wife freaks me out. I want it to be "our bed" but he says that the bed is not that old and besides that, it was very expensive. Men don't get it, do they?*

MISTAKE # 29
Squeaky old bed

Have it fixed or get rid of it. There are plenty of tips on the Internet about how to un-squeak a bed. For example, use wax for wood or tighten the bolts. Your kids or neighbors don't need to know when you are having sex.

Lauren says:
> *My fiancée has a squeaky old bed. I can't make love with all that noise going on. It doesn't bother him, but it does bother me. I can't have an orgasm there so what's the point of having sex to start with?*

MISTAKE # 30
No lock on the bedroom door

If you have kids or live with other people, a lock on the bedroom door is a must. You are entitled to privacy, especially when having sex. Don't let your kids walk in on you in the midst of passion. Lock the door and relax. Having sex while being worried that someone might come in is not fun.

MISTAKE # 31
Age difference

Is age just a number? Some people ask me about the age difference between the spouses. Does it matter? I think it does, and I will tell you why. The research says that the bigger the age gap – the shorter the marriage, and that couples with a 5-year age gap are 18% more likely to divorce, 10-year age gap 39% and those with a 30-year age gap are 172% more likely to divorce (Francis & Mialon, 2014).

I say this: if the age difference is more than a generation, meaning more than 16-18 years then this is certainly not an advantage to you. You may know a couple with a big age gap who are happily married, but generally, the couple is most compatible when they belong to the same generation.

Milestones in history, such as Pearl Harbor (my grandparents), the assassination of President Kennedy (my parents), the first man on the moon (my generation), 9/11 (my grown children) are important because the majority of the people remember when this happened. If you and your partner have the same historical reference points, then you are more likely compatible than two people from different generations are. I am not saying that your marriage will fail. However, you will need to work harder to make it a successful one.

Joan Collins, the British actress, married Percy Gibson, who is 32 years younger than she is. When asked if she was worried about the age difference between them she answered: "If he dies, he dies."

MISTAKE # 32
Marrying for the wrong reasons

Some people get married for the wrong reasons. Let me mention a few:

- **She wants a diamond ring.** Marriage is so much more than a beautiful ring. The ring should be the cherry on the cake, not the cake itself.
- **She is pregnant.** In some cultures/religions, this is a must. However, this should not be the reason to get married, as many of these marriages fail. The highest rate of divorce happens within the first three years of a baby being born.

- **Wanting to have children.** As women get older, and their biological clocks are ticking, many want to get married to start a family. Freeze your eggs if you can but think twice before jumping into a marriage for the wrong reasons.
- **We have been dating/cohabitating for a long time.** So marriage is the next logical step you think.
- **Pressure from family and friends.** Your family wants you to get married. All your friends are getting married.
- **Settling.** There is no one better out there for me.
- **Feeling alone.** Your spouse will not cure your loneliness. Some people feel more alone within the marriage than ever before.
- **Money or fame.** A marriage based on these premises will not last.

Staying in love forever

Real love is so much more than falling in love. Passionate love, the initial infatuation, the high, never lasts for long. After the first idealistic phase, love will always change into a deeper, more mature feeling. At this stage, many people give up and move on to someone else in the search for that emotional high. They repeat the same mistakes over and over again because the answer to real love is not falling in love but being in love. To put it in numbers, passionate love lasts only for a few months, let's say three to four months. The feeling of being in love in a good relationship lasts for approximately two years. After this period, there is a shift toward a different kind of love, the mature love.

Spiritual partnership

Mature love is best described by Gary Zukav when he says, "Spiritual partnership is a partnership between equals for the purpose of spiritual growth." What does it mean? When people get married they promise each other to stay together despite the differences and hardships they may have in the marriage. For some people, a marriage becomes a prison; they feel trapped. They may disrespect each other, abuse the other and generally take things for granted. "A spiritual partnership is between people who promise themselves to use all of their experiences to grow spiritually," says Gary.

Zukav (2012) continues:

When two people in an intimate couple relationship look at their interactions as opportunities to learn about themselves instead of change each other, they are infusing their relationship with the energy of spiritual partnership. If they are married, they infuse their marriage with the energy of a spiritual partnership, and eventually it will become a spiritual partnership. A spiritual partnership is a partnership between equals for the purpose of spiritual growth. Spiritual partners use their delightful experiences together as well as their power struggles to learn about themselves and change themselves. This is a new way to live, a new way to create together, a new way to evolve together.

MISTAKE # 33
Not being equal

You might wonder how to become equal? Gary says that in life we are defined by our personalities and these are not equal. We might be good at something that other people are not good at, and this makes us superior. Or we might feel inferior to other people because we feel less intelligent or whatever. It doesn't really matter because these feelings are based on fear. Some people are stronger, and some people are weaker. Equality is understanding that no one in the universe is more important than you are. Our souls are equal. When you connect to someone, and you feel equal, that is a soul-to-soul connection (Zukav, 2014).

MISTAKE # 34
Not sharing the housework

The importance of equality in happy long-term relationships has been confirmed by research. An Ohio State University study of nearly 1,000 couples, during 20 years, concluded that the low-conflict couples made their decisions collaboratively (Kamp Dush & Taylor, 2012). The happy couples believed in shared decision-making, they had a stronger belief in lifelong marriage than the less happy couples did, and the husbands were helping in the household. Believing in egalitarian marriage and sharing the burden of housework seems to be the key to a successful lifelong union.

12 key factors for a happy long-term relationship

Another study from researchers in New York investigated 274 individuals who were married over 10 years (O'Leary et al., 2011). Those who were still "very intensely in love" reported 12 key factors:

1. **Thinking positively about your partner.** Remembering the good and not ruminating about the bad.

2. **Thinking about your partner when apart.** Having your partner in your thoughts during the day is positive.

3. **Difficulty concentrating on other things when thinking about your partner.** If you can easily forget about your partner during the day, you are not in love. This applies particularly to men.

4. **Enjoying novel and challenging activities.** This one is particularly important to men. Doing exciting activities together strengthens the relationship.

5. **Spending time together.** Sharing the housework, grocery shopping, cooking and gardening together strengthens the love bond for each other. Just as in point 4, this one was more important to men.

6. **Expressing affection.** Express your love in a physical way is important. Kissing, touching and holding hands are good.

7. **Being sexually turned on by your partner.** The sexual chemistry was present in the happily married couples who were still in love after many years. This illustrates that sex is important in successful relationships.

8. **Engaging in sexual intercourse.** Sex is like glue in the relationship. It holds it together. To have sex on a regular basis is important.

9. **Feeling generally happy.** This might be the chicken and the egg story. Are happily married couples happier because they tend to be happy people or are they happy because their good marriages make them happy?

10. **Wanting to know where your partner is at all times.** For men this point is important. Men who are in love want to know where their partner is.

11. **Obsessively thinking about your partner.** For women, this was a sign of love. They didn't want to know the whereabouts of their husbands, as in point 10, but their minds were occupied by obsessive thinking about their spouses.

12. **Having a strong passion for life.** This one is more important to men.

(O'Leary et al., 2011).

"Men marry women with the hope they will never change.
Women marry men with the hope they will change.
Invariably they are both disappointed."
~ *Albert Einstein*

Are we meant to live alone or in pairs?

Some people say that we are born alone, and that we die alone, meaning that we don't need another person in our lives. This is not true because when we are born our mother is there and when we die, most of the time, someone is there with us. So are we meant to live alone or in pairs? What do you think? My view on this is that we need other people to survive. Fear of death is closely linked to rejection (see Chapter 15). In today's society, we can manage to live independently but thousands of years ago, when still living in caves, we needed other people for survival. It seems that social interactions are important to us even today. Happy people report the importance of a support system, either by family members, friends, neighbors, church, merchants or random people they meet in daily life. These human exchanges enrich us mentally and spiritually.

Have you seen the movie *Tuesdays with Morrie* from 1999? You can see it on YouTube. The film is based on a book by Mitch Albom called *Tuesdays with Morrie: An Old Man, a Young Man, and Life's Greatest Lesson* (1997). I highly recommend it. This is a story about a college professor, Morrie (played by Jack Lemmon), and his former student, Mitch (Hank Azaria). Morrie is dying from a terminal illness. Each Tuesday, Mitch travels from Michigan to Massachusetts to meet with Morrie. During the 14 meetings, until Morrie passes away, Mitch gets a lesson on the meaning of life. They discuss love, death, relationships, marriage, family, children, culture, media, disappointments, regrets and many more existential topics. The movie/book is also about aging versus being young and healthy. Regardless of where you are in your life right now, the story will inspire you as you will draw parallels with your own life.

So, to answer the question "Are we meant to live alone or in pairs?" I believe that we are biologically programmed to form a couple to have babies. To raise a child (or a few) is not easy so we need a partner or a village as they say. We depend on others. Once the children leave the nest, do we still need to be together? Is this necessary for our survival? No, it isn't, but as I said before, to have a happy and fulfilling life, we need social interactions and the support from other people. We were not born to live alone or to survive on our own. This is the reason why so many people suffer from isolation.

Irvin Yalom, the great existentialist, lists isolation as one of the four main problems or conflicts in human existence. He refers to them as "the givens of existence" (1980, p. 9) or the ultimate concerns. The other three are death, freedom and meaninglessness. Isolation, or the true aloneness in the world, causes us emotional distress, anxiety, feelings of depression and physical pain, according to Yalom.

I believe that isolation is on par with the fear of rejection mentioned earlier in this chapter (and also in Chapter 15). Both lead to fear of death that is instinctive and innate in humans. The sad thing is that thousands of years ago, the subject of our fear was the danger outside the cave, the wild animals that preyed on humans. These days, it's humans that are the biggest threat to other humans.

How to live a happy life?

One of the longest studies in history is actually on human development and happiness. Since 1938, researchers at Harvard University have followed 724 men. It is called "The Study of Adult

Development." Only 60 of them are still alive today, but the research continues. One of these men became the president of the United States - John F. Kennedy. Another one became the editor of the Washington Post - Ben Bradlee. This careful study involved interviews, medical records, blood samples, brain scans and recently even DNA testing.

What they discovered was that though initially most of these men thought that money, career achievement, and being successful would bring them the most happiness in life, the reality proved to be different. By the end of life, the happiest and healthy people said that their relationships with others; a spouse, family member, or friends, were the reasons for happiness, good health and good quality of life. So close, intimate relationships are crucial to our wellbeing and happiness, just like Morrie said.

People who are socially connected at old age are happier and live longer. People who are married are happier as well, unless they argue all the time. However, if the marriage is not a happy one, it is better to divorce because these people were less happy than single people were. Their health suffered as well. A stable and supportive marriage is the best option for a long and happy life followed by close relationships with others. Or as John Lennon said "All you need is Love."

CHAPTER 4

LOSS OF LIBIDO, MISMATCHED DESIRE
SEXUAL DYSFUNCTIONS
PREMATURE EJACULATION
ERECTILE DYSFUNCTION
VIAGRA, WHO NEEDS IT?

One of the most common problems in couples therapy is the desired frequency of sexual intercourse. Usually, one partner wants more sex than the other does. Clients often mention the beginning of their relationship, when they used to have sex almost every day, and now, some years later, they have sex once per month, if even that. So what happened? How can we alter this dilemma? And how important are hormones when it comes to sex? In 1998, a pill for erectile dysfunction (or impotence) called Viagra became the fastest selling prescription drug in history. Today, we have a few more similar drugs, two of them called Cialis and Levitra. Originally developed for cardiovascular disease, these drugs expand the blood vessels in the penis resulting in stronger and longer erections. You might think that only older men with erectile problems use Viagra. However, the majority of my male clients, regardless of age, have tried the drug. Most of the time, the wife/girlfriend is unaware of his recreational Viagra use. Some men take it "just in case" resulting in prolonged painful erections when the sex doesn't happen. Women use Viagra as well but for entirely different reasons, which I explain in this chapter. What can we learn from a high-end London escort? Moreover, why would a man have his penis amputated? Let's find out.

Hormones and sexual arousal

Sex hormones in humans, androgens and estrogens, are mainly produced by the endocrine glands – in females, ovaries and in men, testes. Both sexes produce testosterone, estrogens, and progesterone but in different quantities. A man may have 20 to 40 times more testosterone than a woman does, and women produce more estrogens than men do. Another hormone, oxytocin, a neuropeptide, sometimes called the "love hormone" that is produced in the brain by the hypothalamus, also affects our erotic, emotional and sexual arousal.

Testosterone, in both men and women, is necessary for the libido and sexual functioning. Low levels may influence sexual pleasure and sensitivity of the genitals, even erectile function. In females, testosterone levels play an important function regarding sexual desire and arousal, as well as the frequency of sexual activities. Several studies of postmenopausal women with testosterone deficiency have shown that shortly after administrating testosterone tablets, the subjects reported increased genital arousal, sexual desire, the frequency of masturbation and sexual fantasies.

According to Crooks and Baur (2011), the most common signs of testosterone deficiency in both men and women are:

- Decrease in one's usual level of sexual desire.
- Reduced sensitivity of the genitals and the nipples to sexual stimulation.
- Overall reduction in general levels of sexual arousability, possibly accompanied by decreased orgasmic capacity and/or less intense orgasms.
- Diminished energy levels and possibly depressed mood.
- Increased fat mass.
- Decreased bone mineral density, which can result in osteoporosis in both sexes.
- Reduced body hair.
- Decreased muscle mass and strength.

Estrogens in women affect overall well-being as well as sexual desire, pleasure, vaginal lubrication and intensity of orgasms.

However, it should be administered in the correct dose, as too high of a level may lower the sexual desire and even cause breast cancer, though research in this field has been unclear and conflicting (Crooks & Baur, 2011).

Another important sex hormone is oxytocin, often called the "cuddle hormone" because it is increased by sexual arousal and orgasm. The biological function of oxytocin is found in breastfeeding and bonding between the mother and her baby. Between sexual partners, levels of oxytocin and serotonin spike during lovemaking and orgasm, and stay high for several hours afterward, thus, making the couple feel relaxed and calm. This might be one of the reasons that men often fall asleep while women want to cuddle after climax. Another hormone called prolactin that men release during orgasm causes sleepiness and drowsiness.

Research has shown that autistic children, so often having problems in forming social attachments, have lower levels of oxytocin, confirming that humans need this hormone in facilitating social interactions (Crooks & Baur, 2011).

New research from Holland stated that men are not as empathetic and communicative as women are because they have higher levels of testosterone (Bos et al., 2016). The research study concluded that when women were administered high doses of testosterone, their ability to identify emotions was drastically lowered. This could also be seen on MRI brain scans where women who were given even low doses of testosterone showed fewer connections in the regions of the brain that affect emotional processing. The researchers speculated that people with autism had similar brain scans, thus, probably the reason for their autism spectrum disorder was exposure to testosterone in the womb during pregnancy (Bos et al., 2016).

Why do you think men have lower empathy levels than women? Could this be a survival mechanism from long ago when men were the hunters and providers? Killing animals is not an easy task. What other reasons can you think of?

MISTAKE # 35
Testosterone is a male hormone

Testosterone is a hormone produced in both women and men, though men produce 20 to 40 times more of the hormone than women do. They also produce estrogens but in much lower quantities than women do. Testosterone has been linked to sexual desire and sexual functioning in both sexes. Castrated men lack sexual desire and activity. Thus, we can assume that the hormone plays a major role in human sexuality.

Total testosterone levels in men vary from 300-1,200 ng/dL and in women between 20-50 ng/dL (nanograms per deciliter). These are conventional units used in the U.S. In Europe, Canada and rest of the world, we measure testosterone levels in SI units (comes from French - Système International d'Unités), and in nmol/L (nanomoles per liter), also called the metric system. The equivalent amounts in SI units for men are 10-42 nmol/L and for women 0.6 to 1.2 nmol/L (Winters, 1999).

When it comes to sexual behavior and libido, the free testosterone should be measured. Free testosterone, which is approximately 3% of total, is not bound to albumin or sex hormone-binding globulin (SHBG). These two proteins transport the testosterone in your body. Once they reach their final destination through the blood stream, they free the testosterone, thus, making it biologically active.

Testosterone levels in men have steadily declined during the years (Travison et al., 2007). Measurements made decades ago showed higher levels of testosterone levels in American men. The same applies to sperm quality. It is still unclear what factors have contributed to this decline. Testosterone is the primary male hormone for maintaining muscle and bone mass in men. It peaks in the late 20s and then declines from age 30 onward.

Testosterone levels in men

Laboratory Ranges (adapted from LabCorp)
Total Testosterone for Males
Age
7 months to 9 years   Less than 30 ng/dL (< 1.04 nmol/L)
10–13 years   1–619 ng/dL (0.04–21.48 nmol/L)
14–15 years   100–540 ng/dL (3.47–18.74 nmol/L)
16–19 years   200–970 ng/dL (6.94–33.66 nmol/L)
20–39 years   270–1,080 ng/dL (9.00–37.48 nmol/L)
40–59 years   350–890 ng/dL (12.15–30.88 nmol/ L)
60 years and older   350–720 ng/dL (12.15–24.98 nmol/L)

Reference Intervals for Free Testosterone
(free is about 2-4% of total)
Age
20–29 years old   9.3–26.5 picograms/mililiter (pg/mL)
30–39 years old   8.7–25.1 pg/mL
40–49 years old   6.8–21.5 pg/mL
50–59 years old   7.2–24.0 pg/mL

Testosterone in ng/dL × 0.0347 = Testosterone in nanomoles per
liter nmol/L.

The table above shows laboratory ranges of total and free testosterone in American males. These are the average levels and not the optimal levels for good health. Experts believe that the optimal level for healthy sexual functioning should be minimum 600 ng/dL (20 nmol/L) for total testosterone and approximately 20 pg/mL (700 pmol/L) for free testosterone.

MISTAKE # 36
Low hormone levels

Low testosterone levels have been linked to medical conditions such as diabetes, obesity, high blood pressure, heart disease, depression, anxiety, erectile dysfunction and low libido, among others.

Every man and woman should have their hormones checked when young and healthy. Testosterone levels are highest in the morning so the blood test should be done at this time. Women should make three blood tests during their menstrual cycle; on day one, 14 and 20 (Vliet, 2001). These tests should be saved for the future and serve as a baseline as we grow older. If you are a woman over 35, I highly recommend Dr. Elizabeth Lee Vliet's book *Screaming to be Heard: Hormonal Connections Women Suspect, and Doctors Still Ignore*. There, she explains everything you should know about hormones and how they affect our health.

Treatments for low testosterone

There are several treatments available for low levels of testosterone in both men and women. The most common ones are transdermal gels and skin patches, orally disintegrating tablets, and muscular injections or implants. Oral testosterone is also available but avoided because it may damage the liver.

Testosterone replacement therapy should only be considered after confirming the levels by a blood test and evaluating the symptoms by a physician. The common symptoms in men are: low libido (sex drive), erectile dysfunction, hair loss, decreased muscle mass, poor energy levels, depression, difficulty concentrating, irritability and low sense of well-being.

The risk of taking too much testosterone should not be ignored. Side effects could include heart disease, stroke, prostate cancer, blood clots or sleep apnea. The natural way to boost testosterone levels is changing the diet, exercising and losing weight. Obesity, alcohol, smoking and drug use are associated with low testosterone levels. For example marijuana reduces testosterone levels in men and lowers libido in both males and females (Crooks & Baur, 2011).

Freud and hormones

Not many people know that Sigmund Freud had a vasectomy when he was 67 years old while suffering from oral cancer. He used to smoke up to 20 cigars per day, even after being diagnosed with squamous cell carcinoma of the palate. In 1923, after several operations where parts of his jaw were removed, Freud opted for a "rejuvenation" procedure performed by Austrian endocrinologist Eugen Steinach (1861-1944). Steinach believed that a vasectomy would increase sexual potency in men. By halting sperm production in one of the testicles (he performed unilateral – one sided – vasectomy) he would increase hormone production in that testicle. This new boost of hormones would have a beneficial effect on overall well-being in aging men. At that time, sex hormones were not discovered yet, so Steinach's work was described as endocrine research on sex glands.

Originally, Steinach experimented on male rats by performing bilateral (both sides) vasectomy. He noticed that the senile rats that were almost dying were underweight and lethargic before the operation. Within a few weeks, they came back to life, gained weight, developed shiny fur and became sexually active, copulating up to 19 times per day. His next step was to experiment secretly on humans.

He performed three vasectomies on his patients without their knowledge while operating for other reasons. He noticed that within 18 months the patients manifested visible changes to their physique, and their overall vitality increased noticeably (Sengoopta, 2003).

Steinach was nominated six times for the Nobel Prize in physiology (1921 to 1938) but never received it. His rejuvenation procedure was discredited in 1935 when scientists discovered testosterone. Freud lived another 16 years after his vasectomy though he said that the procedure did nothing to improve his vitality.

SEXUAL DYSFUNCTIONS

Sexual dysfunction is rather common in society. Statistics say that almost 50% of women and 30% of men have some sexual dysfunction. Premature ejaculation is most common in younger men and erectile dysfunction in older men. Female orgasm disorders are discussed in Chapter 5. You will see some references to DSM-5 and ICD-10 in the disorder descriptions:

DSM-5 *Diagnostic and Statistical Manual of Mental Disorders*, Fifth Edition is the standard classification of mental disorders used by mental health professionals in the United States.

ICD-10 is the 10th revision of the *International Statistical Classification of Diseases and Related Health Problems* (ICD), a medical classification list by the World Health Organization (WHO).

Erectile Disorder (ED)

Whoever said that "laughter is the best medicine," never suffered from erectile dysfunction. Erectile disorder, dysfunction or simply impotence - from Latin impotentia coeundi - will happen to any man at least once in his lifetime.

Curtis (41) says:
>*This has never happened before. Last week we tried to have sex but I couldn't rise to the occasion. My wife was very disappointed. She believed it was her fault. It wasn't; it was me. I'm worried that this will happen again.*

MISTAKE # 37
Erectile dysfunction happens only to older men

According to DSM-5 (APA, 2013), 20% of young men are afraid of impotence when having sex for the first time. However, 8% did experience problems that hindered penetration during their first sexual experience. Between 13% to 21% of men who are 40 to 80 years old report occasional problems with erections. In the older group of men, those between 60 to 70 years old, 40% to 50% may have major problems with erections (APA, 2013).

Diagnostic criteria for Erectile Disorder (ED) according to DSM-5:

A. **At least one** of the three following symptoms must be experienced on almost all or all (approximately 75%-100%) occasions of sexual activity (in identified situational contexts or, if generalized, in all contexts):

1. Marked difficulty in obtaining an erection during sexual activity.
2. Marked difficulty in maintaining an erection until the completion of sexual activity.
3. Marked decrease in erectile rigidity.

B. The symptoms in Criterion A have persisted for a **minimum** duration of approximately **six months**.

C. The symptoms in Criterion A cause clinically significant distress in the individual.

D. The sexual dysfunction is not better explained by a nonsexual mental disorder or as a consequence of severe relationship distress or other significant stressors and is not attributable to the effects of a substance/medication or another medical condition.

According to recent research from the Netherlands, 40% of men 50 to 75 years old reported having difficulties with an erection (Schouten et al., 2010). ED is a very sensitive subject. Thus many men feel embarrassed to mention it to their doctors. The word impotence has a social stigma attached to it, a social taboo.

There are many causes of ED. Physical causes include:

- Cardiovascular disease - heart disease.
- Hardening of the arteries - clogged blood vessels (atherosclerosis).
- Stroke - a serious condition that occurs when the blood supply to the brain is interrupted.
- High cholesterol.
- High blood pressure - hypertension.
- Diabetes - affects blood supply and nerve endings in penis.
- Obesity.
- Kidney failure.
- Metabolic syndrome - a condition involving increased blood pressure, high insulin levels, body fat around the waist and high cholesterol.
- Parkinson's disease - a condition that affects the way the brain coordinates body movements, including walking, talking and writing.
- Multiple sclerosis - a condition that affects the body's actions, such as movement and balance.
- Peyronie's disease - development of scar tissue inside the penis.
- Prescription medications including antidepressants, diuretics, antihistamines and medications to treat high blood pressure, pain or prostate conditions.
- Tobacco use - restricts blood flow to veins and arteries, can cause chronic health conditions that lead to ED.
- Alcoholism and other forms of substance abuse. Especially long-term drug use or heavy drinking.
- Sleep disorders.
- Prostate surgery, radiation treatment for cancer, treatments for prostate cancer or enlarged prostate.
- Surgeries or injuries that affect the penis, the pelvic area or the spinal cord.
- Severe head injuries, 15-25% of people have problems with ED.
- Prolonged bicycling, which can compress nerves and affect blood flow to the penis, may lead to ED.

Source: Mayo Clinic (2016).

Hormonal conditions that can cause ED:

- Hypogonadism - causing low testosterone levels.
- Hyperthyroidism - an overactive thyroid gland.
- Hypothyroidism - an underactive thyroid gland.
- Cushing's syndrome - affects the production of cortisol.

Psychological conditions that can cause ED:

- Stress.
- Anxiety, especially performance anxiety.
- Depression.
- Poor communication.
- Relationship problems.
- Mental health conditions.

Erection starts in the brain. A man who has experienced ED in the past will automatically feel anxious about his next sexual encounter.

Travis (35) says:
> *My father died last year, and a few months ago, I lost my job. I feel depressed and anxious about the future. Last time my wife and I had sex, I couldn't sustain an erection. Since then I don't feel like sex at all.*

Treatments for ED:

- Psychological counseling - psychotherapy, couples and marriage counseling, and **sensate focus** exercises (see page 213).
- Oral medication - Viagra, Cialis, Levitra, Stendra.
- Penile injections - produce an erection that last one hour.
- Suppositories - put inside the penile urethra for erection.
- Testosterone replacement therapy.
- Penis pumps.
- Penile implants.
- Blood vessel surgery.
- Losing weight and eating a balanced diet.
- Start exercising - improves the blood flow to the penis.
- Quit smoking.
- Stop drinking.

- Stop taking illegal drugs.
- Sleep more.
- Stress less.
- Pelvic floor muscle exercises - Kegels (see page 219).

MISTAKE # 38
Smoking

The American Journal of Epidemiology published a study of 7,684 Chinese men aged 35 to 74 years (without clinical vascular disease) that found the more cigarettes the men smoked per day, the higher was the risk of impotence (He, 2007).

Premature (early) ejaculation (PE)

According to research, an average sex act lasts three to seven minutes. Premature ejaculation is when a man ejaculates within one minute of vaginal penetration (APA, 2013) or before he wishes to ejaculate. The ICD-10 places the cut-off time at 15 seconds (WHO, 1992). PE is the most common male sexual dysfunction that affects 20% to 30% of men, 18 to 70 years old (APA, 2013). PE is very common during first time intercourse, but if it continues, it can be seen as a sexual problem. Some men will ejaculate even before anticipated penetration or before their penis is fully erect, which can cause severe problems in the relationship.

Causes of PE:

- Psychological factors – early sexual experiences, religious confines, cultural aspects, secretive and hurried masturbation, guilt feelings.
- Childhood trauma related to sex.
- Sexual inexperience.
- Anxiety about sexual performance.
- Relationship problems.
- Novelty of a new relationship.
- Diabetes, high blood pressure and other health problems.
- Erectile dysfunction.
- Abnormal hormone levels and other biological problems.
- Stress.

Treatments for PE:

- Behavioral therapy (Kegels, squeeze technique and start-stop technique, edging). See below for details.
- SSRIs (antidepressants). These inhibit arousal and help with ejaculation control. Prescription is required. Side effects.
- Viagra, Levitra, Cialis - they can control and delay ejaculation. Side effects should be considered.
- Topical anesthetics, delay gels, creams and sprays, that desensitize the penis. These can spread to the partner though so using condoms is recommended.
- Condoms with Benzocaine (anesthetic that numbs the glans).
- Regular condoms can help to desensitize the penis.
- Penile injections. Only by physician.
- Masturbating few hours before intercourse.
- Thinking of something unsexy during sex. Works for some but not for all.

The squeeze technique

Masters and Johnson developed the squeeze technique for premature ejaculation. They stated that 98% of men with PE were helped with this exercise. The man should masturbate until he is close to orgasm. Then, just before ejaculation, he should firmly squeeze his penis, thus, stopping the orgasm. This exercise should be repeated several times, first alone and then with a partner. It has proven to be a successful tool in treating PE.

Start-stop method

This is a very common technique for PE. The man should masturbate until he is close to orgasm. Then, just before ejaculation, he should stop and relax, then start again. This exercise should be repeated several times until he can't hold it and must ejaculate.

Edging

Edging is a type of orgasm control. It involves building up the excitement and then stopping just before coming, then starting again and repeating the whole process several times. It can be done both by men and women, when masturbating or during intercourse. As women need more time to achieve an orgasm, from 20 to 30 minutes, men are rather quick to have one. By prolonging his time to her requirements, both can enjoy an orgasm instead of him coming first and her feeling frustrated. Unfortunately, this is a very common scenario and one of the main reasons that women are not interested in having sex.

Kegel exercises for men

You might have heard of Kegels for women (see page 219), but men can also do these exercises. The pubococcygeus (PC) muscle is located in the pelvic region. It stretches from the pubic bone to the tailbone (coccyx). This is the muscle that you use when you want to stop the urine flow. Practice next time when peeing to see exactly which muscle stops the flow. Next, try to clench and release this muscle several times, let's say for 10 seconds (or 10 times), then relax for 10 seconds and repeat. The next step is to contract the PC muscle for a longer time and more often. The goal is to hold it for 30 seconds several times per day. Men can also do this exercise with an erection. Put a small towel over your erect penis and try to lift the towel up by using the PC muscle. Finally, use these exercises during intercourse for better ejaculatory control. Kegels can also help with incontinence and overactive bladder.

MISTAKE # 39
An uncircumcised penis is more sensitive than a circumcised penis

Some people say that an uncircumcised penis is more sensitive than a circumcised one, therefore, more prone to PE but this is not what the research says. A study of sexual problems in traditionally Islamic countries, where circumcision is the norm, revealed that 39% of men in these countries suffer from premature ejaculation (Yasan & Gurgen, 2009). This ties to the notion that strict sexual upbringing, religious confines, secretive and hurried early masturbation, combined with anxiety and guilt feelings, can significantly contribute to PE.

Interview with an escort

A high-end (London-based) escort talks about her clients:

- Arab men can't hold it for long. Most of them suffer from premature ejaculation, as they usually come within 30 seconds. They also have daddy issues because they drop everything when their father calls.

- Japanese men can hold it a little longer, but they also suffer from premature ejaculation. They are very polite though and are a pleasure to work with.

- Asian men have small penises; African men have the longest penises. Too big is not good; it hurts. The average client has small to medium penis size.

- Russian guys are obnoxious. They drink a lot and are very ignorant. Germans come next in the loathsome department.

- Most of my clients are married men with children.

- One client used to send me all over the world to meet with him though we both live in London. One time he saw me for two hours in New York, but he paid for three days, hotel, round trip, all included. All I had to do was to wait for his call.

- I don't do anal, and I always say it upfront. However, I have had requests for some weird stuff like peeing on a client. Or a guy who stuck his penis into a Nutella jar and asked me to lick it. Another one would lick my feet for two hours and never take off his clothes or have sex with me.

- Some men don't want to have sex; they only want to talk or take me out to dinner. The rate is the same, though.

- A few clients wanted to marry me, at least they said so.

- Once a woman hired me to seduce her husband. She wanted to divorce him and needed evidence that he cheated on her. So I went to his work, but he was not interested. Back in my car, I called the wife to tell her that her husband was a good guy that probably would never cheat on her. While talking to her, I saw him coming out to his car and told her so. She asked me to follow him. He drove to a nearby park to meet up with a young woman who pushed a stroller. They started to kiss. I took some pictures with my phone and sent them over to the wife. She was shocked. The woman he kissed was their nanny.

Hypoactive Sexual Desire Disorder (HSDD)

Hypoactive sexual desire disorder (HSDD) is a sexual dysfunction in both men and women. In the new DSM-5, it has been replaced and divided into two separate disorders: Female Sexual Interest/Arousal Disorder and Male Hypoactive Sexual Desire Disorder. Research indicates that HSDD affects 43% of women and 31% of men in the United States (Laumann et al., 1999).

There are different subtypes of HSDD. It can be acquired or lifelong and general or situational. Acquired means that it started after a period of normal sexual desire and lifelong means, that the person always had low or no desire for sex. General means that the low desire is overall the same in all situations. Meanwhile, situational means it is only with a current partner.

HSDD affects mostly women though many men also seek help in therapy or counseling. It is the most common form of female sexual dissatisfaction (FSD) and often caused by relationship conflicts, lack of intimacy, lack of trust, anger and communication problems. Stress in daily life, fatigue, poor self-image and other sexual difficulties also contribute to HSDD.

Other factors such as medication use, menopause, hormone levels or depression can lower the libido. Recreational drugs such as marijuana, cocaine, amphetamines, barbiturates (tranquilizers or sedatives), alcohol and smoking tobacco, affect libido as well. Many common drugs such as antidepressants and birth control pills may affect sex drive and ability to reach orgasm. Menopausal women should check their hormone levels regularly, especially testosterone, which is directly linked to the libido, and should be over 20 nanograms per deciliter.

The main psychological factors that contribute to HSDD are sexual abuse or trauma, religious or cultural factors, life-event factors, relationship conflicts, conditioning/modeling patterns and body image issues. Marital conflict seems to be the main cause of HSDD.

Delayed ejaculation (DE)

According to DSM-5 (APA, 2013), only 75% of men ejaculate each time they have intercourse and 1% of men report problems with ejaculation, so delayed ejaculation (also called impaired ejaculation) doesn't seem to be such an issue to most men. The prevalence stays constant until the man reaches approximately 50 years, and then increases with age. Once they reach their 80s, the men report twice as many problems with ejaculations comparing to men below 59 years old (APA, 2013). Some men can only ejaculate when masturbating, either alone or with the help of a partner. There is no specific time according to APA (2013) for diagnosis of DE but, if a man needs 30 minutes or more to ejaculate, we can assume that he has a problem. Anejaculation is when a man is not able to ejaculate at all.

Several drugs and medications can contribute to delayed ejaculation. Cocaine (coke), methadone, alcohol, antihistamines (for allergies), antidepressants, anti-anxiety drugs, high blood pressure medication, Viagra, motion sickness pills, diuretics and gastrointestinal medications can cause ejaculation problems. Psychological factors such as anxiety, depression, stress, fear of pregnancy, religious taboos, relationship conflict, and porn addiction may cause DE as well. If you have this problem, see a urologist or a sex therapist for help.

VIAGRA – WHO NEEDS IT?

Viagra, Cialis and Levitra are drugs used for erectile dysfunction. They expand the blood vessels in the penis resulting in stronger and longer erections. In 1998, when Viagra was first introduced to the public, 40,000 prescriptions were made in the first 14 days, making it the fastest selling prescription drug in history. Viagra, which is produced by Pfizer, the second largest pharmaceutical company in the world after Swiss Novartis, generates almost two billion dollars of revenue per year. Pfizer's Viagra patent will expire in April 2020 but already in December 2017, generic Viagra will be available made by Teva Pharmaceuticals USA Inc., an Israeli company that made a deal with Pfizer, letting Teva be the first one to produce it. The patent on Cialis, made by Lilly, will expire in May 2018. The new generic

Viagra should become much cheaper than the original one that can cost up to 275 dollars for 10 tablets (50 mg). Viagra comes in 25, 50 and 100 mg tablets. Actually, a cheaper version of Viagra has already been available, but not many people know about it. A drug called Revatio, used for treating pulmonary arterial hypertension (PAH), contains 20 mg of sildenafil, the same component used in Viagra. Revatio costs much less than Viagra, approximately 30 dollars for 30 tablets, and in addition, should be covered by insurance, so the price is substantially lower. You could save hundreds of dollars per month by asking your doctor for a Revatio prescription instead of Viagra. Sildenafil should not be prescribed to patients who are on nitrate therapy, have any heart problem or have low blood pressure. Mixing Viagra with nitrates will widen the blood vessels and lower the blood pressure drastically. You could pass out or even die.

MISTAKE # 40
Viagra is only used by older men

You might think that only older men with erectile problems use Viagra. However, the majority of my male clients, regardless of age, have tried the drug. Most of the time, the wife/girlfriend is unaware of his recreational Viagra use. Some men take it "just in case" resulting in prolonged painful erections when the sex doesn't happen. Even men as young as 18-20 years old have tried Viagra with the aim to prolong the erection and to control the time of ejaculation. The refractory period, 20 minutes or longer in healthy men, can be shortened by 10 minutes on Viagra. The refractory period is the time after ejaculation when another erection is not possible.   Viagra should never be mixed with other recreational drugs or large amounts of alcohol.

Timothy (19) says:
> *All my friends have tried Viagra at least once. I like it because it gives me confidence and because I can hold it much longer before coming. I can also have another go shortly after.*

We don't know much about drug dependence regarding Viagra. Long time recreational use may lead to erectile dysfunction, even in younger men. Tolerance to the drug is another issue, as you might need larger doses with time for the same effect. I have noticed that there is a psychological dependence that is worrisome. Young men should not use Viagra unless really in need. Furthermore, there are many side effects of the drug.

Possible side effects of Viagra:
- Headache
- Flushing in the face, neck, or chest
- Feeling hot or irritable
- Rash
- Dry mouth or dry throat
- Upset stomach, indigestion, diarrhea
- Blue-tinted vision
- Difficulty to differentiate between the colors green and blue
- Abnormal or blurred vision
- Risk for double vision and temporary vision loss
- Loss or decrease of hearing
- Nasal congestion, sneezing
- Back pain
- Muscular pain or tenderness
- Nausea
- Dizziness, drowsiness
- Numbness of arms and legs
- Vertigo

Serious side effects of Viagra:
- Stroke
- Heart attack
- Heart palpitations
- Heartburn
- Shortness of breath
- Lightheadedness
- Chest pain or irregular heartbeat
- Arrhythmia (irregular heartbeat)
- Cardiomyopathy (enlarged heart)
- Change or loss of vision
- Ringing in ears or hearing loss
- Swelling in the feet, ankles, and hands

MISTAKE # 41
Viagra is an aphrodisiac

It is important to remember that Viagra is not an aphrodisiac; it will not make you sexually aroused by itself. You will need sexual stimulation for Viagra to work. The tablet should be taken 30 minutes to one hour before sex, and it should work for approximately four hours. It doesn't mean that you will have an erection for four hours, but that the ability to help produce an erection begins to wear off after four hours.

MISTAKE # 42
Overdosing on Viagra

Overdosing on Viagra can be fatal. This happened to a man who wanted to impress his girlfriend so much that instead of one blue pill he swallowed the whole box. Unfortunately, he died of a heart attack shortly after. Viagra should not be taken more often than once per day and only one dose. This medication is for men with erectile dysfunction and should not be used for recreational purposes.

Prolonged erections - Priapism

Erectile dysfunction drugs (Viagra, Levitra, Cialis, and Stendra) can cause prolonged, persistent and painful erections. This condition is called priapism and can last for several hours or even days. It requires urgent medical treatment, often involving aspiration of blood from the penis. The word priapism comes from Greek mythology. Priapus, the well-endowed God of fertility, son of Zeus and Aphrodite, had a constant oversized erection. His enormous erect phallus has been depicted in several frescos and paintings.

There have been reports of men who had their penises amputated due to Viagra overdose. Once gangrene starts in the penis, the doctors have no choice but to amputate it to prevent the gangrene from spreading to other parts of the body. Gangrene is dead tissue caused by an infection or lack of blood flow. It usually starts in toes or fingers but in this case, it affects the erect penis. If your erection lasts longer than four hours, you should contact a physician. There is a high risk of erectile dysfunction if the erection persists after 4-12 hours. Gangrene can set in after 24 hours of priapism, so it is imperative to see a doctor immediately. Between 2006 and 2009 in the United States alone, 32,462 men visited emergency rooms presenting with priapism (Roghmann et al., 2013).

MISTAKE # 43
A good lover can hold it for a long time

This is another belief due to the porn industry and men's bragging; the super-stud with a large penis who can stroke it away for over one hour (or whatever the length of the movie). Most women don't like prolonged thrusting. They need direct clitoral stimulation to achieve an orgasm, preferably by oral sex. Ask your partner what she likes before assuming things. Furthermore, prolonging intercourse can be painful to the woman. It can lead to tearing, vaginal abrasions, even urinary tract infections (UTI), and yeast infections. Some women will fake an orgasm to get it over with faster.

MISTAKE # 44
A full bladder causes morning erections

Morning erections, nocturnal penile tumescence (NPT) also called "morning wood" or "morning glory" are healthy and experienced by most men. They are not caused by a full bladder, as many people believe. They occur several times per night during periods of rapid eye movement (REM) sleep, though men older than sixty may have them during non-REM sleep as well. In the morning, REM sleep is longer than during the night. Therefore, most men wake up with an erection that typically goes away within a few minutes after awakening.

If a man does not experience morning erections, he may have an erectile dysfunction problem. A healthy man will have between three and five erections per night. On average, they last between 25 to 35 minutes. Think of this as penis exercise that goes on all night.

Morning erections may be caused by specific neuroreflexes, which are stimulated during REM sleep and are connected to testosterone and norepinephrine hormones. The nerves in the penis free nitrous oxide that expands blood vessels and increases blood flow to the penis as well as the man's heart rate.

Most men will have nightly erections during their life, and the awareness of them may vary. Not all men will wake up with an erection in the morning, though their penis may stay erect up to two hours during the night, so the "morning wood" expression is not correct and has nothing to do with time, but rather the a person's stage of sleep.

MISTAKE # 45
Only men use Viagra

VIAGRA FOR WOMEN

Women have been using Viagra for several years, not for sexual arousal but to increase fertility. When inserted vaginally (never orally), Viagra improves the blood flow to the uterus, thus, thickening the endometrial lining. The thickness of the lining is very important in achieving a pregnancy. Viagra suppositories can be produced by a pharmacist and administered at the beginning of the menstrual cycle. Viagra therapy has been proven effective in IVF treatment. According to research done by Dr. Sher (SIRM), after one cycle with Viagra, 70% of women with previous IVF failures and thin endometrial lining improved the thickness of their lining, 45% gave birth to a baby and 9% miscarried.

FEMALE VIAGRA
FLIBANSERIN - ADDYI

In August 2015, the U.S. Food and Drug Administration (FDA) approved a drug for low sexual desire in premenopausal women called Addyi. This is the first drug for hypoactive sexual desire disorder (HSDD) ever approved by the FDA. Flibanserin was originally used as an antidepressant, but it failed to be approved as such. One of the side effects of this drug was that some women reported a slight increase in sexual desire after using it for depression.

Viagra for men works by increasing the blood flow to the penis. Flibanserin, on the other hand, operates on the brain, increasing dopamine (feel good hormone) levels. However, the desired effect of increasing sexual desire works only on 10% of women, meanwhile

Viagra works on almost all men. Furthermore, men take Viagra only when they want to have sex but women need to take Addyi every day, and it takes several weeks to see any results. The worst part is the side effects of Addyi: dizziness, sleepiness, nausea, fatigue, insomnia and dry mouth. Also, the drug can't be taken together with alcohol so the woman taking it must stop drinking altogether. Being such a new drug there is no information about the long-term risks involved. The question is whether Flibanserin is worth all the trouble for so little payoff.

Why do nursing homes give Viagra to their male patients?
To keep them from rolling out of bed.

MISMATCHED DESIRE

As we already established earlier, one of the most common problems in couples therapy is the desired frequency of sexual intercourse. Very often, the libidos don't match, especially after a year or so into the relationship. Research concluded that the longer the relationship progressed, the less sex the women wanted while men's desire stayed the same (Klusmann, 2002; Murray & Milhausen, 2012). Research also shows that in happy relationships couples have sex at least once per week. The more sex the couple has, the more marital satisfaction there is (Frederick et al., 2016). The conclusion of this could be that the desire disparity leads to marital dissatisfaction, conflict and distress in relationships.

Barbara says:
> *I don't feel like sex anymore. The more he nags, the less sex we have. I prefer to use my vibrator when he is away.*

Marcus says:
> *I feel alone in my marriage. She has rejected me so many times that I don't even try to initiate sex anymore.*

Some happy couples have sex once a month or a couple of times per year, but as long as they both agree with this, thus their desires match, all is good. Approximately 30-40% of couples complain about desire discrepancy, and 50% are not happy with their sex life.

Derek says:

> *We used to have sex every night. Since the baby was born, we have sex 2-3 times per week. That's not enough for me. We should have it more often.*

MISTAKE # 46
He wants sex "all the time"

This is a common complaint that I hear from my female clients. Some men want to have sex every day, some two to three times per week. For most women this is too much. Unless you are at the beginning of your relationship when sex happens all the time, having sex once or twice per week is sufficient. This is what happily married people in long-term relationships do. Couples with small children have sex less often than other people. In Derek's case, I was really surprised that he expected to have more sex than two to three times per week. His wife was exhausted, still breastfeeding their six-month-old baby and getting up almost every night when the baby cried while Derek "needed his sleep" because he was working long hours.

MISTAKE # 47
Saying "NO" to your partner

If you haven't had sex for a long time and your partner initiates it, consider doing it though you might not be in the mood. Sometimes, just like going to the gym, you don't feel motivated at first, but once there, it feels great. You might need to push yourself a little. Remember that consensual sex is good for both of you. I am not saying that you should put out for him, as both of you should have full enjoyment from the encounter.

MISTAKE # 48
Rape within marriage

Marital or spousal rape is non-consensual sex that happens within a marriage. Needless to say, this is wrong and should never happen; however, it does happen every day. In many countries, marital rape is tolerated and not considered a crime. In the Unites States (all 50 states), it has been illegal since 1993. The prevalence of spousal rape is 30% in the U.S., and only 3% of the victims report the crime to the police. As many as 70% of the victims will be raped again by their spouse. If you are one of the victims, get help. See pages 186-187 for more information.

MISTAKE # 49
Too stressed or tired for sex

Men and women are different when it comes to stress and sex. Men want to relieve their stress by having sex. Women, on the other hand, need to deal with the stress first and then have sex when they are feeling more relaxed. In today's busy society, most women are stressed out. By the time we go to bed at night, we are exhausted. Our brains are occupied with planning the next day's activities. A better alternative is to have sex in the morning. Set the alarm 30 minutes before your usual time and see what happens. Men's testosterone levels peak in the morning so you might be pleasantly surprised. I would advise you to get up first, pee and brush your teeth before jumping back into bed again.

Another alternative would be to have afternoon sex on weekends. Interestingly enough, women tend to ovulate in the afternoon, meaning that the optimal hormone level for female sexual desire happens at that time.

If you are a woman, you can also deal with the stress by "switching off" your brain for let's say 30 minutes and concentrating on your sexual pleasure, with either your partner or masturbating alone.

MISTAKE # 50
The pill

Birth control pills and other hormonal devices may lower your libido. Another form of birth control to recommend would be an intrauterine device (IUD) or coil, in some countries also known as a spiral. Make sure to use the copper one and not the hormonal one that might affect your hormone production. It is important to mention that an IUD will not stop you from contracting sexually transmitted diseases (STDs) or sexually transmitted infections (STIs). Using a condom is the best option if you are not in a committed monogamous relationship.

MISTAKE # 51
Medication

Though medication may be necessary for your health, it is important to know that several kinds of meds can lower your libido. For example, antidepressants, also called selective serotonin reuptake inhibitors (SSRIs) increase serotonin levels in the brain, thus lower oxytocin, which is a hormone directly connected with sexual response and orgasm in both women and men. Prozac, Luvox, Zoloft, Paxil and Lexapro are a few known SSRIs. These are proven to lower libido in 60% of people, therefore a better option is to switch to Wellbutrin or Celexa as they have less sexual side effects (Berman & Berman, 2001). Testosterone and dopamine, on the other hand, stimulate and increase the sexual desire in both sexes.

Benzodiazepines, anti-anxiety drugs such as Xanax, anti-seizure drugs and some beta-blockers (for the heart) can lower the libido. Statins such as Zocor and Lipitor, drugs that lower cholesterol in the blood, reduce the ability to achieve an orgasm and may cause sexual dysfunction according to a study from San Diego School of Medicine, California, that included 1,016 men and women (Golomb & Evans, 2008).

Other medications such as antihistamines, found in allergy and cold medicines, may cause vaginal dryness, making intercourse painful, therefore lowering the libido. Vaginal dryness is often seen in older women, more about that in Chapter 14. Using a lubricant could help with this issue. One should always remember that medications often come with side effects.

MISTAKE # 52
Drinking alcohol

Alcohol is associated with low testosterone levels in men, inhibiting the production in the testes, thus lowering the libido and sexual performance. It also lowers vasopressin and oxytocin levels, which are involved in penile erection. Psychologically, alcohol reduces inhibition, which may lead to increased sexual behavior. However, physiologically, it decreases sexual arousal, lowers sexual performance, and the ability to orgasm declines. In women, alcohol increases sexual arousal, thus, acting as a sexual disinhibitor. Men know this too well; Champagne - makes girls dance and drop their pants (Masquerade, 1988).

MISTAKE # 53
Marijuana, Cannabis, Pot, Weed

Cannabis (marijuana, pot, weed) is the most commonly used illegal drug in the world. Marijuana reduces testosterone levels in men and lowers libido in both men and women (Crooks & Baur, 2011). The Internet is flooded with testimonies from marijuana users who swear that smoking pot is enhancing their sex drive. What the drug does for some people is to lower their inhibitions, relax the muscles and increase their sensitivity to touch, thus enhancing the sexual experience. Yet, for others, it hinders their sexual performance.

Recent animal and in vitro studies found a link between cannabis and sexual dysfunction (Shamloul & Bella, 2011). Another study from Fred Hutchinson Cancer Research Center in Seattle, Washington, found a link between marijuana use and the most aggressive form of testicular cancer (Daling et al., 2009). Men who smoke marijuana had a 70% higher risk of testicular cancer, a specific type called nonseminoma that mostly affects young men between the ages of 20 and 35. This study included 1,348 males between 18 to 44 years old. Another study from Buffalo University concluded that long-term marijuana use damages the sperm (Burkman et al., 2003).

Many people can only have sex when they are either drunk or stoned. Daily use of marijuana, according to a Chicago study, has a measurable effect on the brain. Researchers found that two years after stopping marijuana, the subjects manifested brain changes similar to schizophrenia-related brain abnormalities, possibly indicating long-term effects (Smith et al., 2013). The earlier the marijuana use started, the more abnormal brain changes were reported. Another study from the University of Minnesota on adolescent brain development found that there is a connection between repeated exposure to cannabis and brain resting functional connectivity, intelligence and cognitive function. Lower intelligence quotient (IQ) and slower cognitive function were measured in these individuals (Camchong, 2016).

MISTAKE # 54
Using drugs

Recreational drugs such as cocaine, amphetamines, barbiturates (tranquilizers or sedatives), and opioids (Vicodin, OxyContin, and Percocet), morphine and codeine are not only addictive but lower the sex drive as well. They can cause erectile disorders and inhibit orgasms in both women and men.

MISTAKE # 55
Poor diet

We all know that a healthy lifestyle contributes to a better sex life. Eating greasy fast foods, burgers and fries is not a good idea. The trans-fatty acids found in fried foods decrease the libido and cause abnormal sperm production in men. You can boost your testosterone production by changing your diet to a healthy one. The fatty foods can cause hardening and narrowing of arteries (atherosclerosis) causing erectile dysfunction in men. Cutting out the junk food and eating more vegetables and fruits is a good start.

A study from Australia published in the *Journal of Sexual Medicine* concluded that obese diabetic men improved their erectile function, sexual desire, testosterone levels, and urinary symptoms by losing 5% to 10% of their bodyweight over eight weeks time (Khoo et al., 2011). They were put on a low-calorie diet (approximately 1,000 calories per day) and a low-fat, high-protein reduced-carbohydrate diet, prescribed to reduce their daily intake by approximately 600 calories per day.

MISTAKE # 56
Too much sugar

Consuming vast amounts of sugar lowers both the total and free testosterone levels (Caronia et al., 2013). You might not think about it, but sugar is everywhere so read the labels carefully. Sugar increases insulin in the blood, which makes your testosterone levels drop, lose muscle mass and store belly fat. Body fat and especially stomach fat stores the hormone estrogen in men, causing them erectile dysfunction, low libido and man boobs (gynecomastia).

MISTAKE # 57
Licorice

Licorice contains glycyrrhizic acid, which is known to reduce testosterone levels in both men and women. It also makes you gain weight. Several studies have confirmed that especially men should not consume licorice because it lowers interest in sex and causes erectile dysfunction.

MISTAKE # 58
Vitamin and iron deficiency

Women need more iron than men do because they lose blood each month during menstrual periods. Iron deficiency or anemia leads to fatigue and consequently lowers the libido. Your body needs vitamins and minerals to produce testosterone, mainly vitamin A, B (3,6,12), C, D, E and minerals selenium and zinc.

Vitamin A increases sex hormone production in both men and women. In men, it is vital for sperm production. Vitamin A is a fat-soluble vitamin, so it needs to be consumed together with fat for optimal absorption. Vitamin A can be found in sweet potatoes, carrots, dark leafy greens such as kale and spinach, squash, lettuce, dried apricots, cantaloupe melons, bell peppers, sweet red peppers, tomatoes, mangos, watermelons, tuna fish, liver and all tropical fruits.

Vitamin B is beneficial to sex drive, testosterone production, erectile function and intensity of orgasms. Vitamin B can be found in bananas, avocados, eggs and many more foods. Vitamin B12 can be found in milk products, eggs, cheese, fish, meat, shellfish and poultry. Vegans, people who don't eat animal products, need supplementation of vitamin B12 cobalamin.

Folic Acid/Folate is a B vitamin crucial to fertility not only for women but also for men because it increases sperm quality. We all know the benefits of folic acid in preventing birth defects especially spina bifida (neural tube defect) and anencephaly (abnormal development of the brain). If you are planning to get pregnant then supplementing folic acid is a must. Folic acid deficiency can also lead to depression (Coppen, 2005). Foods such as grain products, cereals, pasta and bread are often fortified with folic acid in the United States but not in Europe. Food fortification is a controversial subject. For example, in 2004, Denmark banned Kellogg's from adding vitamins and minerals to their products. Other sources of folic acid are green vegetables, asparagus, avocados, cauliflower, nuts, sunflower seeds, beets, carrots, celery, oranges, bananas, corn, dairy products, eggs, poultry, meat, seafood and fruits.

Vitamin C is widely known for its benefits to general health. It strengthens the immune system, and it aids in the production of sex hormones. A study from Dubai that included 13 infertile men, ages between 25 to 35 years, confirmed that twice-daily supplementation of 1,000 mg of vitamin C, for two months, improved sperm count, sperm motility, and sperm morphology significantly (Akmal et al., 2006). Vitamin C can be found in citrus fruits, kiwis, strawberries, papaya, Brussels sprouts, broccoli, cauliflower, sweet potatoes and sweet peppers.

Vitamin D is necessary for estrogen production in women and testosterone production in men. It boosts your libido so if you feel friskier in the summer, this is the reason. Lack of vitamin D can lead to depression; thus, many people feel moody in the dark winter months. Read more about vitamin D on page 77 and page 198.

Vitamin E also called the "brain vitamin" because it reduces the risk of stroke and Alzheimer's disease is essential for sperm production and sperm motility. Lack of vitamin E can cause erectile dysfunction, low libido and infertility; therefore, it is often used in infertility treatments. Vitamin E can be found in sunflower seeds, almonds, spinach, Swiss chard, avocados, peanuts, turnip greens, asparagus, beet greens, mustard greens and vegetable oils.

Selenium has an important role in sperm production. Almost half of the selenium in men's bodies is stored in the testes and seminal ducts. Couples that are trying to conceive should take selenium supplements because this mineral improves sperm motility and regulates thyroid function. Selenium can be found in nuts and seeds, seafood, beef, liver, lamb, chicken, turkey, eggs, pork, mushrooms, onions, wheat germ, oats and barley.

Zinc that is required for the production of sperm in men and testosterone in both men and women can be found in seafood, beef, lamb, wheat germ, spinach, pumpkin and squash seeds, nuts, chocolate, pork, chicken, beans, mushrooms, garlic and brown rice. Zinc is also necessary for prostate function so zinc deficiency will affect your sex life.

Magnesium is an aphrodisiac that improves the libido and sexual performance in both sexes because it boosts testosterone and estrogen production. You will find magnesium in bananas, dark leafy greens, seeds, nuts, avocados, dark chocolate, dried fruit, yogurt, beans, whole grains, fish, rice and more.

MISTAKE # 59
Lack of sun and vitamin D

Most people living in northern latitudes are vitamin D deficient, especially during the winter months (Ginde, Liu, & Camargo, 2009). Even during the summer, we don't get enough vitamin D because we are scared of the UV rays causing us skin cancer and premature aging. Though too much sun can be damaging to the skin, 20 to 30 minutes daily of direct sun exposure is needed for good health.

Vitamin D is essential for estrogen production in women and testosterone production in men. It boosts your libido so if you feel friskier in the summer, this is the reason. Lack of vitamin D can lead to depression; thus, many people feel moody in the dark winter months. Vitamin D is essential for calcium absorption in the body. Read more about vitamin D on page 76 and page 198.

MISTAKE # 60
Lack of exercise

By exercising and losing weight, you can improve your sex life. There is a direct link between obesity and sexual dysfunction in men. Men with a waistline larger than 40 inches (102 cm) have a much higher risk to develop erectile dysfunction than men with smaller waists. Exercise improves circulation in the body, and that includes the blood flow to your genital area, consequently increasing the desire and lifting your mood. The fact is that any reduction in weight, however small, in obese individuals contributes to better sexual performance.

MISTAKE # 61
Skewed body image

Body image and sexual satisfaction go hand in hand in both men and women. Men want more muscles and women are obsessed with thinness. Some women don't want to have sex because they think that they look fat. This is regardless of whether she weights 50 kg (110 lbs) or 75 kg (165 lbs). Even those with only a few kilograms to lose feel sexually unattractive and suffer from low self-esteem. The eternal chase for a perfect body is ruining people's sexual desires.

Alexandra says:
> *I gained three kilos (seven pounds) since Christmas so right now we are not having sex. I need to lose weight first.*

Erika says:
> *I hate my post-pregnancy body. I will never have sex again.*

Julie says:
> *Look at my thighs! They are huge. No amount of exercise can fix them. I need liposuction.*

Amanda says:
> *I broke my leg last year and gained weight. I don't want to date until the extra pounds are gone and I feel better about myself.*

All four women are absolutely gorgeous. They are smart and highly intelligent. If you saw them on the street you would think that they were beautiful, confident young women; yet, they all feel insecure when it comes to their body image. In the age of social media, where daily selfies are the norm, and every photo is retouched, edited, manipulated with filters and so on, it's hard to know what is real and what is fake. The thigh-gap, the empty space between the upper thighs, has become an unrealistic body ideal, an obsession for millions of young women.

We live in a world where the most beautiful models are not good enough to be portrayed in the media, as they need to be photo-shopped first. How crazy is this? How much pressure is this causing on the "normal" women out there to live up to the perfect image of a sexy and desirable female? If you feel insecure about having sex because your body is not perfect, then think again. Don't deprive yourself of sexual pleasure with your husband, boyfriend, partner. It's a waste of time. Embrace your body as it is and have great sex - now. Life is too short. Don't wait until you have the perfect body because that might put you off another few years - or decades. One day you will wake up in your fifties or sixties and realize that you wasted all these years chasing the ideal body image. It's not worth it. It's about living in the here and now with any shape or form of your beautiful body because every woman is beautiful in her unique way. Love your body; love yourself.

MISTAKE # 62
Sleep deprivation

Research shows that sleep apnea is linked to lower libido, lower testosterone levels, and sexual dysfunction, in not only men but women as well. Men with restless legs syndrome (RLS) are 78% more likely to have erectile disorder. Even for young men in their twenties, lack of sleep (five or fewer hours per night) lowers testosterone production (Leproult & Van Cauter, 2011).

Veronica says:

> *My husband snores really loud - every night. His snoring drives me crazy. I try to poke him so he will change his position. Sometimes it works and sometimes not. He can turn over but still continues to snore. I have tried earplugs, noise machines and sleeping on the sofa. I could still hear him in the living room!*

Snoring is a big problem in relationships. The National Sleep Foundation website states that 67% of U.S. adults snore. Many couples decide to have separate bedrooms due to snoring. This leads to less intimacy and less sex. According to the British Snoring & Sleep Apnea Association (BSSAA), 31% of couples sleep in separate rooms. Sleep is essential to our health so having separate bedrooms is a good short-term solution; however, doing something about the origin of the problem is better.

Sleep apnea is a common and serious condition; therefore, it requires medical attention. Continuous positive airway pressure (CPAP) therapy is the best treatment for obstructive sleep apnea. This is a mask that you wear during the night while you sleep. It opens the airway and eliminates the breathing pauses, thus stopping the snoring and choking noises. Sleep apnea has been linked to cardiovascular disease and cancer (Martínez-García et al., 2012; Nieto et al., 2012).

MISTAKE # 63
Sex is boring

So make it more fun. Are you one of those couples that settle down in the relationship? You find your comfort zone; you trade sexy lingerie for leggings and oversized t-shirts. He starts to wear sportswear around the house and doesn't shave on the weekends. How sexy is that? When familiarity sets in – the passion moves out. Just like the Mistake # 17 "Lack of mystery" on page 33, too much familiarity kills sexual desire. You need to change things, to spice up your mundane sex life and stop the "duty sex" attitude. Start dating each other again; start flirting.

Make an effort with your appearance. If you are a man, then shave for her. Put on nice clothes so she can see how sexy you are. The two of you are supposed to be lovers, not siblings. Compliment each other when you look nice; notice when your spouse makes an effort. Validation is important to the relationship. Praise and flattery are ego boosting; they motivate people. Self-confidence is sexy so help your partner to feel good.

Try to make sex more spontaneous by changing the time and place. Have sex in the morning or during lunchtime. Try new places to have sex, maybe on the sofa, in the car or on the kitchen countertops? Or how about the back row of a movie theater? Be careful though because sex is illegal in public places. Dare her to go out without her panties on. Try role-playing; dressing up and pretending to be someone else can be fun. Meet up in a bar and pretend that you just met or hire a babysitter and rent a room instead of going out to dinner. Order room service and have your dinner in bed after you had sex. Have a bath together. Be inventive, have fun. Don't take life too seriously. Happy couples know how to laugh together.

MISTAKE # 64
Not enough mental foreplay

Good sex starts in the mind. Setting the mood for sex is important, especially to women. I am talking here about the mental foreplay that happens days in advance, not the one that you have just before sex. Make sure to be attentive to your partner. Small gestures and nice comments are significant to setting the right mood for sex.

I often hear of women who wait all day long for the husbands to get back home from work. She prepares dinner, she anticipates the interaction when he gets through the door, what she is going to tell him about. She imagines what will happen after the dinner; she even feels frisky. Then, the moment he gets home, he makes some stupid comment about her dinner choice or the way she looks, or something trivial about her day, ruining her mood completely. Just because you bring home the bacon doesn't mean that you can behave in this manner. Mutual respect and appreciation will get you more sex than finding flaws in your partner.

Ella says:

> *I had my hair and nails done yesterday, then rushed to the store to get his favorite beer, then spent two hours cooking. He entered the door 30 minutes late, no apology, and the first thing he did was to ask if I got his suit back from the cleaners. He didn't notice my new haircut or the new lipstick I was wearing. A total turn off for me.*

Jeffrey says:

> *I was in meetings all day yesterday. Someone spilled coffee on my suit; there was an accident on the road and by the time I got home, I was exhausted. I had another meeting this morning, so I needed my suit back from the cleaners. Is it too much to ask? She has all day long for herself. Meanwhile I have to work so we can pay the bills and go on fancy vacations. Who is the victim here?*

There is no need to play the victim. You are a team. Focus on the positives in your relationship. Make it a routine to have a moment with your wife when you enter the door. Look into her eyes, kiss her and ask her about her day. It only takes a minute but makes such a difference for the rest of the evening. It may even save your marriage.

MISTAKE # 65
Lack of sexting etiquette

About the above-mentioned mental foreplay, flirting and sexting can be fun. It builds the anticipation. Men are visual creatures so text him something like, "Missing your hands on my bum," or "I love it when you kiss my neck, just behind my ear." This should get him into a frenzy of lust. If you are a guy, try this: "I can't stop thinking about you," or "I love the taste of your lips (or other parts of her)." Do NOT send her a photo of your penis. Moreover, make sure your text doesn't go to your parents or your kids by mistake. Double check before pressing the send button.

MISTAKE # 66
No romance

Lack of romantic gestures is a big problem in long-term relationships. Many men have no clue what romance is about. Here is a list of things that women find romantic:

- ✓ Say I love you several times per day and before you fall asleep.
- ✓ Buy me flowers for no reason.
- ✓ Plan my birthday, our anniversary and Valentine's Day in advance; don't wait to the last minute.
- ✓ Look in my eyes and kiss me.
- ✓ Kiss me in public.
- ✓ Make out with me without expecting sex.
- ✓ Rub my feet or my back without me asking for it.
- ✓ Touch me because you love me, not because you want to have sex.
- ✓ Hold my hand when you walk with me.
- ✓ Surprise me with a small gift.
- ✓ Court me.
- ✓ Take me out to dinner.
- ✓ Watch a girly movie with me.
- ✓ Write me a note and hide it inside my bag.
- ✓ Listen to me.
- ✓ Tell me that I am beautiful and amazing.
- ✓ Compliment me.
- ✓ Watch the sunset with me.
- ✓ See the stars with me.
- ✓ Text me or email me, for no reason, just to say you miss me.
- ✓ Help me in the kitchen.
- ✓ Make dinner sometimes.
- ✓ Clean the dishes.

- ✓ Ask to help; even if I say no, ask again.
- ✓ Wash my car.
- ✓ Clean out the garage.
- ✓ Make me a cup of tea or coffee.
- ✓ Fold the laundry with me.
- ✓ Kiss me again and say that you love me.

SEX WHEN TRYING TO CONCEIVE

When trying to conceive, the beginning is always fun, but soon enough the problems start. Sex on demand is not fun. Regardless of whether you are tired or not, sex becomes a pre-ovulatory chore. When a couple is going through infertility, the focus stays on the ovulation, thus eliminating the spontaneity.

Patricia says:

> *We have been trying to get pregnant since last year. Each month is worse as the tension around my ovulation destroys the relationship. We both get very anxious. Sex is so mechanical now. The only reason to have sex is the sperm deposit.*

Many men who never had a problem in the past suddenly develop performance anxiety and might not be able to rise to the occasion or ejaculate. This creates conflict in the relationship because timing is crucial to conception.

Tammy says:

> *We are going through IVF treatment. Yesterday, my husband was required to give his sperm sample at the hospital. He was not able to ejaculate. He said he couldn't do it in that room. I was furious with him.*

Suddenly, a lifetime of protected sex, when avoiding getting pregnant was a priority, turns into a baby-making mission. Women who spent years on contraceptives unexpectedly find themselves infertile. This can be a huge blow to the couple as the stigma and shame of infertility is still around us. People around us can be very judgmental, often having negative attitudes toward artificial reproductive technologies. Relatives might ask insensitive questions.

Coworkers and friends are telling you that they understand what you are going through but unless they walk a mile in your shoes, no, they don't understand and they never will.

Angela says:

> *Everyone at the office is getting pregnant. I can't stand it anymore. I want to be happy for them but inside I'm crying. The pain is unbearable.*

Catherine says:

> *I see babies everywhere; in the shops, at the doctor's, on the bus, they are everywhere! I see the ads for Pampers, for baby food and for toys. Happy mothers with beautiful babies. I wonder if I ever will be one of these mothers. Why is God punishing me? What have I done wrong?*

The reality is that infertility is a lonely journey. You and your partner might not want to share your struggle with family or friends. The details about his sperm count or quality of your eggs are private. Remember, it is your human right to have a baby so never apologize to anyone or feel that you have to explain your choices. Try to maintain a strong relationship with your spouse as you work through the emotional and physical issues of infertility. Good luck on your journey.

CHAPTER 5

THE BIG O AND THE MULTIPLE O'S,
CAN I HAVE IT ALL?
THE "G" SPOT – DOES IT EVEN EXIST?
FEMALE EJACULATION AND FEMALE PROSTATE

There are many misconceptions about the female orgasm. From faking it to having multiple orgasms, I will explain it all here. And yes, men are faking it too. In this chapter, I also discuss the importance of female anatomy, the G-spot, female ejaculation, the sexual response cycle and simultaneous orgasms. The importance of Kegel exercises, detailed instructions on G-spot stimulation and a multiple "O" practice guide are also included in this chapter. Finally, I explain how men can have multiple orgasms.

What is an orgasm?

Sexuality helps to strengthen the bond between partners. Not only intercourse alone but through kissing, touching and lusting after each other. When we feel attraction for someone, our heart rate increases. Blood levels of the stress hormone cortisol and adrenaline rise. Then dopamine and serotonin follow, both neurotransmitters that have effects similar to amphetamine and cocaine, bringing on an intense high of pleasure.

An orgasm, or the big "O," is the body's climactic physiological reaction to sexual stimulation (climactic means "forming a climax"). It releases the neurohormones oxytocin and vasopressin. During orgasm, activity in the cerebral cortex slows. The cerebral cortex rules the conscious layers of the brain such as awareness, attention, memory and thought process. Conversely, activity increases in the limbic area of the brain that controls the unconscious part of the mind. This is the reason that orgasms cause uncontrolled vocalizations and body movements (Crooks & Baur, 2011).

Interestingly, scientists believe that oxytocin, a hormone released during orgasm, and vasopressin deepen feelings of attachment, but not equally in men and women. While women get the oxytocin rush fully; in men, their high testosterone levels counteract the oxytocin neurohormone, thus, lowering its effects. So, by achieving an orgasm, a woman bonds with the man stronger than he bonds with her. It seems that women are genetically predisposed to form an attachment to their spouses and children.

Therapists encourage couples to have frequent sex, stressing the importance of sexual bonding. Vasopressin also plays an important role in long-term relationships. Genetic variation in vasopressin receptors has been connected to fear of commitment in several studies (Walum, 2008).

What is the purpose of orgasms?

The orgasm has evolutionary value for men and probably for women in increasing the pleasure of sexual intercourse and thereby increasing the likelihood that one's genes will be spread into future generations. The orgasm also increases pair bonding between the man and woman.

MISTAKE # 67
Sex without orgasm

Orgasm is a major source of enjoyment for both men and women. It is the climax of the sex act for many, and those who do not achieve orgasm (mostly women) often feel they are missing out on full sexual enjoyment. Though we can enjoy the sex act even without orgasm because the intimacy and closeness with the partner feel so fulfilling, there is no reason why we should settle and stop trying to have one. Statistics say that 95% of men reach orgasm when having sex with a partner, but only 69% of women do the same (Richters et al., 2006).

Those women who achieved orgasm did so due to the help of other practices than vaginal intercourse such as oral sex and manual stimulation of the clitoris. If oral sex is performed skillfully, almost all women can climax, as lesbian couples report the highest sexual satisfaction and orgasmic response. According to the DSM-5, 10% of women will never experience an orgasm in their lifetime due to *female orgasmic disorder.*

Lucy says:
> *I was married for over 30 years to a selfish guy. Only now in my 50s have I learned how to enjoy sex and how to have multiple orgasms, thanks to my current lover. I will never again compromise my sex life. Having wonderful orgasms brings us close together.*

Why can women have multiple orgasms?

Giving birth hurts like hell, so God compensated women by bestowing them the possibility of extra pleasure. It's a shame though that he didn't leave instructions (and the stamina) to all men on how to perform oral sex long enough for the woman to have multiple orgasms. Luckily, some men have learned the skill and the rest who didn't can follow my detailed instructions on page 215.

How to have multiple orgasms?

We all know that Federer didn't wake up one morning and decide that today he would win Wimbledon without first spending several years learning how to play tennis. He trained more than anyone and perfected his game long before he could hold the Wimbledon trophy. The same applies to sex and multiple orgasms, as no one was born with fully learned skills. It takes time and practice to master the technique. Fortunately, most of us can win the "multi O" trophy if we try hard enough.

The problem is that women are too embarrassed to ask for what they want. Men are not mind readers, so you need to tell your partner what to do. Give him the "multi O" GPS by first learning about your anatomy, what feels good and how you achieve your best orgasms by masturbating. Then teach him how to please you, but not during sex, as this can put him off. Men can be very insecure and take any remarks as criticism. Try talking to him about this book that you are reading right now. On page 215 there is an oral sex exercise called "G-spot stimulation" that may give you a multi-orgasmic experience. Ask your partner to try it with you. Don't put too much pressure on him and most importantly - have fun together. You might not succeed in having multiple orgasms the first time you try the exercise, not even the first five times, but don't give up; keep on trying. Think of Federer with his Wimbledon trophy and keep practicing. Don't think of him *during* the exercise though ☺.

Venus Butterfly

If you are old enough you may remember the television series called *L.A. Law,* a legal drama that ran for eight seasons on NBC, from 1986 to 1994. One particular episode that aired in November 1986 was called "The Venus Butterfly." In this episode, lawyer Stuart Markowitz, played by Michael Tucker, is defending a client who has great success with women though his appearance, behavior and personality are highly unimpressive. Markowitz is intrigued by his client's popularity and asks him about his secret. The client discloses to his lawyer a sexual technique he practices on women called the Venus Butterfly. The audience never learns what the technique entails. However, we get to see Markowitz in bed with his fellow lawyer girlfriend Ann, played by Jill Eikenberry. She seems very satisfied with this technique that Markowitz just performed on her. Following that episode, they became a long-term couple.

After the episode aired many people contacted the producers asking for more information about this mystifying technique. Even in Sweden, there I lived at the time, everyone talked about it. Magazines and newspapers wrote about it, speculating which technique it could be. The truth is that the writer, Terry Louise Fisher, made it up. The technique implies performing oral sex with a twist. Since then, a few books have been written that use the term Venus Butterfly as an umbrella for several techniques that have one thing in common: oral stimulation of the clitoris combined with simultaneous G-spot stimulation, hopefully resulting in multiple orgasms. See my description of the technique on page 215.

The sex toy industry is using the term Venus Butterfly for all-in-one vibrators that stimulate the clitoris and G-spot at the same time.

Multiple orgasms in men

Some men are able to experience multiple orgasms. Before going further, let me explain how the human sexual response cycle works.

Masters and Johnson male sexual response cycle

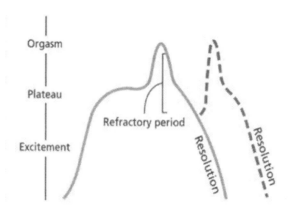

Here above is the male sexual response cycle according to Masters and Johnson. A man's excitement and plateau phases are usually faster than a woman's are (see next page). The plateau phase can last from a few seconds to a few minutes. After the orgasm/ejaculation, a man experiences a refractory period when another erection is not possible. This period can last from several minutes (in younger men) to several hours. The older a man gets, the more difficult it is to achieve a second erection and orgasm. Some men can have multiple orgasms before they ejaculate. This requires an understanding of male physiology and takes some training to achieve.

MISTAKE # 68
Orgasm and ejaculation are the same thing

It is important to understand that orgasm happens first, and ejaculation follows. With training, a man can have several orgasms first and then ejaculate when he is ready to do so. The multi-orgasmic experience in men refers to several orgasms before ejaculation-refractory period-resolution as shown in the above graph. The reason for a man's refractory period is believed to be the hormone prolactin that peaks during ejaculation. Prolactin causes a man to lose his erection. Some men don't produce enough prolactin, therefore, can have subsequent orgasms/ejaculations (Haake et al., 2002). However, most men are not as fortunate, therefore, need to wait some time for the erection to resume. Let's compare the male sexual response cycle to the female cycle.

Masters and Johnson female sexual response cycle

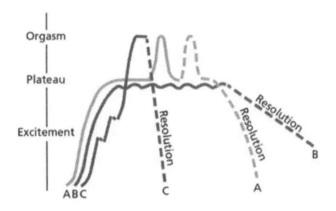

Here above is the female sexual response cycle according to Masters and Johnson. Letters A, B and C represent three different women or one woman on three separate occasions. Woman A moves smoothly from excitement phase to plateau then reaches her orgasm (or has multiple orgasms), then transits to the resolution stage. Woman B reaches the plateau phase but doesn't orgasm on this occasion. Woman C transitions differently (and faster) through excitement to orgasm. In general, women need more time to reach an orgasm then men do, from 20 to 30 minutes or even longer is common.

MISTAKE # 69
Men can't have multiple orgasms

If you separate the orgasm from ejaculation then men can have several dry orgasms before ejaculating. As mentioned before, men with low prolactin levels can experience subsequent orgasms/ejaculations. Men with normal prolactin levels can achieve multiple orgasms with training. Because an orgasm occurs a few seconds before ejaculation, the key is to stop the emission of semen by clenching the pubococcygeus muscle, also called the pelvic floor muscle or PC muscle. The PC muscle is the one that stops urine mid-stream. The next time you urinate, check the muscle by stopping the flow. You should be able to feel your pelvic muscles tightening and pulling upward toward the stomach. If you can't stop the flow then you need to practice Kegel exercises that can be found on page 219. Kegels are beneficial to both men and women.

The procedure for male multiple orgasms

The best way is to practice first by masturbating. At "the point of no return" you should experience genital contractions that last a few seconds, this is the orgasm. At this point contract your PC muscle just like you did when peeing. Some men with weaker muscles need to press the perineum, the space between the testicles and anus, with their fingers. The perineum is often referred to as the male G-spot. This needs to be done quickly; otherwise, you might experience retrograde ejaculation - when the semen goes into the bladder. The point is to stop the ejaculation altogether.

Once you stop the ejaculation, relax a few seconds and then continue masturbating. Another orgasm will come shortly. This time, you do the same as before; clench your PC muscle to stop the ejaculate. If all goes well, you will be able to experience multiple orgasms. With practice, you will gain control and the orgasms will become progressively more intense. Once you learn this technique by masturbating, you will be able to apply it when having intercourse with your partner. It is similar to the start-stop method and edging described on page 59.

As with female multiple orgasms, this technique takes time, patience and determination so don't get frustrated and give up. At first, you might contract the muscle too late and ejaculate. You might do it too early and not have the orgasm. Finally, you will master it just like the Chinese Taoists did thousands of years ago. You can find more information on the Internet by searching "male multiple orgasms" or "how to have multiple orgasms" or "how to have non-ejaculatory orgasms."

MISTAKE # 70
Simultaneous orgasm is the goal

For many people, simultaneous orgasm (when both climax at the same time) seems to be the ultimate sexual experience, the Holy Grail of sex. This performance-based view of sex might bring a lot of pressure to lovemaking. As we already established, a man can ejaculate within minutes; the woman needs much longer time to reach an orgasm. Additionally, she needs clitoral stimulation. So while climaxing together can feel exhilarating, pleasing her first should be a better option. For example, the man can perform oral sex until she is ready to climax and then have penetrative intercourse. There are many ways to enjoy sex, so limiting yourself to the same ending scenario may bring on disappointment when synchronization doesn't happen. A good lover makes her come first.

MISTAKE # 71
Vaginal orgasm

You might have heard of vaginal and clitoral orgasms in women. Freud believed that a vaginal orgasm was superior or more "mature" to clitoral orgasm. This assumption is far from the truth because we know today that there is only one physiological orgasm in women. The majority of women need clitoral stimulation to achieve an orgasm. This means that thrusting your penis inside a vagina without paying attention to her clitoris will not make her climax. Some women might orgasm during sleep or by touching their nipples, or even contracting their pubic muscles. However, this is very rare.

Freud's misconception led many women to feel inadequate because they couldn't climax during intercourse. They believed that there was something wrong with them. The truth is that most women can achieve an orgasm by stimulating the clitoris. Men should know that.

Uterine orgasm

Not much is said about the uterine contractions during orgasm. The uterus contracts to suck up the sperm in the vagina through the cervix. This function is not necessary though because sperm swims up anyhow, with orgasm or without. If the female orgasm was needed for conception, half of the world's population wouldn't be here today.

The intensity of uterine orgasms vary from woman to woman. Most women don't think about their uterus contracting until they have a hysterectomy (removal of uterus – see more about it on page 191). Women who have had their uterus removed are missing the intense orgasmic feeling. Think twice before agreeing to hysterectomy as alternative solutions are possible (see Chapter 14).

MISTAKE # 72
Faking it

It is difficult to say how many women are faking orgasms. Some surveys revealed that more than half of women have faked it. The reason given was not to disappoint the partner, tiredness or a wish to end the intercourse sooner. Another recent study from Oakland University, concluded that the main three reasons were:

- to improve the partner's experience (i.e., increasing the quality of the sexual experience for the partner),
- deception and manipulation (i.e., deceiving the partner or manipulating his perceptions for other gains), and
- hiding sexual disinterest (i.e., sparing the partner's feelings about the woman's lack of sexual excitement).
(McCoy et al., 2015)

The problem with faking is that once you start you will remain in "no orgasm land" forever because your guy thinks that he can easily satisfy you. You will play along to keep up the charade, not wanting him to disappoint you. He will believe that every time you have sex, your orgasm is a given. This may make him complacent in his lovemaking and lead to your resentment.

I have seen a couple where the wife disclosed in therapy that she rarely had orgasms while having intercourse and needed to masturbate when the husband went to work. The man felt devastated after her confession. Many years of faking led to marital breakup, as he was utterly disappointed in her. He said that he would never trust her again. Honesty is important in relationships. It is better to be honest and say that you need a longer time to achieve an orgasm, that you need clitoral stimulation or whatever else you fancy.

Men like to please their women so give him a chance to please you. Experiment together and have fun.

MISTAKE # 73
Men can't fake it

Yes, they can, and they do. Several surveys found that 30% to 35% of men had faked an orgasm in the past. The reasons given were tiredness, stress, lack of mood, feeling under pressure, feeling anxious, low self-esteem, wanting to please the partner, wanting to achieve simultaneous orgasm or just being unable to climax. When it comes to younger men, delayed or retarded ejaculation is a rather new phenomenon. This happens due to excessive cybersex addiction (more about it in Chapter 10).

Jonas says:
> *I had to fake it last night. I was tired, but Kristina insisted on having sex. I didn't want to disappoint her, so I went down on her, and she had an orgasm rather quickly, but when I inserted my penis into her vagina, I knew it would take a long time for me to come. So I faked it. It was easy to do because I wore a condom. She didn't notice anything wrong, and she was happy.*

Wearing a condom is one way to cover up the lack of semen when faking ejaculation. A quick trip to the bathroom and the condom is gone, out of sight. Women can produce vast amounts of vaginal secretions during intercourse. The more aroused she is, the more mucus is produced. An orgasm can release extra fluids so she might not notice the absence of semen.

For more on female ejaculation, squirting or gushing see page 96.

MISTAKE # 74
There is no such thing as a G-spot

The Grafenberg Spot, named after Dr Ernst Grafenberg, who in 1950 noticed a sensitive area inside the vagina, is located approximately five centimeters or two inches from the vaginal anterior (up toward the clitoris) entrance. When a woman is sexually aroused the G-spot swells in size and feels like a spongy ball. The debate on the existence of the G-spot has been ongoing for many years. Masters and Johnson noticed that the roots of the clitoris expand inside toward the vagina. Sometimes, these roots are called bulbs. So the clitoris is not a single button but a tip of an iceberg so to speak, as you only see the top of it. Just like the penis with it's glans, the clitoris is the female glans, and its roots can be compared to the penile shaft but instead of one trunk, they split into several branches.

As you will see in the next chapter, penises come in different shapes and sizes. The same applies to female anatomy and the clitoris. Each woman has a distinctive clitoris and characteristic roots that may vary in sensitivity. This has been confirmed by autopsies of female cadavers (O'Connell et al., 2005). Interestingly, the clitoral nerves, which are at least two millimeters in diameter, can also be seen in female infants.

The roots expand to the anterior vaginal wall where the G-spot or area is located. Though most women need direct clitoral stimulation to climax, some women may achieve an orgasm by only concentrating on the G-spot. Imagine a man masturbating without stimulating his glans, only the shaft of his penis. Though he might reach an orgasm in this way, he would prefer to concentrate on his glans, where all the nerve endings are located, thus, having the most fulfilling and pleasurable experience. The same applies to women.

A combination of clitoris and G-spot stimulation is the best option (see the G-spot exercise on page 215) but not the only one. Most women concentrate only on the clitoris when masturbating because it's easily reachable compared to the G-spot. If you want to explore on your own, there are several G-spot massagers or vibrators on the market today that make it easy to access the anterior wall of the vagina.

G-spot enhancement, amplification or augmentation, has become very popular in the last decade. The objective is to inject hyaluronan (a type of collagen) into the G-spot area inside the vagina to enlarge the area, thus, increasing sensitivity and sexual pleasure. Mostly done by plastic surgeons (but also by some gynecologists), this procedure has been controversial. Some women report increased pleasure and some not; it seems to be quite an individual experience. The effect is only temporary, as the human body absorbs these fillers within three to four months.

The people who say the G-spot doesn't exist because women can't have vaginal orgasms are missing the point here. The G-spot is not solely responsible for female pleasure; it's a complement to the clitoris. This is teamwork so to say. And to the women who feel disappointed that they can't find the G-spot, I say that Columbus didn't discover America in one day, so keep searching.

Female ejaculation and female prostate

MISTAKE # 75
Only men can ejaculate and only men have a prostate

Research shows that half of women have experienced ejaculation during orgasm (Pastor, 2013). Ejaculation, squirting or gushing refers to a liquid that is expelled either from the urethra or Skene's glands, also called the female prostate. Most women can squirt during a G-spot orgasm (when applying pressure to the G-spot and simultaneously stimulating the clitoris). The reason they don't is because they believe that they need to urinate, thus, stop the stimulation before the orgasm and ejaculation can occur. Next time you practice, empty your bladder before, put some towels on the bed and when the moment comes, let it go; don't hold back.

Skene's glands are located close to the urethral opening. Another set of female glands called Bartholin's glands or greater vestibular glands, are located at the lower entrance to the vagina. Their function is to lubricate the entry of the vagina and to aid the penis to enter smoothly. When the woman is aroused, they excrete a small amount of whitish lubricant or mucus. These glands may become blocked or infected, causing bartholinitis or a Bartholin's cyst, a very painful condition that needs to be drained surgically.

Skene's glands produce milky fluid that is similar in composition to prostatic fluid in men (minus the sperm). This liquid includes proteins, enzymes, glucose, prostate specific antigen (PSA), prostatic acidic phosphatase and prostate specific acid phosphatase (Moalem & Reidenberg, 2009). Its function is believed to lubricate the urethral opening and may protect the urinary tract from infections with its antimicrobial properties.

It was long believed that female ejaculation was caused by incontinence. This is not the case because although some amount of urine may be present in a large ejaculate, when examining the liquid in the lab, researchers found not only much lower levels of creatinine but other components that are not found in urine, as mentioned on the previous page. Though female ejaculation is a healthy and normal sexual response, many women feel ashamed when it happens. They may believe that they suffer from urinary incontinence, or their gynecologist may say so. If there is no leakage during coughing, sneezing or strenuous activities, there is nothing to worry about. Most importantly, educate yourself and your partner, and enjoy your lovemaking.

CHAPTER 6

SIZE DOES MATTER
(MOSTLY TO THE OWNER)

Over 50% of men are dissatisfied with their penis size (Lever et al., 2006) but when we ask their partners, 84% of women are happy with the size. Why the huge gap? Where is this coming from? Genital plastic surgery is on the rise. Both men and women feel insecure about their bodies. What is normal and what is abnormal?

What is the average penis size?

According to The Kinsey Institute the average erect penis size is approximately 14 to 16 cm (5.5 - 6.3 inches). The average girth for an erect penis is 12 to 13 cm (4.7 - 5.1 inches).

Flaccid length averages from 7 to 10 cm (2.8 - 3.9 inches).

Flaccid circumference/girth averages from 9 to 10 cm (3.5 - 3.9 inches).

Master and Johnson reported that the erect penis size varies from 12.5 cm to 17.5 cm (4.9 to 6.9 inches).

When is a penis too small? According to the Journal of Urology when the flaccid length is less than 4 cm (1.6 inches), and erect length is less than 7.5 cm (3 inches).

According to a recent review of 17 past studies conducted by researchers from King's College London Medical School, involving 15,521 men aged 17 and older, the average length of a flaccid penis is 9.16 cm (3.6 inches) and 13.24 cm (5.21 inches) when stretched.

When erect, the average penis length is 13.12 cm (5.16 inches). There is a minor correlation between the man's height and erect penis length. The average penis girth is 9.31 cm (3.66 inches) when flaccid and 11.66 cm (4.59 inches) when erect (Veale et al., 2015).

The Ansell/Cancun (2001) study of 300 young American college men resulted in the following penis measurements: 14.9 cm (5.88 inches) the average erect penis length, and 12.6 cm (4.97 inches) the average erect girth (circumference at mid-shaft). Only 25% of these men had an erect penis that was larger than 15 cm or 6 inches. Only 10 men out of 300 had penises longer than 17.8 cm or 7 inches. The majority of men (59%) had penises between 13.3 cm (5.25 inches) to 15.2 cm (6 inches).

To measure your penis size, put a ruler on top of your penis and measure from the pelvic bone to the tip of the penis. To measure the circumference/girth/width, take a measuring tape and put it around your penis at the thickest part of the shaft. For your reference, the size of this book is 6 x 9 inches or approximately 15 x 23 cm so the average erect penis is shorter than the width of this book.

MISTAKE # 76
My penis is too small

A study by researchers at UCLA and Cal State LA concluded that 84% of women are happy with their partner's penis size, 14% wanted it to be bigger, and 2% would prefer a smaller size. The poll included 26,437 women 18 to 65 years old (Lever et al., 2006). The same study included 25,594 men who stated that their penis was small (12%) though only 6% of the women said that. Fifteen percent of men who rated their penis size as small said that they were shy to undress in front of their partner, and 8% of the average size said the same. Interestingly, the researchers noticed that men with smaller penises rated themselves as less attractive on overall body image satisfaction as well as face satisfaction and swimsuit comfort.

The fact is that many men are worried about their penis size. In the above study, 45% of men desired a larger penis. There was a correlation between taller or thinner men with a larger penis size. Shorter or heavier men had a smaller penis. Men with larger penises were more confident, and men with smaller penises were insecure.

When men compare their penises in locker rooms, they may not be aware that small flaccid penises can expand into rather large ones during erection and that the long looking ones often don't get so much bigger when erect.

So what do women say?
What is the best penis size for them?

Amy says:
> *I have noticed that guys with large dicks are not as good in bed as guys with average or smaller ones. They try harder to satisfy you.*

Tiffany says:
> *It's not the length per se but the girth that matters. I like them thick.*

Angela says:
> *I don't like when they are too big. It hurts.*

Nicole says:
> *To be honest, size does matter. I prefer larger size.*

Julie says:
> *You need to feel it and not have to ask if it's in yet.*

Holly says:
> *I had a three-year relationship with a well-endowed guy but never came once.*

Alicia says:
> *Don't like them small and don't like them big. Just average is good for me.*

Research on women's preference of penis size

A 2015 poll conducted by Cosmopolitan magazine of 1,100 readers (96% women, 4% men; between the ages of 18 and 34), revealed that 89% of women said they were not worried about their boyfriend's penis size. When asked to rate their partner's penis size, 56% said average, and 33% said large. Almost 60% of women were not satisfied in the bedroom but would not change anything about the man's penis. Penetration was not important to most women as 62% stated that they rarely or never orgasm from penetration alone.

Another recent research study from the University of California Los Angeles and the University of New Mexico Albuquerque concluded that women like larger penises for one-night stands and slightly smaller for long-term relationships (Prause et al., 2015). They wanted 6.4 inches or 16.3 cm in length and 5 inches or 12.7 cm in girth/circumference for one-time sex and 6.3 inches or 16.0 cm in length and 4.8 inches or 12.2 cm in girth/circumference for long-term sex. These numbers correspond to the the average penis size found in men. Larger penises were not preferred, as they come with a possible injury to the sensitive vagina. This was a rather small sample of 75 women (18 to 65 years old, average age 25).

What is a good-looking penis?

A Swiss study with the above title was conducted in 2015 by researchers from Zurich (Ruppen-Greeff et al., 2015). They asked 105 women ages from 16 to 45 about penile appearance. The women rated eight different aspects of a penis on a 5-point scale.

The results were:
1. Importance of general cosmetic appearance.
2. Importance of appearance of pubic hair.
3. Importance of shape of penile skin.
4. Importance of penile girth.
5. Importance of shape of glans.
6. Importance of penile length.
7. Importance of appearance of scrotum.
8. Importance of position and shape of the meatus (urethra opening).

The researchers concluded that women find penis length less important to overall appearance and that most women are satisfied with their partner's penis size.

MISTAKE # 77
Comparing yourself to porn stars

Porn is a multibillion-dollar industry that caters to male fantasies. The actors you see in these movies are not the average person that you meet on the street. These guys usually do have larger than average penises and the women larger than average breasts. These men last longer due to film editing, taking drugs and using numbing creams/lotions on their penises. According to research, an average sex act takes three to seven minutes. Premature ejaculation is when a man ejaculates within one minute of penetration or sexual stimulation. The fact is that the majority of women need direct clitoral stimulation to achieve an orgasm so thrusting your penis inside her vagina for a long time is not that important after all. Many women prefer oral stimulation on the clitoris. Ask your partner what she likes. Communication is important in relationships.

MISTAKE # 78
Ejaculating on her face

What is common practice in porn movies doesn't apply in reality. If you want to have sex again with her, don't ejaculate on her face, or it will be your last time. Women don't like this; it's a male fantasy that guys like to watch in porn movies.

GENITAL PLASTIC SURGERY

Penile Enhancement

Fillers

Women have been injecting their lips with fillers for a long time. Now men do the same with their penises. Penile enhancement by hyaluronic acid (a dermal filler) is done by injections directly to the penis. It will not make it longer but thicker, especially when flaccid. The effect is only temporary, as the human body absorbs these fillers within a few months. Some plastic surgeons use body fat to inject into the penis. Another filler is polymethylmethacrylate (PMMA). It usually contains 20% tiny PMMA microspheres (microscopic synthetic polymer beads) and 80% purified bovine (cow) collagen gel. This filler is not approved by the FDA for penal (soft tissue) augmentation. Several cases have been reported with uneven, lumpy, disproportional and deformed penises. Complications are common so don't do this.

Dermal fat grafts

Dermal fat grafts have proven to last longer than injections and give better results, increasing the penis circumference by one to two inches (2.5 to 5 cm).

Implants

Penile prosthetic implants are often used for erectile dysfunction. Internal penile pumps that can be activated before intercourse are also available for men with ED.

Surgery

Penis enlargement surgery involves cutting the ligaments that attach the penis to the pelvic bone, thus making it longer as it hangs free. One of the side effects is that the erection will point down and not upwards as before. Furthermore, these operations are risky as several complications like infections, reduced sensitivity, nerve damage, and erectile dysfunction may happen. According to a study published in the European Urology, half of the men who had this procedure wanted another surgery, as they were not happy with the results, only 35% were satisfied (Li et al., 2006).

Weight loss

Losing weight will make a penis look longer. Guys with belly fat may have a "hidden" or "buried" penis. Liposuction can help as well.

Pubic hair trimming

Removing or trimming the pubic hair is a good idea as most women like the appearance of a groomed pubis. And yes, it will make him look longer, about one inch or so.

Designer vaginas – Labiaplasty

Vaginoplasty refers to any surgery related to the vagina and vulva. The most common plastic surgery of the vagina is labiaplasty, to either labia majora or labia minora. This procedure is the fastest growing plastic surgery for women with a 50% rise from 2013 to 2014 in the United States. The two labia, inner and outer vaginal lips, are usually made smaller during such an operation. Reduction of the clitoral hood (the skin that covers the clitoris – the prepuce) and liposuction of the pubic mound are also common. As women come in different shapes and sizes, so do their vaginas. There is no ideal look for a perfect vagina; however, because of the growing porn industry that is easily available on the Internet, the trend for total hair removal, by either waxing or laser, made the genitals more visible to the general public.

MISTAKE # 79
Wanting a child-looking vagina

Grown women want to have a five-year-old girl lookalike vaginas. Any skin folds (that are perfectly normal) are considered as ugly. Especially after childbirth, or with age, the labia might stretch or change their shape, thus causing self-conscious women some discomfort.

Interestingly, in some parts of Africa, having long vaginal lips is highly desirable and considered a benefit to sexual pleasure for both partners. Women there practice labia stretching or pulling, often using weights for faster expansion of the vaginal lips. What looks like hanging skin in daily life gets engorged with blood during sexual arousal, thus changing the shape and size, and adding to the sexual satisfaction.

As in any surgery, there are certain risks involved in labiaplasty. Infections, bleeding, edema, scarring and nerve damage with decreased or increased sensitivity are a few of them. A study published in 2011 by the Journal of Sexual Medicine concluded that 90-95% of women were generally satisfied after the procedure, rating the post-operation sexual satisfaction to 80-85% (Goodman, 2011).

It seems that the pressure for designer vaginas comes from the women themselves and not so much from men. Regardless, if any man doesn't like the look of your vagina, he shouldn't be allowed to look at it in the first place. The man who criticizes your private parts should be banned from visiting them.

Vaginal tightening

Vaginal plastic surgery involves tightening of the vaginal walls. Vaginal rejuvenation is often requested following childbirth or by older women who feel that their vaginal muscles start to become loose (more about older women in Chapter 14). Pelvic floor exercises, also called Kegel exercises, can help with the tightness of the vagina (see page 219 for details).

G-Spot enhancement

G-spot enhancement, amplification or augmentation, has become very popular in the last decade. The objective is to inject hyaluronan (a type of collagen) into the G-spot area inside the vagina to enlarge the area, thus, increasing sensitivity and sexual pleasure. Mostly done by plastic surgeons (but also by some gynecologists), this procedure has been controversial. Some women report increased pleasure and some not; it seems to be quite an individual experience. The effect is only temporary, as the human body absorbs these fillers within three to four months. Read more about the G-spot in Chapter 5.

Hymen restoration

Hymen repair (hymenoplasty) or hymen reconstruction is often performed by plastic surgeons or gynecologists to women who want to restore their "virginity." The procedure involves stitching the edges of the outer vagina opening, usually at the same place there the original hymen was located. Some cultures put a high value on the presence of hymen on the wedding night. The fact is that the hymen can be easily broken by inserting a tampon, riding a bicycle, exercising or horseback riding. A vagina is never completely closed because the menstrual blood needs to come out. The hymen looks like a half moon shaped thin membrane that usually covers less than half of the opening at the lower end of the vaginal entrance.

Anal bleaching

Anal bleaching or lightening is a relatively new trend. Thanks to pornography that popularized genital hair removal, either by waxing or laser, women realized that once the hair was gone the skin underneath was darker than the rest of the body. This is normal and nothing to worry about. However, as the porn stars started to bleach their anuses the mainstream followed. One might think that only gay men would be interested in this procedure, but the fact is that nine out of ten customers are women. Whitening is done by creams or lotions that contain bleaching acid. Hydroquinone creams were used in the past, but these have been banned in many countries due to their toxicity and dermal carcinogenicity (causing skin cancer). Skin irritation, allergic reactions, and patchy skin discoloration have been reported as well. Unless you work in the porn industry and need to show your anus on the big screen, I see no reason for anal bleaching whatsoever.

MISTAKE # 80
Pornography is the norm

We need to separate pornography from reality. We have a new generation of young people that learn about sex from the Internet. Our children rely more on the Internet than on us. How can this be? Why is talking about sex with your kids still a taboo but watching porn is acceptable? Because everyone does it? Boys, as young as 9-10 years old are already watching porn online. They don't have to search for it, as many times these sites are just popping up out of nowhere. These boys are conditioned to sexual violence and disrespect toward women. They assume that group sex, anal intercourse and ejaculating on women's faces are normal. Young men masturbate while watching porn, but when it comes to sex with a real person, the problems are endless. Read more about masturbation and sex addiction in Chapter 10.

CHAPTER 7

IT TAKES TWO TO TANGO – THREE IS A CROWD (AND OTHER SEXUAL FANTASIES)

We all have sexual fantasies and erotic dreams. Should we share them with our partner? Should you tell your wife or girlfriend that a threesome with her best friend is at the top of your list? What is normal? How far can we go? Why the hype about the mile-high club? And sex in public places, is that okay? Can we live out our fantasies? Here, I give examples from my private practice, and I think that I have heard it all.

SEXUAL FANTASIES

According to research, 93% of men and 86% of women have erotic dreams at night (Schredl et al., 2004). Nocturnal orgasms can happen to both men and women though they are more common in men. The term *wet dream* is typically used when a man unknowingly ejaculates during sleep. Erotic fantasies were reported by 95% of both men and women (Crooks & Baur, 2011).

Researchers from Canada investigated the most common sexual fantasies by asking 1,517 people to answer an online sex fantasy questionnaire (Joyal, Cossette, & Lapierre, 2015). The subjects were 799 women and 717 men with an average age of 30. They stated their sexual preference to be heterosexual (85%), homosexual (4%) and neither sexuality (11%). You can see the list of the 20 most common fantasies for each gender on the next two pages.

Having a threesome with two women was fantasized about by 85% of men and 37% of women, having a threesome with two men by 45% of women and 31% of men, anal sex by 64% of men and 32% of women, taking part in oral sex by 88% of men and 79% of women, and having interracial sex by 61% of men and 28% of women. Both genders fantasized equally about having sex in an unusual place (82%) and about feeling romantic emotions during a sexual relationship (92% for women and 88% for men).

Interestingly, 66% of men and 57% of women fantasized about making love openly in a public place, 83% of men and 66% of women having sex with someone they know other than their spouse, 73% of men and 49% of women having sex with an unknown person, 52% of women and 46% of men being tied up by someone in order to obtain sexual pleasure, 36% of women and 29% of men being spanked or whipped to obtain sexual pleasure and 40% of men and 13% of women having sex with a prostitute or a stripper.

The least wanted fantasies were - my sexual partner urinating on me; 10% of men and 4% of women, urinating on my sexual partner; 9% of men and 4% of women, sex with an animal; 3% of men and 2% of women and finally, sex with a child; 2% of men and 1% of women.

Most common sexual fantasies for women:

1. Having sex in a romantic location such as on a deserted beach. (84.9%)
2. Having sex in an unusual place, such as in the office or a public toilet. (81.7%)
3. Taking part in fellatio or cunnilingus. (78.5%)
4. Giving fellatio. (72.1%)
5. Being masturbated by my partner. (71.4%)
6. Masturbating my partner. (68.1%)
7. Having sex with someone who I know other than my spouse. (66.3%)
8. Being dominated sexually. (64.6%)
9. Making love openly in a public place. (57.3%)
10. Having sex with more than three people, both men and women. (56.5%)
11. Being tied up by someone in order to obtain sexual pleasure. (52.1%)

12.   Having sex with a star or a well-known person. (51.7%)
13.   Having sex with an unknown person. (48.9%)
14.   Dominating someone sexually. (46.7%)
15.   Watching two women make love. (42.4%)
16.   Tying someone up in order to obtain sexual pleasure. (41.7%)
17.   That my partner ejaculates on me. (41.3%)
18.   Having homosexual sex. (36.9%)
19.   Having sex with two women. (36.9%)
20.   Being masturbated by an acquaintance. (36.8%)

(Joyal, Cossette, & Lapierre, 2015).

Most common sexual fantasies for men:

1.   Taking part in fellatio or cunnilingus. (87.6%)
2.   Having sex with two women. (84.5%)
3.   Having sex with someone who I know other than my spouse. (83.4%)
4.   Having sex in an unusual place, such as in the office or a public toilet. (82.3%)
5.   Watching two women make love. (82.1%)
6.   Ejaculating on my sexual partner. (80.4%)
7.   Having sex in a romantic location such as on a deserted beach. (78.4%)
8.   Giving cunnilingus. (78.1%)
9.   Masturbating my partner. (76.4%)
10.   Having sex with more than three people, all women. (75.3%)
11.   Having sex with an unknown person. (72.5%)
12.   Being masturbated by my partner. (71.7%)
13.   Having sex with a woman with very large breasts. (68.6%)
14.   Making love openly in a public space. (66.1%)
15.   Masturbating an acquaintance. (65.9%)
16.   Being masturbated by an acquaintance. (64.7%)
17.   Having anal sex. (64.2%)
18.   Watching someone undress without him or her knowing. (63.4%)
19.   Being masturbated by an unknown person. (62.5%)
20.   Masturbating an unknown person. (62.4%)

(Joyal, Cossette, & Lapierre, 2015).

It is important to remember that the above-mentioned Canadian study was based on self-reports and that the subjects were rather young (20 to 40, average age 30) therefore, not representative of the general population.

MISTAKE # 81
Living out a sexual fantasy

For many people, a fantasy is just that, a fantasy, and not something that they would like to experience in reality. Some women may fantasize about being raped, but this doesn't mean that they really want it to happen. Other fantasies such as having a threesome, an orgy or wife swapping may seem exciting but are highly dangerous to the relationship (see more on page 162).

Lori says:
> *My boyfriend suggested a threesome with my friend. He was drunk when he said it, but I felt very hurt by that. I love my friend but not in a sexual way. We both thought my boyfriend was a douchebag.*

Brandon says:
> *My wife told me once that she would like to have sex with two men at the same time. She said it as a joke, but I think that she meant it. I feel that she is not happy with our lovemaking, that she wants something that I can't give her.*

MISTAKE # 82
Sharing a sexual fantasy

Odd or explicit erotic fantasies, especially involving other people, should be kept private. Your partner might feel hurt if you disclose to him something specific such as you fantasizing about Brad Pitt when having sex with him. Likewise, you might be hurt by him saying that your behind reminds him of Nicki Minaj's booty.

Robin says:
> *My husband told me once that when he was young, he would masturbate while looking at a Pamela Anderson Baywatch poster. I wish he would never have told me that because sometimes I feel like Pamela is in bed with us.*

MISTAKE # 83
Making a sex tape

This can be fun to do, and both of you may enjoy your masterpiece next time you are having sex. However, what was fun when things were good between the two of you may become a problem once the relationship ends. Who will keep the tape? Should it be destroyed? And can it be used against you by a scorned lover who is looking for revenge? Harassment, cyber-stalking, blackmail and extortion have happened to other people in the past so don't let this happen to you. If you already have a sex tape, then keep it in a safe place.

MISTAKE # 84
Sex in public places

Sex is illegal in public places. Having said that, according to a recent Internet survey conducted by a sex toy company, 52% of adults have tried it at least once. The respondents were 600 Americans age 18 and up. The most favorite location were parked cars (80%), the woods (55%), a park (44%), beach (42%), office (25%), public bathrooms (22%), movie theater (16%) and airplanes (7%). Interestingly, a church (5%) and taxi (2%) were mentioned as well.

MISTAKE # 85
Sex in an elevator/lift

Elevators have security cameras. Aside from that, they are fast. Stopping the elevator between floors by pressing the stop button might work. However, don't press the emergency button by mistake or knock the phone off the hook.

MISTAKE # 86
Sex in the car

Unless you are Jack and Rose on the Titanic, sex in the car can be complicated due to limited space. The back of a limo is fine but if you are driving a MINI Cooper then think twice before getting entangled like a human pretzel.

MISTAKE # 87
Sex on the beach

Since the iconic beach scene between Burt Lancaster and Deborah Kerr in the movie *From Here to Eternity* (1953), sex on the beach has been included on many fantasy wish lists. The reality is that having sex on sand is not a good idea, as sand gets everywhere it's not supposed to be. So unless you are lying down on a towel or a sun bed, don't do it. Remember that sex is illegal in public places.

MISTAKE # 88
Sex in the water

Sex in a pool, hot tub, sea, river, lake, etc. is possible, however, not advisable because there is plenty of bacteria in these places. You may end up with a yeast infection or urinary tract infection (UTI). A thrusting penis inside the vagina can push particles in the water up through the cervix and into the uterus. Chlorine and seawater can irritate the delicate walls of the vagina, even cause some damage.

MISTAKE # 89
Sex at work

Not a good idea. You could get fired (unless you work in the porn industry of course) or be accused of sexual harassment. Hookups at work are common, as we spend most of the time there. Many companies have specific no-sex rules. Respect them. Office gossip will get you in trouble.

THE MILE-HIGH CLUB

The mile-high club refers to having sex on a plane at a high altitude. It doesn't apply if the plane is on the ground. The idea behind it is that the vibrations of the plane combined with high altitude, thus, a lower oxygen level, may heighten the intensity of the orgasm. Another factor is the risk involved. If you get caught, and it happens, you might end up in prison or pay a hefty fine. This happened to a British couple in 1999. They were sitting in business class on a transatlantic flight from Dallas to Manchester. After several alcoholic drinks, things got cozy between them. The interesting part was that both were married to other people and on top of that, they were strangers to each other before the flight. They were arrested by the police at arrival and publicly humiliated by the press. Both lost their jobs in the aftermath of the offense.

MISTAKE # 90
Sex on a commercial flight

Before 9/11, in the good old aviation days, sex in the lavatory was not such a big deal. If you were on a long-haul flight, preferably during the night when the lights were usually dimmed or completely off, sneaking out to the toilet for a quickie was doable. Today, people are watching. Any unusual behavior will be reported to the crew. Besides that, having sex in a smelly or dirty toilet is no fun. The water you see on the floor is not water, if you know what I mean. The walls are thin so any noise or movement can be detected outside. Aside from that, you never know who is watching. With the new security measures that allow camera surveillance everywhere, unbeknownst to your knowledge, you might become the new hot couple with a sex tape on the Internet.

Several airlines have launched improved business and first class suites that include beds, even beds for couples. Is sex allowed there? Probably not but would the crew interfere if this was the case? As long as you are discrete, they might not react. The new planes even have walk-in showers in the first class where you can lock the door behind you and indulge in some steamy action. Etihad Airways, the United Arab Emirates' national carrier, is the first one to introduce The Residence – a three-room suite with a living room, double bed, and a private bathroom with a full-height shower. For the price of $32,000 you get a one-way ticket from New York to Abu Dhabi, private butler included. If having sex up in the sky is on your bucket list then this option, though costly, sounds like the best one, unless you happen to know someone who owns a private jet and is willing to lend it to you.

In my opinion, the mile-high club is highly overrated. Sex in public places is against the law. Lavatories on planes are considered public places. There is no law forbidding two people to enter a lavatory together. However, by doing so, you might draw attention from the crew or other passengers. In 2002, two British men tried to have sex in the toilet on a transatlantic flight to John F. Kennedy Airport. The incident was reported to the captain who promptly warned the ground control at JFK. Two F-16s were summoned to escort the American Airline 747 into the airport. The men were arrested and deported back to the UK.

MISTAKE # 91
Sex in the shower/bathtub

Sex in the shower or bathtub can be dangerous due to slippery surfaces. Invest in non-slip safety shower stickers or an anti-slip mat to prevent falls and injury.

MISTAKE # 92
Sex on a washing machine during the spin cycle

This can be fun. However, the spin doesn't last forever so speed up your lovemaking or restart the spin cycle. This is listed as a mistake due to the risk of accidents. You could fall down in the midst of passion so be careful.

MISTAKE # 93
69ing

This is not a race so why not enjoy it one at a time and fully focusing on the pleasure?

MISTAKE # 94
Talking dirty

If you both like talking dirty in bed, then all is fine. However, if one person likes it and the other gets offended by it, not such a good idea. Calling her "slut" or "bitch" (or the c-word) can be offensive to her. Some women may like it and for some, it's a turn-off. You need to talk about it before you have sex. I know several women who stopped seeing a guy because they hated his profanities during sex.

CHAPTER 8

BROKEN PENIS AND OTHER ACCIDENTS DURING SEX, PAINFUL INTERCOURSE, VAGINISMUS

Not many people are aware that an erect penis can break in half, just like a human arm or leg. Penis fracture is a painful injury that needs urgent medical intervention. Surgery is usually required to repair the damage. Dyspareunia is the medical term for painful intercourse. Though it affects mostly women, men can also have this problem. Vaginismus and vestibulodynia are female conditions that cause severe pain inside the vagina. How do they happen and what are the remedies for these conditions? I explain it in this chapter.

Accidents during sex do happen. Here are some examples:

MISTAKE # 95
Breaking the penis

Penile fracture is usually a very painful and traumatic experience. As there is no bone in the penis, you might wonder how this can happen. It occurs when a man is thrusting his penis in and out of the vagina and at some point misses the entrance on the return. He may hit the pubic bone or the side of her vagina. If the woman is on top and lands with her body weight on his penis, the damage might be severe. Another scenario I heard of many years ago was a man who had sex on the stairs. He slipped out and then hit the hard edge of the staircase. They both heard the crack when his penis broke. He needed emergency surgery and happily recovered after six weeks. Since then he has fathered three children, so all is well in that department. You can see some real life testimonies on YouTube showing swollen purple penises looking like eggplants.

The penis is a vascular organ that contains three parallel tubes of spongy tissue. These tubes fill with blood when the man is sexually excited, resulting in an erection. Penile fracture is the traumatic rupture of these tubes. Vigorous masturbation can also cause penile fracture, but this happens rarely. Any fracture or damage to your penis should be immediately reported to a physician. Failing in doing so may cause permanent damage to your penis resulting in erectile dysfunction, bent shape, painful intercourse or damaged urethra.

In 2005, a man sued a woman for breaking his penis during consensual sexual intercourse (Doe v. Moe). The U.S. court ruled that she was not to blame for his fracture as she was neither reckless nor negligent and the sexual act was consensual. She was on top of him when the accident happened.

MISTAKE # 96
Breaking the prepuce

Prepuce or foreskin is the fold of skin that covers the head of a penis – the glans. Women have a prepuce on their clitoris. Damage to the prepuce can cause extreme pain and a vast amount of bleeding. Usually, this is not a serious condition, but you should avoid sex including masturbation until the tear heals (approximately two weeks). Some men may need surgical intervention, but this is rare.

MISTAKE # 97
Twisting of the testes

Twisting of the testes or testicular torsion is a very painful condition that affects mostly adolescent males, statistically one in 4,000. Surgery is often required to quickly restore blood flow to the testicle. This should be done within six hours as the testicular tissue may die and the testicle may need to be removed.

MISTAKE # 98
Stuck object in the rectum or vagina

This is a quite common scenario in emergency rooms. Ask any surgeon working in ER what weird things he had to retract from people's (mostly men) rectums. Vibrators, dildos, tubes, bottles, perfume bottles, jars, glasses, eyeglasses, light bulbs (yes, they break inside), phones, keys, toothbrushes, candles, tennis balls, money, toys, pens, hard boiled eggs, carrots, cucumbers and other vegetables. These are called "rectal foreign bodies" that require surgical removal.

MISTAKE # 99
Penile rings or cock rings

Many accidents happen when the rings get stuck on erect penises. Metal rings should never be put on penises because these swell with blood, and as the backflow is blocked, the penis becomes engorged. Men do this to increase penis size and sensitivity of the penis. Some men will use a penis pump, a vacuum pump that forces the blood into the penis while wearing the ring. Unfortunately, these rings get stuck and must be removed by electrical chainsaws in the ER. Permanent damage to penile tissue is common.

MISTAKE # 100
Penis pump

Penis pumps are vacuum devices used to enlarge an erect penis. When used incorrectly, they can damage blood vessels in the penis and even cause penile fractures that will require surgery. Bruising and blistering of the penis are also common.

MISTAKE # 101
Broken penis extensions

Penis extensions are fragile. They can break during sex so be careful if you are using them.

MISTAKE # 102
Injecting liquids or drugs into the penis

You might have heard of men injecting coke or meth inside their urethra? This is a really bad idea so don't do it. Just like women inject fillers into their lips, men use injectables to enhance their penises. You should never inject anything into your penis. Penile enhancement by Restylane (a dermal filler) should only be done by a certified physician. Some plastic surgeons use body fat to inject into the penis. Read more about genital plastic surgery on page 102.

MISTAKE # 103
Penis extension or enlargement surgery

I could write a whole chapter about this one; however, let me say only this – don't do it, it often doesn't help. These surgeries can go wrong, and they frequently do. Penile implants may help men with erectile dysfunction (ED) but using them for penis enhancement is not advisable, as there are too many risks involved.

MISTAKE # 104
Chastity belts

Both men and women have been seen in ERs wearing chastity belts that somehow got stuck on the bearer and needed manual removal, often by using an electric chainsaw.

MISTAKE # 105
Wrong lubricant

Keep your lubricant close by and not in your bathroom cabinet. When in a rush, you might grab another tube by mistake, just like the guy who put mint toothpaste on his penis.

MISTAKE # 106
Penis in a zipper

This could be a painful experience so be careful when you unzip your pants. This happens a lot to small boys but unfortunately also to grown men. Many reports from ER confirm that this is a common accident.

MISTAKE # 107
Penis in a vacuum cleaner

The London fire brigade reports incidents of releasing men's genitals from vacuum cleaners and toasters.

MISTAKE # 108
Lost keys to the handcuffs

This is a classic scenario when the fire brigade is called. They arrive to find an embarrassed couple trapped in handcuffs. Usually, one of them is attached to a bedpost.

MISTAKE # 109
Beds falling apart, frames breaking

Vigorous lovemaking can cause beds to fall apart and frames to break. Invest in a safe bed and when away use common sense.

MISTAKE # 110
Falls in the shower

Falls in the shower are common due to slippery floors, etc. Having sex in the shower comes with risks. Be very careful because several bone fractures have been reported, even fatal injuries.

MISTAKE # 111
Breaking wine glasses

Many accidents have been reported with broken wine glasses in bed. These can cause nasty cuts that may need a trip to the ER.

MISTAKE # 112
Erotic asphyxiation

See page 144 for details about this often deadly sexual practice. The FBI reports that in the United States only there are approximately 1,000 yearly deaths connected to autoerotic asphyxia.

MISTAKE # 113
Overusing erection-enhancing drugs

Overdosing on Viagra can be fatal. This happened to a man who wanted to impress his girlfriend so much that instead of one blue pill he swallowed the whole box. Unfortunately, he died of a heart attack shortly after. Read more about Viagra on page 63.

DYSPAREUNIA

Dyspareunia is the medical term for painful intercourse. Though it affects mostly women, men can also have this problem. A man with an uncircumcised penis can have a foreskin that is too tight to retract over the glans, thus causing pain during sexual activity. If this is a constant problem, minor surgery can be advisable. Infections can also cause painful intercourse and ejaculation. Peyronie's disease involves a scar tissue inside the penis that bends it out of shape and causes painful coitus, sometimes even erectile dysfunction in men. It can be caused by either medical procedures relating to the urethra or traumatic bending of the penis during coitus.

Dyspareunia is more common in women, as it affects up to 20% of females during a lifetime. Some women have it from the first time they have sex and some only sporadically. There are many causes of pelvic pain in women. It can be due to an infection, lack of lubrication, scar tissue, endometriosis, fibroids, torn ligaments from childbirth, or psychological causes.

Vestibulodynia affects approximately 10% of women. This is vulval pain at the entrance of the vagina, the inner lips, that contains the Bartholin's and vestibule glands and the urethra. It is unclear what causes vestibulodynia in women though some doctors believe it originates from an overgrowth of nerve fibers in the area.

VAGINISMUS

Vaginismus can be defined as painful spasmodic and involuntary contractions of the muscles inside the vagina. It makes penetration or medical exam impossible; even insertion of a tampon can be painful. There are several causes of vaginismus; sexual abuse in the past, sexual trauma, coerced or painful intercourse or psychological factors. Women who were married without their consent report 58% of vaginismus according to a study of sexual problems in traditionally Islamic countries (Yasan & Gurgen, 2009). The same study revealed that many men in these countries suffer from premature ejaculation (38.7%). Read more about premature ejaculation in Chapter 4.

Vaginismus can be successfully treated. The best approach is through psychological counseling combined with vaginal dilation exercises. A set of dilators is recommended. They vary in size from very small to a large one that resembles a human penis. If the woman is currently in a relationship, she should perform these exercises together with her partner. If done correctly, intercourse will finally be possible in most cases. Kegel exercises (see page 219 for details) can also help with vaginismus.

CHAPTER 9

ANAL IS THE NEW BLACK
ORAL SEX, ANAL SEX, ANILINGUS
HYGIENE, SEX TOYS

Between 75% and 80% of American adults engage in oral sex (NHSLS). How common is anal sex? If you are watching pornographic movies, then you might think that everyone does it. I have counseled many young women who feel coerced into this practice by their partners. The prevalence for trying anal sex at least once is 41% in the U.S. and 35% globally (Crooks & Baur, 2011). College women report that 32% had engaged in anal intercourse at least once (Flannery et al., 2003). Contrary to common beliefs, gay men do not practice anal sex as much as oral sex and mutual masturbation (Lever, 1994). And why do some women not like doggy style sex? In this chapter, I also talk about sex toys. Are they helpful? Who should use them and why?

ORAL SEX

"Clinton lied. A man might forget where he parks or where he lives, but he never forgets oral sex, no matter how bad it is."
~ *Barbara Bush*

Who knew that Barbara had such a great sense of humor? So what do we know about oral sex? Oral sex is when one partner stimulates the genitals of the other partner by mouth and tongue. When it is done on a man, it is called fellatio, and on a woman, it is called cunnilingus. Research shows that women like oral sex and are most likely to achieve an orgasm during intercourse that involves cunnilingus (Richters et al., 2006). Second, lesbians report the highest sexual satisfaction and orgasmic response. Contrary to common beliefs, gay men do not practice anal sex as much as oral sex and mutual masturbation (Lever, 1994). The most frequent sexual behavior among gay men is kissing on the mouth (75%), followed by oral sex (73%), partnered masturbation (68%) and lastly anal (37%) intercourse (Rosenberger et al., 2011). Oral sex can be done simultaneously, in the 69 position, or individually. Many people prefer to concentrate on either receiving or giving oral sex to enjoy it fully. Between 75% to 80% of American adults engage in oral sex (NHSLS).

As Barbara Bush already established, men like receiving blowjobs and would like their partners to perform them more often. They also like you to swallow the ejaculate.

To swallow or not to swallow?

This is a good question because many women find the taste of ejaculate disgusting. They swallow to please the man, but I have never met a woman who likes the taste. If men tasted their semen, they would be very disappointed. There is a way to change the taste by changing the diet. A vegetarian diet with plenty of fruits is the way to go, however, with the exception of onions, garlic, cauliflower, asparagus, broccoli and cabbage that makes it taste bitter. Coffee, alcohol, smoking cigarettes, red meat, hot spices and junk food should also be avoided. For best tasting semen, try to drink plenty of water and fruit juice. Eating sweets can also make the ejaculate sweeter.

Another thing about asparagus – it makes your pee smell bad. The reason for this is that asparagus contains sulfurous amino acids that once digested, break down into pungent components. Though all people are affected by this process, only 50% can smell the odor in their urine. So even if you can't smell it, your partner might.

How about the taste of a woman's vagina? Just as with men's ejaculate, the vagina smell and taste varies from woman to woman.

The same diet advice applies here. Smoking and alcohol makes it bitter. The pH of the vagina is acidic, around 4, compared to water that is 7. The pH scale is between 0 and 14; anything lower than 7 is considered acidic (citric acid in lemons have pH 2) and above 7 alkaline (baking soda is 9.5). The reason that vaginas are acidic is to ward off the unhealthy bacteria inside. You might have heard the expression that a vagina is like a self-cleaning oven that doesn't require washing inside? This is partially wrong because when it comes to intercourse, the pH of semen is between 7 and 8, much higher than the 4 of the vagina. This disparity in pH may upset the balance for some women and cause irritation or bad smell. Hygiene is very important, especially before and after sex. Regular soap should never be used on female genitals because it's too harsh on the sensitive skin. Buy a special feminine wash for this purpose. Though the majority of gynecologists advise against washing inside the vagina, many women do so anyway, especially after having sex.

Autofellatio

Autofellatio is when a man performs oral sex on his penis. This is quite difficult to achieve unless you have a very flexible spine or are good at practicing yoga. There are several actors in pornographic movies that have performed autofellatio on themselves. They usually have a large penis.

Autocunnilingus

Autocunnilingus is when a woman performs oral sexual stimulation on her genitalia. This is rather difficult to achieve unless you are a contortionist (a person with extreme physical flexibility) or a yogini (yoga master). Another reason to start that yoga class.

MISTAKE # 114
Heterosexual anal intercourse

Let me be very straight with you – don't do it. Why? Because there are many reasons you shouldn't. See the list below. Unless his penis is the size of your little finger, refrain from him pressuring you on going there. Years ago, anal sex was something in which only homosexual men engaged in. Today, thanks to readily available internet pornography, many men see it as an achievement or the Holy Grail, something they can boast about over a beer with their friends.

Pornographic movies are not made for sex education. They are mostly made by men, for men, to masturbate while watching. The porn industry in a multi-billion dollar business. They need to keep the novelty going by inventing new areas of sexual nature. In recent years, this new area has been anal sex. What is next? Putting it in the nostrils? I am not against porn per se because several better quality educational movies may be beneficial for some people. However, I am concerned when young men are learning about sex from these skewed films.

Some women may even like anal sex; I have no problem with that. However, I have counseled many young women who feel pressured by their boyfriends who say, "Try it once, and you will love it" or "My previous girlfriend loved it" or even "If you really love me you will do it." Never do anything that you don't feel comfortable doing. Several women I spoke with had anal sex while intoxicated or drugged, which seems to be the standard approach by men. Get her drunk first, then have fun. What is even more worrisome for me is the fact that these women didn't remember if the guy wore a condom. If you are ever going to try anal sex, the first thing to remember is to wear one. Condoms are not made for anal sex. Therefore, they can break easily if too much pressure is applied so pay attention and be cautious. The second thing is the lubrication; you need plenty of it. Who can forget the butter scene from *Last Tango in Paris* from 1972? Douching or having an enema is also a good idea, so there are no feces close to the anus. This seems to be a common procedure among homosexual men.

Stella says:
> *My husband nags all the time that we should have anal sex. We tried once, and it hurt badly. I love him dearly, but this is a deal-breaker for me. What shall I do?*

Reasons why you should not have anal sex:

- If you have watched any of the anal sex movies, you might have noticed how dangerous to the human health they are.

For example, you can see a guy putting his penis inside a woman's vagina (so far so good), then it goes into her anus, then out again and into her vagina or straight into her mouth. There is a copious amount of bacteria inside an anus that gets transferred to the vagina, mouth or the partner. This can cause vaginal or urinary tract infections among others.

- Sexually transmitted infections or diseases (STIs or STDs) are also transferrable through the anus. HIV (that causes AIDS), chlamydia, gonorrhea, infectious hepatitis, anal warts (also known as condyloma acuminata), human papillomavirus (HPV) and many more might enter the bloodstream because the thin lining of the anus breaks or tears easily. The tissue on the inside is much more vulnerable than the vaginal tissue.

- Anal cancer has been linked to human papillomavirus (HPV), the same virus that causes cervical cancer in women. There are several subtypes of HPV. HPV is believed to cause anal cancer as well as cervical, vaginal and penis cancer in men. Both men and women can get throat cancer from HPV. Another link to anal cancer is the human immunodeficiency virus (HIV). People with HIV infections are more likely to get anal cancer. Anal cancer is more prevalent in women than men.

- The anus is not made for friction or penetration. It does not have the natural lubrication like the vagina has. Studies have shown that the risk of contracting HIV is 30 times higher through anal sex than vaginal sex.

- The anus is a muscle, called the anal sphincter, that holds in the feces. It opens only when it needs to defecate. Forcing a penis or an object inside is not a good idea. This muscle is so tight that penetration is painful. Though men might like the tightness of the anus on their penises, they can also be hurt in the process. Speaking of objects that people put up their butts – ask any surgeon working in an emergency room what weird things he had to retract from people's (mostly men) rectums. Vibrators, dildos, tubes, bottles, perfume bottles, jars, glasses, eyeglasses, light bulbs (yes, they break inside), phones, keys, toothbrushes, candles, tennis balls, money, toys, pens, hard-boiled eggs, carrots, cucumbers and other vegetables. These are called "rectal foreign bodies" that require surgical removal.

- You can still get pregnant from anal sex; semen can leak out and get into the vagina.

- The anus is an exit, not an entrance. We are not meant to have anal sex. Fecal incontinence, bleeding and hemorrhoids are common in homosexual men practicing anal sex.

- It is rare to achieve an orgasm through anal intercourse. Most women need clitoral stimulation.

- Menstruation and preserving virginity are common reasons for practicing heterosexual anal intercourse. Are these reasons worth the risks involved?

- It hurts.

If you are a woman, don't be afraid to say NO. Do not fall for his arguments or his begging. If he loves you, he will respect your wish. I hear stories from women that are hair-raising, so don't become one of them. He might tell you that everyone is doing it. That's a lie. And if you are a man, do not succumb to peer pressure. It is not cool to have anal sex. I would guess that your penis is larger than your pinky. If not, then you are excused.

ANILINGUS

Anilingus is erotic oral stimulation of the anus, also called rimming or a rim job. Anal stimulation can be very pleasurable, but there is a health risk involved with this practice because the mouth can come in contact with human feces. Bacteria, viruses and parasites from the anus can be transmitted to the mouth, not only to the person performing anilingus, but both partners are at risk. Moving from the anus to vagina can spread sexually transmitted infections or diseases (STIs or STDs), even cause urinary tract infection. Some people advise to use a dental dam, a plastic sheet that dentists use, or plastic food wrap (a.k.a. plastic film, cling film, Glad wrap, Saran wrap, folie, foil), but this rarely is used during sex.

MISTAKE # 115
Doggy style

For those who are new to sex, doggy style is a position where the woman gets down on her knees and hands, and the man puts his penis inside her vagina from behind. This is a subject that often comes up in therapy. Men love it, and women hate it. Why is that? Let me list the facts.

Why men love doggy style:

- It is primal sex, the way animals do it.
- He is in control over his partner.
- He dominates his partner.
- He controls the pace.
- He likes what he sees (her bum, not her face).
- He is emotionally disconnected from his partner and can concentrate on his own pleasure.

Why women hate doggy style:

- All of the above to start with.
- It hurts (the position of her uterus and cervix might not agree with a thrusting penis).
- I am not a dog so stop treating me like that.
- Look into my eyes when you make love to me.
- I want to see your face.
- I want to touch you.
- I want to kiss you.
- I want to connect during sex; there is no connection here.
- My boobs are hanging down.
- It feels uncomfortable; my knees are hurting.
- It feels degrading to me.
- I feel used.
- My clitoris is not stimulated.

Communicate with your partner before engaging in something that you don't like. And just to make this clear, some women do like this position, however, many don't. It's a personal choice. The most common and most preferred sexual position is still the missionary – man on top of the woman, face-to-face. It allows for close body contact, eye contact, intimate communication, kissing and talking.

SEX TOYS

There is not much reliable research done on sex toys, but several polls concluded that approximately 50% of women have used a vibrator in their lifetime. It is also believed that women who use vibrators report higher levels of desire, greater sexual satisfaction and reach an orgasm easier. The vibrator is mostly used by women in their thirties and by those who are in relationships. Most women use them for clitoral stimulation and not for penetration, as some would presume.

The popularity of the rabbit vibrator soared after being featured in a *Sex and the City* episode called "The Turtle and the Hare" from 1998. The name refers to the part of the vibrator that is intended for clitoral stimulation because it looks like rabbit ears. The central part of the vibrator looks like a penis with a rabbit head attached to the shaft. The dual action sex toys, stimulating both the clitoris and the inside of the vagina at the same time, are the most popular selling sex toys. They offer several speeds of rotation and patterns of clitoral stimulation. It has been noticed that older women might need a stronger clitoral stimulation than young ones do. Therefore, it is a good idea to test the vibrator on your hand in the shop before buying it. Most sex toys are sold online, though, so make sure that you can return your purchase if you are not satisfied with the performance.

MISTAKE # 116
Not cleaning your vibrator

Any objects that come close to your genitals need to be properly cleaned, before and after. Dildos, plugs and vibrators, if not cleaned, can harvest disease-causing bacteria and even transmit it to your partner. You should never put anything inside your vagina that previously was inside or around your anus. This can cause infections.

CHAPTER 10

MASTURBATION AND SEX ADDICTION, HOW MUCH IS TOO MUCH?

How do we define sex addiction? Is masturbating once per day an addiction? Is watching Internet pornography on a daily basis an addiction? What is the official diagnosis? Should I be concerned? In this chapter, I explain the criteria for compulsive sexual behavior and give advice on how to deal with the problem.

MASTURBATION

Masturbation, or self-stimulation of the genitals to achieve an orgasm is very common. Men masturbate more than women do, as 95% of males and 89% of females reported that they have masturbated. The frequency of masturbation is also higher for men. Several studies concluded that college men masturbate approximately three to four times per week. As the male body produces sperm continually, it is expected that these sperm need to get out every few days. Masturbation is common even when a person has a sex partner and doesn't mean that the relationship is in trouble.

There is no official diagnosis for sex addiction in the DSM-5 so having sex or masturbating every day is regarded as okay. However, many mental health practitioners know that compulsive sexual behavior is a real problem in today's society. We see male clients who masturbate several times per day regardless of whether they are at home or at work. This is not healthy.

CYBERSEX ADDICTION

It is estimated that at least one-third of Internet users visit sexually oriented-websites. Though men are mostly responsible for surfing for sex it has been noticed that women do the same but in much lower numbers. While men are more visual and like to watch pornographic films, women like to engage in sexually explicit chat rooms.

MISTAKE # 117
Masturbating at work

If you need to masturbate outside of the privacy of your home, then you have a problem and should see someone to get help. Some people who work from home have even a bigger issue with cybersex addiction and compulsivity. The easy access to pornographic content on the Internet is causing problematic sexual behavior.

Antonio says:

> *I have a big problem. I work from home designing websites for other people. Last year, I didn't have many assignments so I started to watch porn. I got hooked, and now I don't know how to stop it. The biggest problem though is having sex with my wife. I can't ejaculate when I'm inside her. I need to stimulate my penis by hand, and it takes a long time for me to come.*

Phillip says:

> *I work for the government. Sometimes, my work is very stressful but most of the time it's boring. I don't watch porn on my work computer, but I watch it on my phone with the headphones on, usually in the toilet cubicle so no one can see me. I also masturbate there. Lately, it has been every day, sometimes two times per day. I am worried about it, as sex is on my mind all day long.*

Is your husband a cybersex addict?

More and more women who seek therapy for marriage counseling are worried that their husbands are addicted to Internet porn. They may have seen the evidence in the browsing history of his computer or walked in on him unexpected in the midst of the deed. They say that their spouse is emotionally detached from them. Stonewalling is common in these situations. The husband may say that this is not such a big deal, as everyone is doing it these days.

Paula says:
> *I walked in on John yesterday when he was masturbating. He forgot to lock the bathroom door. He was sitting on the toilet seat with his iPad on his lap. I didn't see what he was watching, but I could hear the sex noises, the moans so typical to porn movies. I felt disgusted so I promptly closed the door. He came out few a minutes later to apologize.*

Paula's husband doesn't see his behavior as an addiction but as a recreational activity that enhances his sex life. John thinks that his viewing of erotica is healthy and that watching porn together would spice up their lovemaking. Paula doesn't like pornographic films because they are degrading to women. Would Paula be willing to compromise and watch soft porn films that were made by women for women? She said that she would think about it.

Two weeks later, Paula came back to therapy and announced that she would not watch pornography and that she wanted John to stop masturbating altogether. The fact that he was doing it secretly was having an adverse effect on the relationship, she said. She believed that John was addicted to porn just like an alcoholic is addicted to booze so the best way to deal with the problem was to stop it altogether. John was not happy, but he said that he would try.

After another two weeks had passed, John said in therapy that he had stopped masturbating. Therefore, he needed more sex with Paula. He more or less demanded that they have sex at least three times per week compared to the weekly weekend sex they were having. This was not acceptable to Paula, as once weekly was already a big effort to her. Finally, they found a compromise; John was allowed to masturbate in front of Paula but not when alone.

What would you do if John were your husband? Can a wife forbid her husband to masturbate? Do you consider John to be a sex addict?

Differences in sexual desire are common in relationships. He may want to have sex every day and she only once per month. You can read more about mismatched libidos in Chapter 4.

MISTAKE # 118
Sex addiction

Sex addiction is not the same as Internet porn or cybersex addiction. The first one requires real people to have sex with, the latter requires an Internet connection and a screen. Sex addiction is not included in the DSM-5. However, it is included in the ICD-10 under "excess sexual drive" - code F52.8. Does it mean that people in Europe see sex addiction as a problem and Americans don't? It's not that simple. The debate on compulsive sexual behavior has been ongoing for many years. The experts are not able to agree on how to describe and diagnose the disorder. What is normal and what is abnormal? For example, the media have labeled Tiger Woods and Charlie Sheen as sex addicts. Would you say that they are or not? Some clinicians say that sex addiction should be called impulsive bad behavior and not classified as a disorder. Other people say it's a legitimate excuse to cheat on your spouse. Whether you pathologize the behavior or not, the phenomenon is real.

MISTAKE # 119
Cybersex addiction

Cybersex addiction is a big problem these days and it's not going away. On the contrary, it's increasing. Gone are the days when you had to go to a sex shop to buy a video. Now, you are only one click away from a pornographic website that is available 24/7 and it's free. For the first time in history, young men are reporting erectile dysfunction, ejaculation problems and low sexual desire when with a real-life partner. Depression, social anxiety, low motivation and procrastination are often the main reasons they come to therapy. However, the common denominator for these men is often Internet porn.

Research shows that high-speed Internet porn is changing the brain the same way other addictions do such as drugs, eating junk food or playing video games. In the book *Your Brain on Porn: Internet Pornography and the Emerging Science of Addiction* (2015), the author Gary Wilson describes what Internet porn does to the brain. You can also check out his website yourbrainonporn.com where he has combined hundreds of resources such as the latest research, brain scans and graphs to illustrate his point that porn on the Internet is highly addictive and damaging to your health. His Tedx presentation on the subject from 2012 has been seen on YouTube over six million times. It's called "The great porn experiment | Gary Wilson | TEDxGlasgow." He says there that most young boys with Internet access seek pornography by age 10 and that their brains are fascinated by sex.

Today's porn is far more compelling than it was in the past due to the unending novelty. It's not the nudity but the novelty that is exciting. He shows a graph with copulating rams (his website has another one with rats) that maps the time to ejaculation on one side and number of females on the other. If the ram copulates with the same female, his ejaculation takes longer each time he copulates. So from 2 minutes in the beginning, it takes him up to 16 minutes after a few times. However, if the ram is presented with a new female each time, the ejaculation time stays constant (2 minutes). This is called the Coolidge Effect – the automatic response to novel mates. Could the popularity of Tinder be attributed to this?

When the guy is clicking on pornography websites, his brain is producing dopamine surges. Each time he sees a new mate his dopamine spikes. The constant novelty, the shock and surprise rewire his brain. Gary asks if we are the first generation to masturbate left-handed.

The overproduction of dopamine causes the brain to release Delta-FosB, a protein that activates genes involved with addiction and binging. Delta-FosB rewires and changes the brain just like drug addiction does, making the person crave more consumption. The pleasure-reward system concentrates on porn, and nothing else counts because everything is boring except porn. Gary shows brain scans of drug addicts and compares them to porn addicts' brains.

Addiction-related brain changes:

1. **Sensitization** or Pavlovian conditioning. Several recent brain studies on porn users assessed sensitization, and all reported the same brain response as seen in alcoholics and drug addicts.

2. **Desensitization** often manifests as the need for greater and greater stimulation to achieve the same buzz ("tolerance"). Some porn users spend more time online, prolonging sessions

through edging, watching when not masturbating, or searching for the perfect video to end with.

3. **Hypofrontality.** Alterations in frontal-lobe gray matter and white matter correlate with reduced impulse control and the weakened ability to foresee consequences. Hypofrontality shows up as the feeling that two parts of your brain are engaged in a tug-of-war. The sensitized addiction pathways are screaming "Yes!" while your "higher brain" is saying, "No, not again!" While the executive-control portions of your brain are in a weakened condition the addiction pathways usually win.

4. **Dysfunctional stress circuits** can make even minor stress lead to cravings and relapse because they activate powerful sensitized pathways.

Source: http://www.yourbrainonporn.com/doing-what-you-evolved-to-do

Symptoms of Internet porn addiction:

- Distress about escalation to more extreme porn.
- Difficulty maintaining an erection while putting on condom.
- Delayed ejaculation (DE).
- Growing erectile dysfunction (ED), even with extreme porn.
- Inability to reach orgasm (anorgasmia).
- Decreased sensitivity in the penis.
- Loss of libido.
- Copulatory impotence (can get it up for porn, but not partners).
- Devaluation of real-life partners.
- Frequent masturbation, little satisfaction.
- Uncharacteristic, worsening social anxiety or lack of confidence.
- Morphing porn tastes that don't match sexual orientation.
- Uncharacteristic fetishes.
- Inability to concentrate, extreme restlessness.
- Depression, anxiety, brain fog.
- Impulse-control and concentration problems.

Source: http://www.yourbrainonporn.com/doing-what-you-evolved-to-do

Rebooting - Rebalancing the brain

So what can a hardcore porn addict do to reverse this dilemma? How can we cure the addiction? The solution is to give the brain a rest from porn and masturbation. This is a difficult task for an addict, as sex is part of our physiological makeup, thus, hard to give up. The good news is that you don't need to give it up forever. A few months is enough for your brain to rewire itself. Gary says it takes four to five months for a young guy and two months for older men. The reason for the disparity is that older men didn't start to have problems until they got high-speed Internet. Meanwhile, the young teens start on the high-speed Internet at a time when their brains are at peak dopamine production and brain neuroplasticity. Another vulnerability factor is that teen brains gradually strengthen heavily used circuits and prune back unused ones so by the age of 22 a man's sexual taste is set in the brain.

You can quit your porn addiction by stopping the intense artificial sexual stimulation that the Internet provides. At first, you may experience a flat-line in your genital response but after a few months, the brain resets itself. However, going back to porn is not an option, as your brain has a sensitized porn pathway that remains vulnerable and can be easily reactivated.

"Insanity is doing the same thing over and over again
and expecting different results."
~ *Albert Einstein*

CHAPTER 11

ODD FETISHES AND KINKY SEX
CAN I BORROW YOUR BRA HONEY?

One of my clients, a married man with children, could not sustain an erection unless he was wearing his wife's bra. Is he a pervert? Absolutely not. Just like human imagination, fetishes come in different shapes and forms. Role-playing, BDSM (i.e., bondage, discipline, dominance, submission, sadism, masochism) has become a common knowledge since the bestseller book *Fifty Shades of Grey* hit the shelves a few years ago. Also called "mommy porn" because it appealed mostly to married women over thirty, the book has sold over 125 million copies worldwide and has been translated into 52 languages (by June 2015).

In this chapter, I also write about self-strangulation or autoerotic asphyxia – a dangerous, often deadly form of sexual play (it kills over 1,000 men in the U.S. each year) that involves reduced supply of oxygen to the brain to heighten sexual arousal.

Who was Peeping Tom? And Lady Godiva? What do they have in common with paraphilias? And what is groping? Did you know that 50% of women are exposed to exhibitionists in their lifetime? And that up to 30% of women have been sexually abused as children? Incest and pedophilia are explained in this chapter as well.

Who was Marquis de Sade? Was Hitler a pervert? And what happened in the book and movie *The English Patient* that is so disturbing? Let's find out.

Paraphilia

First used in 1980 in the DSM, the word *paraphilia* is supposed to be less offensive or judgmental than *perversion*. It comes from Greek "para" which means aside or beside, and "philia," which means love or affection. Paraphilia refers to uncommon and atypical sexual behaviors often involving objects or deviant (abnormal) situations.

DSM-5 lists eight paraphilic disorders:

- Voyeuristic disorder (spying on others in private activities);
- Exhibitionistic disorder (exposing the genitals);
- Frotteuristic disorder (touching or rubbing against a nonconsenting individual);
- Sexual masochism disorder (undergoing humiliation, bondage, or suffering);
- Sexual sadism disorder (inflicting humiliation, bondage, or suffering);
- Pedophilic disorder (sexual focus on children);
- Fetishistic disorder (using nonliving objects or having a highly specific focus on nongenital body parts);
- Transvestic disorder (engaging in sexually arousing cross-dressing).

Paraphilias listed in the DSM-5 under Other Specified Paraphilic Disorders are:

- Telephone Scatologia (obscene phone calls to unwilling recipients),
- Necrophilia (intercourse with a corpse),
- Zoophilia (sex with animals),
- Coprophilia and Urophilia (feces or urine involved sexual arousal), and
- Autoerotic Asphyxia (strangulation or oxygen deprivation, mentioned in DSM-5 under Transvestic disorder).

There are several more unnamed "other specified and unspecified paraphilic disorders" in the DSM-5.

Latest research on the prevalence of paraphilias

In January 2016, Canadian researchers from Quebec published the study "The prevalence of paraphilic interests and behaviors in the general population: A provincial survey" (Joyal & Carpentier, 2016). They asked 1,040 people about their sexual practices. Half of the respondents had an interest in at least one paraphilia listed in the DSM-5, and one-third said that they had experienced the paraphilia at least once. The most common paraphilias were; voyeurism (35%), frotteurism (26%), fetishism (20%), and masochism (19%). Both men and women reported interest in these paraphilias. So, if 50% of people are interested in paraphilias and 35% have experienced it, why is it called deviant sexual behavior?

MISTAKE # 120
My husband is a pervert

Natasha had been married 12 years when she one day came home unexpectedly. She was astonished to see her husband wearing her bra and panties. He was sitting in front of his computer, watching porn and masturbating. "I was shocked," she said. "I just stood there and didn't know what to say. Before that day, I never saw it coming." Richard, a handsome man in his forties, was an alpha male with no homosexual tendencies or toward cross-dressing. They were both professionally successful, had three children in private schools, two dogs, a chalet in the mountains – they were the perfect couple who had it all. Looking back at that day, Natasha says that she was furious at Richard for wearing her expensive La Perla bra. Being much bigger than her, Richard had stretched the bra to its bursting point. "You ruined my bra!" she shouted. "What the hell were you thinking?!"

Richard was deeply ashamed of himself. He apologized to Natasha and promised to buy her another bra, which infuriated her even more. "You are a pervert!" she screamed. "Why are you doing this? Are you gay?"

Richard is not gay. He is a heterosexual male who gets sexually aroused by wearing female lingerie. In other words, he is a fetishist. There are many kinds of fetishism. Some people (they are mostly male) are sexually attracted to body parts such as feet or breasts.

Some like shoes, boots or socks. Then some like wearing women's underwear, just like Richard.

The origin of fetishism is hard to pinpoint. We can only speculate that it comes from childhood or early puberty. In Richard's case, we believe it was his early masturbating habits that formed the bond with women's underwear. When Richard was 12 years old, his parents hired a live-in nanny to take care of his little sister. Richard remembers her as a beautiful young woman with a drawer full of sexy lingerie. He would spy on her getting dressed or having a shower. He remembers "borrowing" her bra, getting aroused and masturbating in bed, hidden under the covers.

By the time he was 17, he had started to date girls. The excitement of bras and panties subsided remarkably when he could have real sex with his girlfriends. He doesn't remember needing the bra stimulus until a few years into the marriage to Natasha. At some point, he says, sex with Natasha became boring. There were times when he couldn't get or sustain an erection, so he experimented with Viagra (more about erectile dysfunction and Viagra in Chapter 4). One day when masturbating, he came to think of his teenage years and the nanny. He went to his wife's closet, took her bra and put it on. At that moment, he knew that this was the solution to his erectile problems, as his penis had never been this hard or large before. The excitement was unbelievable. Unfortunately, his happiness was short-lived because Natasha surprised him that fateful day.

Shortly after, they came to therapy together. Richard was ashamed to tell his story. Natasha seemed extremely confused but also very angry. At first, she wanted a divorce. She called Richard names: a pervert, freak, gay, queer, faggot and idiot, to mention a few. It took us several sessions to investigate Richard's past and to finally connect the dots. Once they both understood how and why his fetishism had formed, they could move on to repairing their relationship.

Would you say that Richard suffers from Fetishistic Disorder? Or Transvestic Fetishism? According to DSM-5, I would say no because to qualify "A diagnosis of fetishistic disorder must include clinically significant personal distress or psychosocial role impairment (Criterion B)" (APA, 2013, p. 701). Criterion B is "The fantasies, sexual urges, or behaviors cause clinically significant distress or impairment in social, occupational, or other important areas of functioning" (APA, 2013, p. 700).

In Richard's case, his behavior does not meet the clinical criteria for Fetishistic Disorder and treatment. It does not hinder him during work, social interactions or other areas of his life except sexual activities. It took a long time for Natasha to come to terms with Richard's "kinkiness." On the positive side, Richard was a good husband and a great father. As he had always been loyal to her and at all times provided for his family, she finally accepted his penchant for women's underwear under the condition that he would buy his own garments. She even helped him to shop online, carefully choosing the correct size, not for the cup but the band size around his chest. We had a few laughs about that.

At the end of the therapy, they started to have sex together, him wearing a beautiful red lacy bra, just like the one he found so many years ago in the nanny's drawers. According to both of them, there was no need for Viagra and sex had never been better.

Transvestic disorder or transvestic fetishism

Transvestic Disorder, engaging in sexually arousing cross-dressing, is listed in DSM-5 on pages 702-704 (APA, 2013). All men who dress in women's clothing don't fall under the transvestic disorder umbrella, only those who get sexual excitement from it. So actors, female impersonators, drag queens or transsexuals are excluded. Cross-dressers are usually heterosexual middle-aged (or older) married men. They don't have issues with their male gender, but they may have urges or sexual fantasies involving wearing female garments. Some say that they enjoy the softness of the fabric on their skin. Some wear stockings and garter belts – the iconic female garments of erotic dressing. Others may find themselves sexually aroused when trying on high heels.

Transvestic fetishism is a rather rare disorder, as APA (2013) reports a prevalence of 3% in the male population. It is difficult to pinpoint the origin of transvestism (the word comes from Latin for "trans," which means "across or over" and "vestere" that is "to wear" or "to dress"), but generally it starts in childhood or adolescence with a trigger of an object paired together with sexual stimulation. For example, in Richard's case mentioned above, he masturbated while touching his nanny's bra. In psychology we call this "conditioning."

So knowing this, would you allow your little boy to cross-dress for fun? Most of the time children's role-playing and dressing up will not lead to abnormal sexual behavior in adulthood. What about the wives and girlfriends then? Because these men are heterosexual, at some point there will be a conflict with their spouses. Many women don't understand this behavior, therefore, becoming highly judgmental, even shocked when confronted with the situation. If you are one of those women, it may be helpful to remember that your guy acquired his penchant for cross-dressing at an early age, much before he met you, and was conditioned into this behavior. It has nothing to do with you or with your sexual attractiveness. Once they discover "the secret," many women learn to live with it but some find it unacceptable. Before you throw in the towel on your marriage, try couples therapy to see if you can save your relationship.

Voyeuristic disorder

Voyeurism is watching unsuspecting persons getting undressed, having sex, or other private nature activities, meanwhile obtaining sexual arousal or gratification from the practice. The word "voyeur" comes from French and means one who looks. DSM-5 estimates the prevalence of Voyeuristic Disorder to be 12% in men and 4% in women. The person needs to be a minimum of 18 years old to be diagnosed because many adolescent men practice voyeurism out of puberty-related curiosity. The Peeping Tom gets sexually aroused by watching people undressing or having sex. This is often done in hiding. He might be walking close to windows at night or cruising the neighborhood by car in hope of seeing something interesting. When the risk of discovery is high, the sexual excitement is high as well.

The expression "Peeping Tom" comes originally from the Lady Godiva legend. Lady Godiva (1010-1067), the wife of Leofric, made a deal with her husband who imposed high taxes on the residents of Coventry, England. He told her that if she rode naked through the streets of Coventry, he would lower the taxes. She took him up on his proposal and naked, just covered by her long hair, she rode the streets of the city. Before doing so, she warned the residents to stay inside and not to look outside the windows as she rode by. Everyone obliged except Tom, the tailor. He was so curious that he drilled a hole in his shutters and secretly watched Lady Godiva as she passed by. He was immediately struck blind.

In later years, new areas of voyeurism have been established. The technology today allows for small hidden cameras (voyeurcams), often installed in changing rooms, showers, bathrooms or hotel rooms that transmit directly to websites on the Internet for everyone to watch. Usually, the victims are young women who unbeknownst to them are being watched by masturbating men.

Exhibitionistic disorder

Exhibitionism or indecent exposure (exposing the genitals to an unwilling observer) is a coercive paraphilia usually performed by men. DSM-5 states the prevalence is 2%-4% of the general male population. A Swedish study (based on self-reports) found that some women reported exposing their genitals for sexual pleasure as well. The number of women was 2.1% and for men 4.3% (Långström & Seto, 2006).

So who is an exhibitionist and why is he doing that? According to DSM-5, it is an adult male who during adolescence or early adulthood became sexually aroused by exposing his genitals to unsuspecting persons. He may show his naked body or only his penis. The classic picture of an exhibitionist is a man opening his raincoat in front of a shocked woman. His intent is to seek attention. He may have an erection or get one later when thinking about the incident. He may masturbate shortly afterward, still excited about what just happened.

These men are often shy and insecure. They have difficulties in their relationships, have low self-esteem and fear of rejection. Usually, they are nonaggressive and will dash off before the woman calls for help. Some of them do this to affirm their masculinity. When interviewed they proclaimed that they were hoping for the women to show their genitals as well. However, if the woman would approach them, they would flee the scene (Murphy & Page, 2008).

Approximately 50% of women have been targets of exhibitionists. What to do if you are a woman, and this happens to you? The best would be not to overreact. Ignore him and simply continue to go about your business, leaving him unaffected by your response. In rare cases, the exhibitionist will expose himself in front of children. This can be a traumatizing experience for a young child.

Frotteuristic disorder

Frotteuristic disorder, touching or rubbing against a non-consenting individual, is quite common, as 30% of adult U.S. men have engaged in this practice (APA, 2013). The name "frottage" comes from French "frotter," which means to rub. Frotteurism usually happens in crowded places such as busses, trams, subways, trains, elevators, concerts or festivals. The man comes close to the woman and rubs his penis against her. He gets sexually aroused while doing so; he may ejaculate there and then or masturbate later.

Touching the woman with a hand, usually genitals, buttocks, thighs or breasts is called toucherism. In Japan, some trains have women-only cars to shield them from the frotteurs. Many women tell stories from visiting crowded places abroad, for example in Africa, the Middle East or Asia while on holidays. They have been groped on their private parts even when the husband was present. This happens very fast, and it's impossible to see where the hand is coming from. Though frotteurism is illegal and falls under sexual harassment, it rarely happens that the offender gets arrested and prosecuted.

Autoerotic asphyxia

Autoerotic asphyxia, also called asphyxiophilia or hypoxyphilia is a dangerous form of paraphilia that is mostly practiced by white men (Sauvageau & Racette, 2006). The idea is to reduce oxygen supply to the brain during masturbation to intensify the orgasm. To achieve the oxygen deprivation the person uses a rope or a belt for self-strangulation. Sometimes, a plastic bag is used. Obviously, this is a very dangerous activity that often ends in death.

MISTAKE # 121
Playing deadly games

The origin of autoerotic asphyxia has been connected to historical deaths by hanging. During executions by hanging, it was noticed that the victims developed an erection, sometimes called a "death erection." People believed that hanging caused sexual pleasure but the reason for this could be a severed spinal cord (Dake, 2015).

The practice of autoerotic asphyxia is highly dangerous as there are many deadly accidents due to loss of control and paraphernalia failure. It is estimated that in the United States there are approximately 1,000 yearly deaths connected to autoerotic asphyxia (Cowell, 2009; Jenkins, 2000). In reality, the number could be higher as the practice is enacted in secret and likely underreported. It is common for coroners to record a verdict of accident or misadventure. Sometimes, the verdict is left open because the bereaved families prefer this (Dake, 2015). As the victims are often found by shocked parents or relatives that may clean up the evidence of sexual play, and the police investigators may not notice the signs of autoerotic asphyxia, the cases are often reported as intentional suicide (Jenkins, 2000).

Some autoerotic asphyxia victims die a non-asphyxial death – such as heart attack, stroke or exposure. In these cases, the coroner reports the manner of death a natural (Dake, 2015). A typical victim is a white Caucasian male (96%) and average age 33.

The DSM-5 mentions autoerotic asphyxia under Transvestic Disorder (on page 704) stating that this behavior is co-morbid with transvestism. In 2009, it was reported that American actor David Carradine, known from Kung Fu and Kill Bill movies, died from accidental asphyxiation in a hotel room in Thailand. He was allegedly found hanging by a rope, naked, with his hands and genitals tied up. Photos taken by the police from the scene are still circulating on the Internet. His two ex-wives confirmed David's penchant for bondage involved sexual practices.

Michael Hutchence, the Australian lead singer of rock band INXS, was found dead in a hotel room in Sydney in 1997. The official cause of death was suicide by strangulation. However, it emerged later that Michael was naked and allegedly died when engaging in autoerotic asphyxia. Each year thousands of women worldwide lose their sons, husbands, brothers and boyfriends to a deadly chase of sexual euphoria. Don't do it; it's not worth it! Even if you have someone to supervise you things can go wrong. Asphyxiation can trigger cardiac arrest and a heart attack. It can also cause brain damage due to oxygen deprivation of the brain. This can happen within a few minutes so successful resuscitation might still leave you brain damaged for life.

BDSM
Bondage, Discipline, Dominance
Submission, Sadism, Masochism

Sexual Masochism Disorder (undergoing humiliation, bondage or suffering) and Sexual Sadism Disorder (inflicting humiliation, bondage or suffering) are listed separately in DSM-5 though they both derive from the same notion of associating pain with sexual pleasure. To qualify to be diagnosed with the disorder, the person must declare anxiety, distress, guilt, shame or psychological difficulties. Most of the time this is not the case, as these people are otherwise functioning normally in the society and see their sexual behavior as an enhancement of their sexuality.

Let's clarify what the words stand for:

- **B&D, B/D, or BD** – bondage and discipline
- **D&s, D/s, or Ds** – dominance and submission
- **S&M, S/M, or SM** – sadism and masochism
- **Sadomasochist** (SM) – a person who likes to inflict sexual pain on others and gets sexually aroused by doing so.
- **Sadist** – a person who derives pleasure through cruelty or pain to others. Not necessarily sexual pleasure. The word comes from Marquis de Sade (1740-1814), a French aristocrat who wrote erotic novels with emphasis on sexual violence and cruelty.
- **Masochist** – a person who enjoys receiving sexual pain from others and gets sexually aroused by doing so.
- **Bondage** – sexual play where the person is sexually aroused by being tied up and restricted from movement.
- **Discipline** – refers to training and punishing the submissive person.
- **Dom, Dominatrix, Domme, Dominant** – a person who exercises control over another person.
- **Sub, submissive** – a person who gives up control to another person who dominates him/her.

Role-playing in BDSM refers to a relationship between a dominant or a top (dominatrix when a woman, dom when a man) and a submissive (sub) or a bottom. We might think that the dominant has all the power in this play, but it is not so. As this interaction is consensual and the submissive has the authority to stop the "scene" by saying a code word or a safe word, he or she is in charge. Usually, the previously agreed on word is not "no" or "stop" but something else out of the context such as "red" or "apple." The relationship is based on mutual trust and is usually negotiated in advance by both partners. Sometimes, they even sign a detailed contract, precisely specifying the boundaries of the game.

This role-play often involves bondage, a type of restriction by either ropes, belts, chains or handcuffs. There are specific rules to follow, especially for the sub. If the sub fails to follow the rules, he or she may be punished (or disciplined) by the dom. The punishment can be corporal, such as spanking, paddling, caning or flogging or psychological humiliation of the sub.

People engaging in the master/slave relationships often belong to a BDSM organization where they socialize and learn from each other. These organizations report that the man to woman ratio is 50/50. However, many married men visit dungeons where they pay for dominatrix services. Dungeons are fully equipped rooms for the purpose of BDSM play. A dominatrix does not have sex with the client, and she always stays fully dressed. Her role is to discipline the client who often gets sexually aroused by being punished or humiliated. Usually, the slave is not allowed to touch his mistress above her knees.

You might wonder who are the clients and why they engage in these practices? When interviewing the professionals (pro-dommes), several interesting facts surfaced. The client can be your next-door neighbor or your boss who is wearing the most expensive suit. They want to play a naughty boy at school who is reprimanded by the schoolmistress. These men are educated, middle- and upper-class people who often work in high positions where they have extensive power over others. They may want to relinquish that power for a short time, thus, relax a little. Alternatively, some clients may have low self-esteem and think that they deserve to be punished. Freud believed that the desire to be a sub derives from the guilt over the desire to want to dominate. He also postulated that a man who wants to be bonded and spanked assumes a passive female role. Other psychologists may argue that sadomasochist tendencies start already in childhood when the child is abused by his or her parents.

However, when asked, many masochists report happy childhoods with no traumas or abuse.

BDSM has become common knowledge since the bestseller book *Fifty Shades of Grey* hit the shelves a few years ago. Also called "mommy porn" because it appealed mostly to married women over thirty, the book has sold over 125 million copies worldwide and has been translated into 52 languages (by June 2015). The story is about Christian Grey, a young, rich businessman, and Anastasia Steele, a sexually inexperienced student. A movie with the same title was released in early 2015. It grossed almost $600 million worldwide, on a budget of $40 million. A sequel that is currently filming in Vancouver is called *Fifty Shades Darker*. Since the release of the first movie, several campaigns have criticized it for having a negative impact on the community by glamorizing sexual abuse and violence against women.

Pedophilic disorder

Pedophilia has been included in the DSM since 1968. In the new edition, DSM-5, that came out in May 2013, it is listed under Paraphilias. Pedophilia comes from Greek "paidi" which means child and "philia," which means love or affection. Pedophilic disorder is classified as "Recurrent, intense sexually arousing fantasies, sexual urges or behaviors involving sexual activity with a prepubescent child or children (generally age 13 years or younger)" (APA, 2013, p. 697). Furthermore "The individual has acted on these sexual urges, or the sexual urges or fantasies cause marked distress or interpersonal difficulty" (APA, 2013, p. 697).

The pedophile must be at least 16 years old and at least five years older than the child. So a 16-year old boy having sex with a 12-year old girl is not classified as a pedophile.

Some pedophiles are sexually attracted only to children and some to both children and adults. Some are exclusively attracted to boys, some only to girls and some to both sexes.

DSM-5 estimates the prevalence of pedophilia from 3% to 5% in men, meaning that three to five men out of every hundred are sexually attracted to children. There are no statistics available for women though it is known that female pedophiles exist as well but in much lower numbers.

Pedophilia usually manifests in puberty, is considered a lifelong condition and by many experts impossible to treat. Therapy can help with containing the person's feelings, thus, not acting out on the urges, but not with the initial sexual attraction toward children. Medication for reducing the sex drive may help and chemical castration for child offenders, though it is a controversial subject.

Not every pedophile is a child molester. They may have sexual urges and fantasies about children but don't act on them. Though masturbation while watching child pornography is common, reaching out to children for sexual gratification may not happen.

The origins of pedophilia are not clear, but many pedophiles were sexually abused as children (Putnam, 2003).

MISTAKE # 122
Not believing your child

Most of the time a pedophile is a white heterosexual man who knows the victim (Salter, 2003). He picks his victim among friends, family, neighbors or at his workplace. He often chooses a profession where he comes in contact with children such as a teacher, sports coach or counselor. Some men will embark on a romantic relationship with women who have children so they can come close to them. As a mother, you need to be observant and responsive to your child's signals. Many mothers refuse to listen to their children, denying the abuse out of convenience or make other excuses to avoid seeing the problem. As a mother, it is your duty to protect your child. Lovers may come and go, but your children only have one mother. Be their advocate and defend your children. Do not live in denial because failing to acknowledge the abuse or to believe your child can cause greater harm than the abuse itself.

Joanna says:
> *My mother pretended like nothing happened to me. She looked the other way. My stepfather would come to my room at night and put his hands on my private parts. I was 11. He told me to keep quiet about it but I finally told Mom. She didn't believe me.*

MISTAKE # 123
Not seeking help

If you are a survivor of childhood sexual abuse don't hesitate to seek help. A skilled therapist will help you to deal with your past experiences and shed some light on how they may affect you in your life and current relationships with people. It is important to remember that it was not your fault the sexual abuse happened to you. Do not feel ashamed or guilty about it. Seek therapy and get help; it is never too late to start healing from your experiences. You are not alone; child sexual abuse is quite common in our society. The statistics speak for themselves. Though it is believed that most of the sexual abuse of children is never reported, a recent worldwide study by Swiss researchers concluded that 8% to 31% of girls and 3% to 17% of boys have been sexually abused (Barth et al., 2012). The study included 24 countries. These numbers are astonishing when taking into consideration that most of the abuse is never reported to the authorities.

The difference between pedophilia and incest

Pedophilia or child molestation is usually considered between nonrelatives. On the other hand, incest refers to sexual contact between relatives, often an adult and a child. It can also be between siblings (both child or adults), first cousins (not in all cultures) or parents, stepparents, uncles, aunts, grandparents and the child.

Should first cousins be allowed to marry?

In regard to first cousin marriages, which are allowed in some countries, the statistics show a much higher rate of child disabilities, recessive genetic disorders, birth defects and infant mortality. Many children die in infancy, and those who survive may develop serious disabilities. Research from the UK shows that cousin marriages in the Pakistani community produce 700 children each year with genetic impairments. When it comes to incest, several studies on incestuous reproduction between parent-child or between siblings have shown up to 50% risk of genetic disabilities or infant mortality in these children.

Klismaphilia

Klismaphilia is mentioned in DSM-5 under Other Specified Paraphilic Disorder on page 705 (APA, 2013). Klismaphilia is a rare paraphilia that involves sexual pleasure from enemas. "Klisma" means enema in Greek. It is practiced both by men and women. The origin of this behavior may come from receiving enemas in childhood. Anal stimulation by a loving mother may have contributed to forming this paraphilia.

Coprophilia

Coprophilia is mentioned in DSM-5 under Other Specified Paraphilic Disorder on page 705 (APA, 2013). Coprophilia is a rare paraphilia that involves sexual pleasure from contact with feces, either by defecating on someone or being defecated on. Some individuals like to taste or eat the feces. The word "kopro" means manure or dung in Greek.

Hitler's fecal attraction

Interestingly, in the book *Hitler was a British Agent*, writer Greg Hallet wrote in the chapter called *Hitler's Sexuality* that Hitler engaged in coprophilia, urophilia, sadomasochism and homosexuality (Hallet, 2008). This revelation was based on statements from August Kubizek, Hitler's close boyhood friend from Linz, who said Hitler "liked to be verbally abused and slapped around, to have his head urinated on, his chest shat on, and to have sex with men." Is there any truth to that? I don't know, but there are several similar reports by the Office of Strategic Services (OSS), a United States intelligence agency formed during WWII. OSS was a predecessor of the Central Intelligence Agency (CIA).

Urophilia

Urophilia is mentioned in DSM-5 under Other Specified Paraphilic Disorder on page 705 (APA, 2013). Urophilia or Urolagnia, sometimes called *watersports* or *golden showers*, is a rare paraphilia that involves sexual pleasure from contact with urine, by either urinating on someone or being urinated on. Some individuals like to taste or drink the urine (urophagia). Some like to watch others urinate. They say that the feeling of warm urine on their bodies feels relaxing to them. To empty a full bladder can also be sexually pleasurable for an urophiliac. Some people say that urinating on someone gives them a feeling of dominance over the person. We can only speculate about the origins of this unusual paraphilia. Could this be a fixation in Freud's anal stage?

Havelock Ellis (1859-1939) was a British physician who studied sexuality. He admitted to being an urophiliac. Ellis recalled watching his mother urinating when he was 12 years old (Bering, 2013). He became fascinated with the urine and years later conducted several studies on bladders and urinary streams (Ellis, 1925). Rumor has it that though he was married, he was impotent until the age of 60 until he discovered that watching a woman urinate made him sexually aroused.

Infantilism

Infantilism, being sexually excited from dressing as an adult baby, is a rare paraphilia that is not mentioned in DSM-5 but was classified as sexual masochism in DSM-IV-TR (APA, 2000, p. 572). This classification was wrong, as the majority of infantilists don't want to be hurt or humiliated. A typical infantilist is a man in his late thirties who wants to regress to infant state by wearing nappies, urinating and defecating in them like a baby, drinking from a baby bottle, sucking a pacifier, sleeping in a large baby crib and talking like a baby. Masturbating while wearing a nappy is common in this disorder. There are different kinds of infantilism. Adult baby (AB) is a person who role-plays being a baby in diapers. Diaper lover (DL) is a person who wears diapers but not necessarily wants to act like a baby. He has a fetish for diapers and gets sexually excited by the diaper. The origin of this disorder is not known.

Zoophilia

Zoophilia, also called bestiality or zoosexuality, is mentioned in DSM-5 under Other Specified Paraphilic Disorder on page 705 (APA, 2013). Zoophilia refers to sexual activity between people and animals. Alfred Kinsey (remember him from Chapter 1?) published a study in 1948 where he reported that 8% of men and 4% of women had engaged in sexual activities with animals. Among men living on farms, 17% admitted to sexual intercourse with animals. Sheep, donkeys, goats, ducks, geese, dogs and cats were the most used animals for sexual activities. Zoophilia may not classify as a lifelong paraphilia as many males (or females) practice it in the absence of a human sexual partner. Women reported more incidents with dogs licking their genitals. Intercourse with dogs was less common, though it did happen in a few cases (Kinsey et al., 1953).

Telephone scatologia

Telephone scatologia or obscene phone calling to unwilling recipients, is mentioned in DSM-5 under Other Specified Paraphilic Disorder on page 705 (APA, 2013). The word "skato" comes from Greek and translates to "skit" or "dung" and "logos" means "speech." Individuals with this disorder are mostly men. They get sexually aroused by calling women and verbally assaulting them with profane sexual language. They may breathe heavily while masturbating during the phone call or masturbate shortly afterward. The scatologist is looking for a vulnerable woman because he usually has low self-esteem and wants to target someone weaker than he is. Hearing her voice may be enough for his sexual excitement, so if you are the victim, the best response is not to react emotionally and to hang up immediately. If he calls again, don't answer. This behavior is classified as sexual harassment and should be reported to the police.

Necrophilia

Necrophilia, or intercourse with a corpse, is mentioned in DSM-5 under Other Specified Paraphilic Disorder on page 705 (APA, 2013). "Nekros" means dead in Greek and "philia" means love or affection.

There is not much research done on this rare paraphilia other than a literature review by Rosman and Resnick (1989). They investigated 122 cases of necrophilia, 88 published and 34 unpublished. They concluded that people engaging in necrophilia were not mentally retarded, psychotic (only 11% were psychotic) or sadistic but 50%

had personality disorders, and 55% had unusual belief systems. These individuals, mostly men (95%), were searching for a sexual partner that would not reject them (68%). More than half of them, 53%, worked in places with dead people like funeral homes, cemeteries, churches, hospitals or morgues, so they had easy access to corpses. Some necrophiles committed homicide (28%). Interestingly, in this group of murderers, 46% had occupational access to bodies; yet, they still killed their victims.

Rosman and Resnick concluded that the typical necrophile has a profound lack of self-esteem, is afraid of rejection, or may be fearful of the dead, thus, transforms his fear into sexual desire for the dead. Being such a rare disorder, it is difficult to pinpoint the origin of necrophilia. Many experts are united in the conclusion that early childhood sexual, physical and emotional abuse actively contribute to this disorder.

Necrophilia in the movies

One interesting case of romantic necrophilia that was highly debated at the time can be seen in the film *The English Patient* from 1996. Based on the book by Michael Ondaatje (1993) with the same title, the story is about a love affair between Almásy and Katherine. When Almásy returns to the cave to fetch the wounded Katherine, she has long been dead.

Ondaatje (1993) wrote:
She was on her back, positioned the way the medieval dead lie.
I approached her naked as I would have done in our South Cairo room, wanting to undress her, still wanting to love her.
What is terrible in what I did? Don't we forgive everything of a lover? We forgive selfishness, desire, guile. As long as we are the motive for it. You can make love to a woman with a broken arm, or a woman with a fever. She once sucked blood from a cut on my hand as I had tasted and swallowed her menstrual blood. There are some European words you can never translate properly into another language. Felhomaly. The dusk of graves. With the connotation of intimacy there between the dead and the living.
(p. 170)

CHAPTER 12

EXTRAMARITAL AFFAIRS, POLYGAMY, SWINGING
CAN A RELATIONSHIP SURVIVE INFIDELITY?
THE REPTILIAN BRAIN

In a study conducted by marriage counselor Gary Neuman, it was estimated that one in 2.7 men will cheat – and most of their wives will never know about it. Twelve percent of men will cheat no matter what and continue to cheat with no remorse. So in practice, you can give him a blowjob in the morning, and he will still cheat in the afternoon. The rest of cheaters say that emotional disconnection and lack of thoughtful gestures from their wives was the main reason why they cheated. Infidelity and sexual dissatisfaction are the two main reasons couples come to see me for therapy. Can a marriage survive infidelity? What are the signs of infidelity? There are 32 signs that your spouse is having an affair. In this chapter, I also discuss swinging couples, polygamists and the reptilian brain.

MISTAKE # 124
Cheating on your spouse

Cheating, also known as infidelity, adultery or having an affair, can be defined as nonconsensual extramarital sex. Though you don't need to be married, being in a monogamous relationship is enough. An affair can be anything from a one-night stand to a full-blown emotional relationship. The majority of people regard cheating as wrong; yet, many practice it. I have seen many marriages fall apart due to infidelity, marriages that could have been saved if the couple came to therapy first. The consequences are disastrous, so think twice before you cheat on your spouse. Once the affair is discovered, the betrayed partner often feels devastated. Feelings of rejection, anger, resentment, shame, jealousy, helplessness, inadequacy, lack of self-esteem and even guilt are common.

So what are the options? Can we do things differently? Talk to your partner about your relationship and the feelings that you might have for another person. Discuss what is wrong and why you might be attracted to someone else. After all, we are sexual beings that will always pick up signals from other people. If you are currently in a committed relationship, you owe it to be honest to your partner. Work on your issues first before taking the leap to the other side of the fence.

"The grass is not greener on the other side,
it's greener where you water it."

MISTAKE # 125
All men cheat

Both men and women cheat, but the research shows that men do it more frequently than women do. In a study conducted by marriage counselor Gary Neuman (2008), it was estimated that 1 in 2.7 married men will cheat – and most of their wives will never know about it. Twelve percent of men will cheat no matter what and continue to cheat with no remorse. So, in practice, you can give him a blowjob in the morning, and he will still cheat in the afternoon. The rest of the cheaters, 88%, say that "lack of thoughtful gestures from their wives and emotional disconnection" were the main reasons why they cheated.

Infidelity and sexual dissatisfaction are the two main reasons couples come to see me for therapy. Most of the time, it is the man who has cheated; though, I have had several cases where the woman was at fault. In my opinion, the reason for this disparity is that women are more often willing to repair the relationship and to come to couples counseling. Many women may believe that a cheating husband is a common practice in our society. Alternatively, if a man has been cheated on, he will most likely leave his wife and move on with his life.

MISTAKE # 126
Men cheat because they want sex

Only 8% of men in Gary Neuman's survey said that sexual dissatisfaction was the main reason for their infidelity. Forty-eight percent rated emotional dissatisfaction as the primary cause. It's a myth that men only want to have sex. For 92% of the men living in the United States, cheating is not mainly about sex. Men need to feel validated by their partners; they need to feel needed and appreciated. They try hard to please and to do the right things but without positive feedback and affirmation from their wives, they feel lost and insecure.

MISTAKE # 127
The other woman is younger and sexier

This is not true; only 12% said that this was the case. The majority of mistresses were not any better looking than the wives were. They were filling an emotional void that the man was feeling at the time, and the sex came along. Men express their loving feelings through sex, so when he feels connected to a woman, sex follows. Seventy-three percent of men waited at least a month to have sex with the other woman. Only 6% had sex the same night they met. So, one-night stands are not the main reason of sexual infidelity. Actually, 40% of mistresses were colleagues at work, where he spends most of his time when not at home. The men felt appreciated by their coworkers. Some worked together on a project, traveled together to conferences and some had work-related lunches or dinners together. Seventy-seven percent of cheating men have friends who cheat, so infidelity seems normal to them. Sixty-six percent reported that they felt guilty about the affair and wished that it never happened. Sixty-eight percent said that they never thought they would be unfaithful, never expected it to happen.

MISTAKE # 128
Being the other woman

A love affair with a married man is a waste of time. You might think that he will leave his wife and kids for you. Some men do, but most of them don't. From the beginning, he might tell you that his marriage is over, that he is not in love with his wife, that he got married for all the wrong reasons, that you are the only one who understands him, that you are his soul mate, that he wishes he met you years ago. You will fall for his sweet talk, the gifts, the romance, the stolen moments in rented hotel rooms. Then you will realize that you will always come second in his life. This is not what you want so the conflict will start, and the dynamic of your relationship will change. You will spend the holidays alone, waiting for his messages. You will suffer when he is not around. Finally, he will break your heart because his wife gets pregnant. How did that happen if they were not sleeping together? Or he will tell you that they decided to give the marriage another chance. This actually happened to a few clients of mine. They were all lovely women who wanted so much to be loved that they believed in miracles.

One of my clients was trapped in such a relationship for 15 years. Her lover always promised to divorce his wife, but there were several "issues" that came up each time. It could be money, work, children (anything from being sick to not wanting to hurt his family with impending divorce), or even a dying relative. The excuses were endless. She wasted 15 years waiting for his divorce. Finally, one day, she came to therapy. She spent the first session crying her eyes out. From being suicidal to finding new love took her five months. Our work together was not easy because once her lover realized that she was on her way out of the relationship, he promptly separated from his wife. The separation lasted four weeks until another excuse came up and he moved back home to his wife and kids. This time around, my client had the courage to end the relationship and move on with her life. It was the best decision she ever made. She is now engaged to a sweet and loving man who wants to marry her. For the first time in her life, she is number one on someone's list.

Finally, let's say that he will leave his wife for you and you start afresh. A new happy relationship can't be built on someone else's misery; remember that. You can call it karma or whatever you fancy, but what goes around, comes around. One day you will argue, and he will tell you that he left his wife and kids for you. You may be called a home wrecker by his children or his extended family members. Statistics show that second-time marriages have a higher divorce rate than first-time marriages do. The latter have over a 50%

dissolution rate; you can do the math and calculate your chances. The risk of you becoming the non-understanding wife and him finding a new mistress is rather high. Soon, he will be filling the void in his life with someone else. You deserve better than that.

MISTAKE # 129
Most marriages don't survive infidelity

Can a relationship survive infidelity? This is a difficult question to answer because it all depends on the circumstances. You have to ask yourself first if the relationship is worth saving. How much have you invested into this relationship? I don't mean money but emotional investment. Do you have children? What will happen to them in the case of a divorce? Most importantly, don't panic. Find a good therapist and go together to counseling. A skilled therapist will work with you and guide you through the process in a non-judgmental and empathetic way. There are certain crucial steps to follow that I will explain next.

Step 1: The affair must end before the work can start. It's useless to have couples therapy if one of the spouses is seeing someone else romantically. Let me be very clear here, no contact and I mean no emails, no texts, no Facebook, no phone calls, nada. Make sure that the mistress/lover understands that you are giving the relationship another chance so please leave us alone; we need to work this out, just the two of us. If they still try to contact you, don't respond and be honest toward your spouse about receiving any messages. Make sure your spouse understands that you are being transparent here. What to do if you work together? Change your job, get transferred, do whatever possible to cease contact with the person.

Step 2: The straying partner must be genuinely remorseful. Otherwise this will not work. A sincere, authentic, heartfelt apology is needed at this stage. A simple sorry is not enough. Your spouse needs to know that you made a terrible mistake and that you really mean it. He or she wants to hear that this will never happen again in the future and that with time you can be trusted again. This apology has to be repeated several times on different occasions. I cannot stress enough how important this stage is, especially for women.

They need to hear the apology over and over again, like a broken record.

Step 3:   Acknowledge the pain of the wronged spouse. I have seen several couples rushing through this step. However, you need to truly feel the pain of your spouse. Infidelity is the most hurtful experience. We feel betrayed, angry and abandoned by our life partners, the people that we trusted most, the people who were supposed to protect us and cherish us. Be patient, listen to your spouse, answer all the questions they need to know and most of all, be empathetic. This step is crucial for the healing to begin. It might take weeks or even months.

Step 4:   Learning to forgive. Forgiving doesn't mean forgetting. Most people will never forget the betrayal as long as they live. Forgiving means letting go of the resentment and the anger. It means not bringing it up again in other arguments or situations, not using it against the straying partner. This is very difficult to do. I know a woman that still after 45 years of marriage reminds her husband of his extramarital affair he had some 30 years ago. The infidelity lasted a few weeks; yet, so many years later they are still fighting over it. This is not a happy marriage.

Step 5:   Rebuilding the trust. The betrayed partner must learn to trust again. He or she should be given access to all correspondence, emails, texts, etc. Total transparency is crucial at this stage. We are not talking some 20 years forward but for the near future, until the trust is restored, the person who cheated is on probation. All extracurricular activities must be explained and approved by the wronged spouse. Be prepared to answer questions about your whereabouts. Make sure you are reachable by phone at all times. Bring home receipts from restaurants or take pictures with your phone to back up your stories.

Step 6:   Building a new relationship. You need a new start. The old relationship will never be the same. You can't rush this process. Imagine that you divorced, went separate ways, met again after a few years and started dating again. Take it slowly. Plan romantic dates, go to the movies or take a weekend trip, just as you did when you first met. During this stage, we need to address any relationship issues that were present before the affair started. What went wrong? Why did the person stray? How was your communication? Any sexual problems? Can we fix this?

Sean says:

> *The affair just happened, it was not planned. She was there for me when I was feeling down. We worked together, so I spent more time with her than with my wife. I changed my job to save my marriage.*

Restoring your love is possible, I have seen it happen and when it happens, I am the most grateful person in the room. A sincere thank you to all my clients for letting me be a part of your journey.

POLYGAMY

MISTAKE # 130
The more, the merrier?

The word polygamy comes from Greek "polygamia," which means marriage to many spouses. Usually, it is the man who marries several wives. When a woman has several husbands, it is called polyandry. Though formerly practiced in parts of China, Nepal and India, it is very rare in today's society. The isolated Zo'é tribe that lives in the Amazon rainforest of northern Brazil practices polyandry. It is common for women to have several husbands, sometimes as young as 13 years old.

Polygamy is illegal in the Western world. However, in the United States alone, there are estimated 30,000 to 50,000 polygamists, mostly Mormons and a growing number of Muslims. In the Middle East and parts of Asia and Africa, polygamy is accepted because of the Muslim religion. Islam permits a man to have up to four wives, but he has to treat them equally, which often proves to be a difficult task. The origin of this law dates back before the Qur'an was even written and the reason given was the frequent wars that left many women widowed and children orphaned. As the number of women was greater than the number of men, it was socially accepted, and encouraged, for a man to take care of more than one woman.

In today's society, things are more complicated. For example, have a look at the Sultan of Brunei. One of the wealthiest men in the world, the Sultan lives in Bandar Seri Begawan – the capital city of Brunei, in a 1,800-room palace especially built for him in 1984. Considered the largest and most modern palace in the world (the floor area is over 2 million square feet or 186,000 square meters), it cost 1.4 billion US dollars to build. No luxury was spared here. The gold you see is real gold indeed. The marble and the chandeliers were flown in from Italy. The exquisite furniture was hand-made in Europe. Even the horses stay in air-conditioned stables. The luxury is mind blowing.

He was born in 1946. In 1965, he married his first cousin. They have six children together. By the age of 21, in 1967, his father abdicated, and he became the ruler of Brunei. He met his second wife in 1980. She was working as a flight attendant on Royal Brunei Airlines. The rumor has it that she spilled a drink in his lap, and when vigorously drying his pants, romance bloomed, and the Sultan was hooked. They married in 1982, had four children, then divorced in 2003. She moved from Brunei to the UK. His third wife was 33 years younger. They met in 2005 in Malaysia while she worked as a TV presenter. Lovely and educated, she charmed the Sultan from day one. They were quickly married in a secret ceremony, but the news soon leaked out, and she officially became the third wife, excuse me, officially the second wife. Two children and a few years later, she also ran away. Both ex-wives were stripped of their royal titles and honors. Despite all his wealth, the Sultan failed to stay married to more than one woman, his first cousin.

There is not much research conducted about polygamous marriages. However, what we know for sure is that women are negatively affected by them. They suffer from depression, anxiety, low self-esteem and less marital satisfaction than women in monogamous marriages do (Al-Krenavi & Slonim-Nevo, 2008).

SWINGING COUPLES

MISTAKE # 131
Swinging will save our marriage

Swinging is a form of consensual extramarital sexual behavior, sometimes also called partner or wife swapping. Usually, the partners are committed to each other but search for recreational sex without any emotional involvement. They form clubs, have meetings either at each other's homes or rented hotel rooms, or even ship cruises that are specially arranged for them. Having 4,000 people on a cruise is not unusual. Some hotels offer vacations for swingers as well.

There are several reasons why a couple would like to participate in this "lifestyle" as they call it. It could be for enhancement or variety of sex, curiosity or a fantasy fulfillment. Interestingly, as you might think that mostly men would be interested in having sex with other women, over 50% of female swingers consider themselves bisexual.

There are some ground rules involved at these gatherings. You always have to ask for permission before engaging with another person. It usually starts with women getting on first and their men watching from the sidelines. Then, if given permission, the men may participate as well. Some people just watch and never touch anyone else, some may masturbate in full view of other people, and some couples have sex while others are watching them.

Several online surveys have revealed that swingers are happier with their sex lives than non-swingers are. They say that swinging keeps them from cheating. So should you consider swinging to improve your relationship? Let's look at the risks here. Even if you have established the rules before, you never know what may happen. How will you react emotionally seeing your spouse having sex with someone else? Swingers say that they are not jealous because this is only about physical sex and no emotions. I strongly disagree. Once it happens, you can't take it back. The picture of your loved one having sex with a stranger will be etched in your mind forever. What if he is better looking than you are and has a bigger penis? And if she is prettier, younger and has bigger breasts? Additionally, there is a risk of sexually transmitted diseases. You might use a condom, but that will not stop you from contracting STDs during oral sex. Human Papilloma Virus (HPV) and herpes can easily be transferred.

The biggest problem, though, is if one of you wants to stop swinging. When that happens, the other person needs to agree, no questions asked. This might be difficult and could lead to resentment. Swinging is addictive so going back to "vanilla sex" might be easier said than done. I know a case there the wife got pregnant and totally lost interest in swinging. The husband was very disappointed, which led to a marital conflict. They are still in therapy.

THE REPTILIAN BRAIN

MISTAKE # 132
Underestimating the
reptilian or reptile brain

Sigmund Freud (Remember him? He was the father of psychoanalysis) theorized that the human psyche consists of three parts (Freud, 1923). The first one is the Id (Latin for it). This is the unconscious human survival and basic instinctual drive of our personality. It controls our bodily needs (including sex drive and aggression) and wants instant gratification. It operates on the "pleasure principle," which means that the person wants everything immediately, here and now, regardless of the consequences. This primitive, impulsive and illogical thinking is necessary for a baby's survival.

The second one is the Ego (Latin for I). As the baby grows and interacts with the external world, it develops the Ego. Ego operates on the "reality principle," trying to mediate between Id's demands and the society. Freud said that Ego is like the rider steering a horse, Id being the horse. Ego is rational, realistic and problem-solving.

The third one is called the Superego (Over I). It develops in the phallic stage of the child (age 3-6 years) and consists of the conscience and the ideal self. This is the moral and ethical part placed on us by our parents or caregivers. Superego contains the rules and regulations and aims for perfection.

So let's get back to the reptilian brain. In the 1960s, American neuroscientist Paul MacLean developed the triune brain theory (consisting of three parts in one). According to him, our brains developed in three stages. The first and oldest one is the reptilian brain. This is the brain part that we share with reptiles. It controls basic functions for survival and procreation (sex drive among others). The fight or flight response is located here (an instinctive physiological response to a dangerous situation – we either fight or run away). This is the smallest part of our brains that begins at the brainstem. It starts where the spinal cord enters the skull and contains the cerebellum. Just like Freud's Id above, the reptilian brain is primitive, impulsive and unconscious.

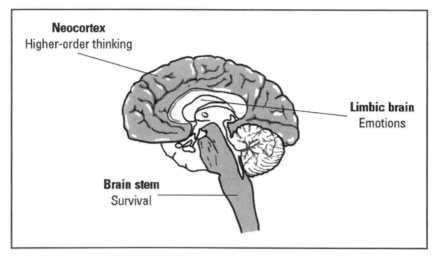

Source: www.ascd.org/publications/books/101269/chapters/A-Walk-Through-the-Brain.aspx

Next comes the limbic brain that is responsible for human emotions. It contains the hippocampus, the amygdala and the hypothalamus. Finally, at the top, we find the neocortex or neomammalian complex that can only be found in mammals. This top layer of the brain that looks like a walnut controls higher-level cognitive thinking. The neocortex is the intellectual, careful, think before you act part of the brain. It develops first at the age of seven (Piaget, 1969).

Obviously, our brains are more complex than the above simplistic description. However, it is important to remember that our basic impulses such as the need for food, sex, pleasure and survival are unconscious. The reptilian brain thrives on excitement, as it loves to indulge in dangerous sports such as skydiving, racing, hang gliding, climbing, bungee jumping or surfing. It likes visual stimulation such as pornography. It is prone to addictions such as drinking, overeating, smoking, drug use and gambling.

Martha says:

> *My husband had an affair with my best friend. How could he do this to me? How could he betray me like this? After 10 years of marriage, two kids, a house and a successful company that we created together? What was he thinking? Why would he destroy my life?*

The answer is that he was not thinking at all. His reptilian, primal brain made him do it. Freud would say that his unconscious motivation did it. His neocortex kicked in from time to time and told him not to do it, but the reptilian brain took over because it usually does win the battle. The reptilian convinced the neocortex that he is smart enough to deny any wrongdoing if the wife finds out (survival instinct). He would get away with it because he is a creative, highly intelligent person. Remember presidents Clinton and Kennedy? Similar situations.

"The reptilian always wins. I don't care what you're going to tell me intellectually. I don't care. Give me the reptilian. Why? Because the reptilian always wins."
Clotaire Rapaille, psychiatrist and marketing consultant.

Does it mean that all men are cheaters? Absolutely not. Several surveys have confirmed that 30% to 50% of men have cheated in their lifetime. However, people lie in the surveys, so it is difficult to know for sure. Gary Neuman (2008) said that 88% of cheaters were not motivated by sex, but the emotional disconnection from their wives made them take the leap. Whatever initiated the practice, sex did follow, and it usually does.

MISTAKE # 133
Women cheat as much as men do

So how about the women then? Do they also act on their impulses? Do they also have a reptilian brain? Yes, they do of course but when it comes to sex women are slightly different. The sex drive is there, just as with the men. However, something else plays a prominent role in the human procreation. Men produce millions of sperm every day. These sperm need to get out. Otherwise, the testicles will overflow so a man needs to get rid of his sperm every few days. The word sperm comes from Greek "sperma," which means seed.

Meanwhile, a man has an abundance of spermatozoa, the woman is born with all her eggs, and she releases only one egg each month. This egg is precious to the woman so she will not give it away on a whim. She will guard this particular egg until a worthy candidate comes around. The man she is looking for should be able to take care of her and the baby. He needs to provide not only through her pregnancy but also after the baby is born. Thus, the mother becomes dependent on the father. This behavior is coded in our DNA. It leads us unconsciously, like an inborn guidance system for survival.

The female reptilian brain can hold back on sexual urges better than the male reptilian brain can. You might think that this theory is untrue, as there are many promiscuous women who sleep around or cheat on their spouses as much as men do. But thousands of years ago when the initial coding took place there were no oral contraceptives or condoms invented yet. Pregnancy was a sure thing back then.

Another factor to add would be the difference between male and female hormones. The importance of oxytocin in human sexual bonding has been researched for years. Oxytocin, also called the "love hormone," is produced by the hypothalamus in our brains. For example, during breastfeeding, the mother releases a larger amount of oxytocin resulting in a stronger bond with her baby. What we know today is that oxytocin is produced in both men and women during sexual arousal and orgasm. The levels peak during orgasm and stay high for a few hours afterward. Interestingly, meanwhile, women get the oxytocin rush fully, in men, their high testosterone levels counteract the oxytocin neurohormone, thus, lowering its impact. So by achieving an orgasm, a woman bonds with the man stronger than he bonds with her. It seems that women are genetically predisposed to form an attachment to their spouses and children. This could be the explanation of the differences in male and female reptilian brains.

Research with oxytocin nasal spray administered to couples in conflict proved to have a positive effect on their communication behavior (Ditzen et al., 2009). When brains of couples married for more than 20 years and still in love were scanned by MRI, the areas of the brain there oxytocin is located were more active than usual (Acevedo et al., 2011). Another study with oxytocin spray for men concluded that the romantic bond for men was stronger when using the spray. The men in the study found their partners more attractive than other females (Scheele et al., 2013). Could this be the solution to male infidelity in the future?

MISTAKE # 134
My spouse will never find out

It has never been easier to discover infidelity than it is today. Checking the phone is a good start. Our lives today depend on technology. Most of the things we do or write are somehow recorded. We have "clouds" safekeeping our information. However, these clouds tend to rain when we least expect it. Several of my clients discovered infidelity when by mistake receiving copies of emails or text messages on family iPads or laptops. If this can happen randomly, imagine what you can find out with a little bit of effort. The passwords to our email accounts are remembered by the browsers. Bank account information is readily available if you are sharing computers. New apps can tell you the exact location of your spouse. Tracking devices can be installed in the car, etc.

Anna says:

> *I would know that he was with her when I called him. His tone of voice would change when he was talking to me. He sounded different. I just knew she was around.*

Tom says:

> *I knew something was up when my wife would take her phone to the bathroom. She never left it unattended, so it was hard for me to check it. One day we were cooking and a message popped up. It was a picture of an erected penis. She said a girlfriend sent it as a joke. I knew it was from him.*

The telltale signs of cheating are endless (see the 32-point list below). He stays glued to his phone, takes it to the bathroom, buys new clothes, pays attention to his looks, comes home late or goes away on frequent business trips. If you live in London, and your guy often travels on business trips to New York, hire a private investigator to follow him. Every city has private detectives. They are costly, and you will need to pay them in advance, but at least you will know what he is up to. They will send you pictures or movies from his rendezvous.

Mimi says:

> *I paid $2,000 in advance to watch my husband kissing another woman on the other side of the globe. I called him immediately. He picked up and said he was in a meeting. I said, "I know you are. She is wearing a blue dress."*

MISTAKE # 135
Ignoring the signs

Below is a list of 32 signs that your spouse is having an affair. It comes from the book *180 Telltale Signs Mates Are Cheating and How to Catch Them* (2003) written by Raymond B. Green, a private investigator, and former police officer, and Marcella Bakur Weiner, a psychology professor at Marymount Manhattan College:

1. Your partner is more attentive to your needs than usual. This is due to the guilt feelings experienced by the cheater in the early stages of his or her affair. The attention will diminish as the affair continues.

2. Your partner begins buying you gifts – a lot of gifts. These are "guilt gifts" purchased because your partner feels guilty about betraying you and showering you with presents makes him or her feel better.

3. Your partner's behavior is causing a gut feeling in you that something isn't right. If this happens, pay attention to your instincts. Ignoring them means you want to blind yourself to the truth. You know your partner's habits, routines and attitudes better than anyone, so be suspicious when these things change.

4. Your partner frequently picks fights with you. Doing this gives him reason to get mad and storm out of the house and, thus, the opportunity to meet his lover. A cheater may also do this because of mixed emotions he is feeling about betraying you.

5. Your partner constantly talks about your relationship ending when you fight or argue. She says things like, "What would you do if our relationship ended?" or "If anything ever happened to us, I would always love you like a friend." In general, she seems very negative about your relationship. Your partner makes these statements because she has a lover to fall back on if your relationship ends. If your partner repeats these kinds of statements often, be

suspicious.

6. Your partner becomes very moody. He or she seems very upbeat and excited when leaving you but acts somber and depressed when around you. If your partner is in a long-term affair, he/she will try to keep both relationships running smoothly. Any problems the cheater has in one relationship will spill over into the other relationship as well. This is inevitable.

7. Your partner never talks to you. You live together but don't interact. He has become cold and inconsiderate of your feelings.

8. Your partner's taste in music suddenly changes. For instance, she always listened to pop music but suddenly starts listening to country music. Your partner might be listening to and growing fond of this new type of music because her lover listens to it.

9. Your partner lacks self-esteem. This doesn't necessarily mean he will go out and have an affair, but an insecure individual often looks to others for guidance. If an insecure person's needs aren't being met, he might find the desired feelings of security and positive feedback in an affair with someone else.

10. Your partner continually criticizes another person. She is trying to make you think that type of individual would never be of interest to her although there exists a secret attraction.

11. Your partner criticizes things about you that he or she once found attractive and appealing.

12. Your partner easily becomes offended at the comments, however harmless, that you make.

13. Your partner stops paying attention to you, your children and home life in general.

14. Your partner begins closing doors when you are around, when before he or she would leave them open. For instance, the Bathroom-Door Rule: Couples in long-term relationships often leave their bathroom doors open while attending to necessities even if their partners are nearby. As affairs develop, the cheaters will close bathroom doors, distancing themselves physically and psychologically from their partners.

15. Your partner stops complimenting you on your looks.

16. Your partner stops saying, "I love you."

17. Your partner acts guilty when you do something nice for him or her. You are supposed to be the person who is making life miserable and the relationship untenable. By doing something nice,

you force the cheater to think about what he or she is doing.

18. Your partner turns the table and accuses you of cheating but has no evidence.

19. Your partner would rather spend time with friends than be with you.

20. Your partner shows no interest in your relationship's future.

21. Your partner stops being affectionate.

22. Your partner is more interested in reading a book or watching television than talking with you or making love to you.

23. Your partner frequently talks about the problems a friend, neighbor, coworker, course instructor or classmate of the opposite sex is having.

24. Your partner begins using new catch phrases or starts to tell types of jokes or express opinions that are unusual for him or her.

25. Your partner pays less and less attention to your children. They seem to sense something is wrong and don't appear to be as emotionally healthy or secure as they once were.

26. Your partner has been acting emotionally distant and withdrawn, but when you ask about it, he doesn't want to discuss it and becomes very protective of his privacy.

27. Your partner seems disinterested and distracted during sex.

28. Your partner talks in her sleep and mentions the name of a particular person on more than one occasion.

29. Your partner seems startled or confused when awakened. This uncertainty may be caused by not being sure which bedroom and which lover's bed he or she is in.

30. Your partner's behavior is such that your friends begin asking you what's wrong. Close friends and family members often will notice tension or discord between the two of you before you are acutely aware of it.

31. Your partner easily becomes offended when you make normal and natural inquiries and may demand to know why you are checking up on him or her.

32. Your partner's sleeping pattern changes considerably from the norm and may include unexplainable exhaustion, restlessness, frequent nightmares and sleep-talking.

(Green & Weiner, 2003).

CHAPTER 13

THE PERSONALITY DISORDERED LOVER

Do you sometimes wonder why certain people are difficult to live with? Why is their behavior so troublesome and unpredictable?

What is a personality disorder?

Personality refers to an individual's "enduring patterns of perceiving, relating to and thinking about the environment and oneself" (APA, 2013, p. 826). A personality disorder is a mental health disorder characterized by long-term unhealthy patterns of thinking and behaving. A person with this disorder has difficulties in functioning socially with other people. Their relationships are often stormy. They have difficulties with everyday stress, either at home or work. They tend to be rigid and inflexible, unable to change or to accept the changes in life. Their contracted view of the world makes it difficult to form healthy relationships.

According to Oxman (2015), the pattern must have developed by early adulthood and must be troublesome and relatively constant across the lifespan. The cause of personality disorders is uncertain. It might be partly genetic and partly environmental, with childhood experiences playing an important role.

There are currently 10 personality disorders listed in the DSM-5 (APA, 2013). DSM-5 *Diagnostic and Statistical Manual of Mental Disorders*, Fifth Edition is the standard classification of mental disorders used by mental health professionals in the United States.

Personality disorders are grouped into three clusters:

Cluster A, the odd or eccentric group includes
· *Paranoid personality disorder*
· *Schizoid personality disorder*
· *Schizotypal personality disorder*

Cluster B, the dramatic, emotional or erratic group includes
· *Antisocial personality disorder*
· *Borderline personality disorder*
· *Histrionic personality disorder*
· *Narcissistic personality disorder*

Cluster C, the anxious or fearful group includes
· *Avoidant personality disorder*
· *Dependent personality disorder*
· *Obsessive-compulsive personality disorder*

Just like any other of the DSM-5 disorders, a personality disorder affects a broad variety of both social and personal circumstances and results in significant functional impairment or distress. Approximately 15% of U.S. adults have at least one personality disorder (APA, 2013) with a high prevalence of other co-morbid mental disorders (Grant et al., 2004; Lenzenweger et al., 2007). The prevalence of personality disorders in psychiatric hospitals and prisons is usually two to three times higher than in the community.

Susan says:
> *We were so much in love before; now, we argue all the time. We can't agree on what movie to see or what to have for dinner. Every single decision is a battle.*

People with personality disorders have more relationship problems than the rest of the population, thus, often seek couple counseling (DiFrancesco, Roediger, & Stevens, 2014). These individuals usually have unstable relationships with others due to their irrational thinking. The most common are the borderline personality disorders (BPD) with their emotional instability and the self-focused narcissists with their narcissistic personality disorder (NPD). Next comes the antisocial personality disorder (ASPD), the sociopaths, with their short-lived and turbulent relationships. The divorce rate is high among the personality-disordered people.

It is important to mention that personality disorders are spectrum disorders that can manifest on a scale from low to high. They are not like a regular sickness that you might either have or not have. Persons with personality disorders can be high functioning with few traits or low functioning with many traits and everything in between.

What is borderline personality disorder (BPD)?

People with borderline personality disorder (sometimes also called emotionally unstable personality disorder), usually live unstable and impulsive lives. They have frequent bursts of anger, chronic feelings of emptiness, unstable social relationships, and are extremely sensitive to rejection (APA, 2013). Their daily lives are filled with severe emotional suffering. They also make frequent attempts at suicide and self-mutilation is common. Life becomes difficult for people with BPD and those living with them due to low stress tolerance, identity problems and fear of abandonment (APA, 2013). Numerous individuals with BPD are either not able to work or do not perform at levels that could be expected of them considering their intellectual capabilities. This disorder accounts for more than one in five inpatient psychiatric admissions and has very high societal and medical costs (APA, 2013).

DSM-5 (APA, 2013) reports that borderline personality disorder is evident in approximately 6% of the overall population and is most common among women – 75%. The prevalence of BPD is possibly five to six times higher than either bipolar disorder or schizophrenia (Nadort et al., 2009). With such a disorder, the person's life is usually unstable and impulsive, which also affects the immediate family members and coworkers.

BPD is often perceived as an untreatable mental condition (Arntz & van Genderen, 2009; Binks et al., 2009). However, psychotherapy has proven to be an effective treatment for BPD. Positive change might take a long time to achieve, though, sometimes including many years of therapy.

Many psychologists and psychiatrists think that BPD results from sexual abuse in childhood. This could be the reason that so many more women than men suffer from this disorder, as more girls are sexually abused. Several recent studies concluded that genetic predisposition is also a substantial factor in BPD (Kendler et al., 2010; Torgersen et al., 2012).

Another cause of BPD could be absent or cold parents (the child was emotionally or physically abandoned), alcoholic parents that neglected the child (child feels abandoned), violent parents with domestic violence incidents (either against children or between themselves, or both), emotional abuse, separation, poor parenting with unsupportive care and other related traumas outside of the family home. Some experts say that borderline people should be diagnosed as trauma survivors, the same as PTSD (post-traumatic stress disorder) patients. They believe that the majority of BDP individuals suffered trauma in their childhood. It is also important to mention that some people diagnosed with BPD lack the above-mentioned childhood factors altogether.

MISTAKE # 136
Marrying a borderline

If you are married to a borderline woman (remember, 75% of BPDs are female) then you will recognize the behavior. I call a borderline "she" because most of the time it is a woman. If your borderline partner is a man, just switch the "she" to "he" when you read the next two pages. The word borderline came about because the disorder was placed on the boundary between neurotic disorders and psychotic disorders, such as bipolar disorder and schizophrenia.

It is important to mention that BPD is a spectrum disorder that can manifest on a scale from low to high. It is not like a regular sickness that you might either have or not have. Persons with BPD can be high functioning with few traits or low functioning with many traits, and everything in between. What follows here are the severe cases.

Jim says:
> *I never know in what mood she will be when I get home from work. Last week she was mad at me because I was 15 minutes late. She threw the food at me and slammed the door behind her. I tried to explain that there was an accident on the way home, but she wouldn't listen. She assumed that I was seeing another woman.*

The borderline woman is emotionally unstable, has an outburst of anger and violence, can't take criticism and has low self-esteem. She either loves you or hates you. She fears that you will leave her for someone else and that you cheat on her all the time. Her paranoia and insecurity will drive you insane. She will depend on you for everything. She might threaten you with suicide or self-mutilation (to manipulate you or get attention). She might engage in excessive drinking or drug use, have an eating disorder (anorexia or bulimia), be preoccupied with her looks or act out with impulsive and risky behavior.

I hate you; don't leave me!

Her fear of abandonment and being alone is immense. As her husband, you are often clueless to what is going on in her head. She might explode at any moment so you are walking on eggshells most of the time. She lives in a world of extremes, seeing others as "all good" or "all bad," black or white, right or wrong, the dichotomy is apparent. She might form a strong attachment to someone but quickly fall out with the person over something trivial, feeling betrayed, never to speak to him or her again.

MISTAKE # 137
Sex with a borderline

Sex with the borderline is very complicated. She might be interested in sex at first, only to bait you in into the relationship. Once you are hooked, then the manipulation and drama will start. Some borderline women engage in promiscuous sex, and some are not interested in sex at all. Overall, they often have sexual problems and your sex life with them will be unpredictable.

The borderline seductress will reel you in through sex. She will pretend that everything you do to her is great by being submissive and up for any sexual fantasy that you might have. She does this to gain control over you because she fears real or imagined abandonment. She is unable to enjoy herself thoroughly during sex because she cannot disconnect from her fear and anger. Naturally, she cannot keep up this charade too long. Soon enough, once she ensnares you, the relationship will change. She will cease to play the role of a sex goddess but play a victim of your "bad behavior." Remember the movie *Fatal Attraction* with Glenn Close and Michael Douglas? The mistress that boiled his rabbit? This is an extreme case of BPD.

Some experts speculate that because the borderline females were often sexually abused as children, they need to regain the control that they lost to their abusers. Being sexually promiscuous or impulsive is another way of taking control over others. Withholding sex can also be seen as control, manipulation or punishment.

Adam says:

> *Last time we had sex was seven months ago. I know because it was my birthday. Since then, every time I initiate sex, she turns me down. Before that it was four months, and before that, eleven months. If it wasn't for our little daughter, we would not be married anymore.*

Sven says:

> *I always thought that once you get married, you will have an immediate supply of sex. Boy, was I wrong! I never had this little sex in my adult life. And I have to beg for it each time.*

MISTAKE # 138
Borderline female with narcissistic male

Just like women who fall for the same type of bad guy over and over again, men repeat their mistakes by falling for exciting borderline females. Often, these males have several issues themselves. Interesting relationship dynamics can be observed in the pair combination of a female borderline and a narcissistic male. They both suffer from similar childhood issues, but they play them out differently. She is insecure and fears abandonment, so by being needy and possessive, she feeds into his ego, which makes him feel special. By creating drama, she concentrates on him, a perfect scenario for the narcissist who thrives on attention. However, most of the time he feels miserable in the marriage. So why are they still married? Because they depend on each other, their respective disorders serve the other, so they form a parasitic bond (Lachkar, 1992). If you remember from above, the two disorders belong to the same cluster B. This is a match made in heaven (or in hell).

BPD wife about her narcissistic husband:

When I want something, I call him my Superman. I say to him that he knows the best, he can fix everything, and he can get me anything. It works each time. If he buys me expensive gifts, then we have sex, not otherwise, because he has to earn it. Men need to appreciate when they get sex.

Even the smartest narcissist will fall prey to the borderline female. He doesn't stand a chance. Like a chameleon, she will change colors and mutate into the perfect woman she thinks he wants her to be. She is on a mission to "own" him, and she will do anything to succeed.

MISTAKE # 139
Marrying a narcissist

The word narcissist or narcissism comes from Greek mythology. Narcissus was a handsome young man who fell in love with his reflection. After gazing at his face for hours in a pool of water, he finally died and transformed into a flower, the narcissus flower, that is named after him. The Narcissistic Personality Disorder (NPD) is prevalent in 6% of the population (APA, 2013).

It is important to mention that NPD is a spectrum disorder that can manifest on a scale from low to high. It is not like a regular sickness that you might either have or not have. Persons with NPD can be high functioning with few traits or low functioning with many traits, and everything in between. What follows here are the severe cases.

A narcissist seldom comes to therapy unless his spouse forces him. I call a narcissist "he" because most of the time it is a man. If your narcissistic partner is a woman, just switch the "he" to "she" when you read the next four pages.

A narcissist thinks that he is the master of the universe and that he knows everything the best. He seldom reads self-help books or listens to advise. He feels superior, special, more important than others, entitled to be above the law, and he acts on his impulses. He genuinely thinks that his opinion matters the most. A narcissist blames everyone else around him for his problems. He is the first one to criticize other people, looking for ways to put them down. This includes his family members, the closest people to him who he should respect and support. He will praise his spouse or his children in front of other people; this is to make him look grandiose in their view, but as soon as he is alone with the spouse or kids, the mental torture starts again. He often indulges in extramarital affairs because he feels special and entitled to do so.

A narcissist is so self-centered that he is unable to show empathy or be truly intimate. He uses people around him for his needs, for his narcissistic supply of excessive admiration. Once he gets what he wants, he will abandon these people and move on to other targets, looking for someone new to worship him and feed his need for omnipotence.

Margareth says:
> *We took our sick daughter to the doctor's office, and my husband asked the doctor to take HIS blood pressure. It was all about him. And still is. I am so happy that we finally divorced.*

I asked Margareth why she married him. She said that her ex-husband was very charming and alluring when they first met. He was charismatic, generous with gifts, smart and funny. He concealed his narcissism well. She fell in love with this charming man who did everything to please her.

In retrospect, she thinks that she was blinded by love and did not realize his true character until her daughter was born, which happened within a year of the wedding. Suddenly, her husband became a Dr. Jekyll and Mr. Hyde, good and evil in one person. The problem was that she never knew which one would wake up in the morning.

Living with a narcissist is very difficult; treating him in therapy is complicated because he doesn't want to change. As I said above, he will not come to therapy unless his wife threatens him with divorce, or he might lose his job, or some other crisis will happen to him.

MISTAKE # 140
Sex with a narcissist

From the beginning of your relationship, he may sweep you off your feet with romantic expressions such as gifts and flowers. He will make you feel special by declaring his undying love for you and wanting to commit quickly. He will tell you that you are the first woman in his life that he has these strong feelings for (though he might have already been married a couple of times before). After the initial honeymoon period, his true colors will come out, his self-centered persona will slowly emerge. His love for you will always be conditional.

Intimacy does not exist for a narcissist though sex is central to him. He will use and manipulate his partner for his selfish needs. He will demand sexual acts that only he enjoys. He will try to control you, make you watch pornography with him, pressure you to have sex when you don't want to, criticize you, cut you off from your family and friends and make you available for his own needs at all times. He will need you to focus on him. You become a sexual object to him, as your needs and desires will be ignored or dismissed. His goal is to dominate and manipulate you by making you inferior to him, thus, reassuring his own specialness and superiority.

The manipulation extends to punishment when you reject his wishes (or commands). He cannot handle rejection. Therefore, he will blame you for upsetting him. He may call you ungrateful, bully you, throw a tantrum, coerce you to do something that you don't want to do or give you the cold shoulder by being passive-aggressive (see page 182 for passive-aggressive lovers). He might call you crazy, and you will seriously think that there is something wrong with you. All this drama is meant to make you feel guilty and to pull you back into his web of manipulation and control.

What a narcissistic husband who cheated on his wife (they were married 21 years) says about his pending divorce:
> *Money talks and bullshit walks. I have the money; it's MY money. I earned it, and I will keep it. She can rent an apartment and move out, but I am keeping the house and the kids.*

Narcissists are often pathological liars. They will invent stories or manipulate you with lies. They will be nice when they want something from you, but they always have their own agenda. Everything they do is calculated for their benefit. They are masters at putting up smokescreens so they can hide the truth or mislead you, or take your attention away from the real reason for their behavior. They will play games with you.

At the time of writing this book, a movie called *Fifty Shades of Grey* has been widely popular at the cinemas. Based on the successful book by E. L. James (or Erika Mitchell), the story is about Christian Grey, a young, rich businessman, and Anastasia Steele, a sexually inexperienced student. A sequel has been announced called *Fifty Shades Darker* that is being filmed in Vancouver as of February 2016. If you have read the book or seen the first movie, it will probably come as no surprise that Christian Grey is a textbook malignant narcissist with sociopathic traits.

Elisabeth says:
> *He bought himself an expensive watch for Christmas though we are behind with our mortgage payments. Who does that?*

Narcissists will spend money on themselves without considering the needs of their spouses and children, as the narcissist and his needs always come first on his priority list. They believe they are so special that they only deserve the best; the best clothes, the best food, the best cars and watches. All material things in life are important to them. They boast about how other people are jealous of them for being so successful, powerful, special, superior and brilliant. The truth is that they feel empty inside, therefore, the need for compensation.

Margareth says:
> *My ex suffered from the Madonna-whore complex. He was jealous and highly possessive. He would criticize my choice of clothes, accusing me of dressing to attract other men. He would call me a WHORE when he was angry. At other times, when in a good mood and in front of other people, he would praise me for being a good mother. His mother was a saint to him, a real Madonna.*

The Madonna-whore complex was first described by Freud in 1912. He called it "psychic impotence" meaning that the man could only sexually desire a whore and not a loving, sweet woman, a saintly Madonna. Freud wrote, "Where such men love they have no desire and where they desire they cannot love" (Freud, 1912; Hartmann, 2009). There are many theories about the etiology of this disorder. However, it is beyond the scope of this book to expand on it or to discuss the origins of narcissism, or how to cope with a narcissist in daily life. It would take another book.

Sexual addicts are often narcissistic (Apt & Hurlbert, 1995). More about sexual addiction in Chapter 10. Narcissists fear losing control by being vulnerable or intimate with someone. They need to be in control because they fear rejection and abandonment. Narcissists also tend to become involved in domestic violence (Ryan, Weikel, & Sprechini, 2008), commit rape (Baumeister et al., 2002; Bushman et al., 2003) and cheat on their partners (McNulty & Widman, 2014), so chose your spouse wisely. The more money he has, the more likely is he going to cheat.

MISTAKE # 141
Sex with a passive-aggressive

The passive-aggressive (negativistic) personality disorder (PAPD) is no longer listed in the DSM-5. Before that, until 2013, it was listed in DSM-IV-TR (p. 789) and in the earlier versions. In the current edition, it is mentioned once under "Other specified personality disorder and unspecified personality disorder" (APA, 2013, p. 646). Nevertheless, many people are affected by this disorder; 2.1% of the general population has it (Livesley, 2001). PAPD has been closely connected to or overlaps with the Borderline and Narcissistic personality disorders (Hopwood et al., 2009) that were described earlier in this chapter.

It is important to mention that PAPD is a spectrum disorder that can manifest on a scale from low to high. It is not like a regular sickness that you might either have or not have. Persons with PAPD can be high functioning with few traits or low functioning with many traits, and everything in between. What follows here are the severe cases.

Passive-aggressive people do not communicate well. They might be angry with someone but will not say it directly. The disorder manifests through negative or pessimistic thinking, procrastination, lateness, forgetfulness, sulking, resentfulness, stonewalling, avoiding problems or issues, self-pity, making excuses and blaming others. This behavior might be a self-defense mechanism because they may have low self-esteem, insecurity, anxiety, fear of rejection or mistrust toward other people.

They will express their anger indirectly by saying "I am not mad" when they clearly are upset, or say "Whatever" or "Fine" with sulky expressions on their faces.

Claudia says:

> *My husband would not have sex with me for a month because I wanted to buy an expensive bag for myself.*

The passive-aggressive lover will use sex as a weapon or a way to manipulate you. In Claudia's case, her husband punished her for being extravagant though it was her own money she wanted to spend. He didn't like the idea of an expensive bag but at the same time, he didn't know how to express his anger without coming across as a stingy person. When she finally gave up on the bag, he initiated sex for the first time in weeks. It was her reward for being "sensible" about it. Before that, he rejected her advances three times by blaming his work, stress or tiredness. This was his way to show her who is the boss in the relationship, his way of controlling her.

Your passive-aggressive spouse may have a fear of intimacy. He or she may be unwilling to share any intimate feelings because they don't want to be emotionally dependent on anyone. To be dependent equals being vulnerable, so the passive-aggressive will go to any lengths to avoid it. You can change this unhealthy relationship dynamic by going to couples therapy together.

Claudia says:

> *Finally, he agreed to come to therapy with me. It took us three months to understand where his anger was coming from, and it wasn't from me. What an eye opener it was. We did schema therapy with Dr. Bea. The schema test revealed our schemas (or lifetraps) that were triggering each other. Now we know better how to avoid the schemas clashing. We learned so much about ourselves; it was very helpful.*

MISTAKE # 142
Jealousy

The DSM-5 mentions two types of jealousy: delusional and obsessional. The main difference between them is that delusional jealousy is a "delusion that one's sexual partner is unfaithful" (APA, 2013, p. 819), and the obsessional jealousy is "characterized by nondelusional preoccupation with a partner's perceived infidelity. The preoccupations may lead to repetitive behaviors or mental acts in response to the infidelity concerns; they cause clinically significant distress or impairment in social, occupational, or other important areas of functioning; and they are not better explained by another mental disorder such as delusional disorder, jealous type, or paranoid personality disorder" (APA, 2013, p. 264).

In plain English, this means that delusional jealousy is a mental disorder (or sickness) that needs to be treated with antipsychotic medication. A person with this disorder imagines and believes the partner to be unfaithful though there is no evidence for such behavior. In some cases, delusional jealousy can be linked to paranoia.

Conversely, obsessive jealousy resembles obsessive-compulsive disorder. The person is obsessing with the possibility that the partner is cheating, constantly looking for evidence and checking on the partner. Obsessive thoughts, ruminations and compulsive rituals that lead to incorrect conclusions are common. A person with this disorder should be treated with psychotherapy alone or combined with antidepressants, depending on the severity of the disorder.

Margareth says:

> *My narcissistic ex-husband was pathologically jealous. He would accuse me of flirting, talking and sleeping with other men. He said that I was dressing like a slut because I wanted attention from other men. He would check on me constantly, even show up at my work with some stupid excuse to see me. He checked my phone and email accounts. This was a mental torture. I felt pity for him at times, as no amount of reassurance could help him. I wish I would have left him earlier. Even now, though he is with someone else, he tells lies about me to our kids. He rewrites the history to his advantage.*

Jealousy comes from insecurity and low self-esteem. A jealous person may feel inadequate in the relationship. Couples therapy can help, but pathological jealousy is very difficult to treat, as it requires many sessions and often needs to be combined with medication.

MISTAKE # 143
Killing for love

Jealousy destroys love. Morbid jealousy also called the "Othello Syndrome," often leads to domestic violence and even homicide. The name comes from Shakespeare's play *Othello*. Othello murders his wife Desdemona because he falsely believes that she has been unfaithful to him.

A crime of passion or crime passionnel in French is an expression for a crime committed due to sudden anger or heartbreak with no opportunity to reflect on what is happening. For example, a husband finds his wife in bed with her lover and kills both of them then and there. Because he acted in the heat of passion, he may be charged with manslaughter instead of premeditated first-degree murder that carries a longer sentence.

Originally practiced in France, crime of passion was legally used in the court of law until 1975 when the French legal system – the Napoleonic Code or officially Code civil des Français – changed the law. Before 1975, a husband who murdered his wife due to adultery could get away with a lenient penalty, sometimes only two years in prison. Meanwhile, if the wife committed the same crime against her husband, she would be punished for murder in the first degree.

Regardless of the verdict, killing in the name of love is a horrible idea. The feeling of being rejected by your lover is one of the most painful feelings we humans experience. I explain that on page 209 under the "Fear of rejection" mistake.

MISTAKE # 144
Cutting off your lover's penis

In 1993, Lorena Bobbitt cut off her husband's penis with an eight-inch kitchen knife while he was asleep. She then got in her car and while driving, tossed the penis out of the car window. She was arrested by the police shortly after. The police found the severed penis by the side of the road. It was surgically reattached and later her husband, John Wayne Bobbitt, proved the success of the operation by taking part in a pornographic movie called *Uncut*.

Lorena, who was 24 at the time, was acquitted of the crime in 1994 by reason of insanity. They divorced in 1995. In a recent interview, she said that after 20 years her ex-husband is still trying to contact her, but she always hangs up on him. Since the divorce, she moved and remarried. In 2008, she founded a nonprofit organization to help battered women and children who are victims of domestic abuse. She said that she had suffered years of emotional and physical abuse at the hands of her ex-husband and that she is happily married to a real gentleman now.

In 2011, another woman in California cut off her husband's penis, put it in the garbage disposal and turned the disposal on, shredding the penis into pieces. She was found guilty and sentenced to life in prison with the possibility of parole after seven years. The reason for her action was her husband's infidelity and him filing for divorce.

Chopping off your cheating lover's penis and making a smoothie of it in a blender might be on your wish list. However, the best revenge is to move on and be happy with someone else. There is no shortage of men out there so why suffer in prison for one jerk?

MISTAKE # 145
Staying with an abusive partner

It is beyond the scope of this book to discuss abusive relationships, but I need to mention it here. Below is a direct quote from the Center for Relationship Abuse Awareness.

WHAT IS RELATIONSHIP ABUSE?

Relationship abuse is a pattern of abusive and coercive behaviors used to maintain power and control over a former or current intimate partner. Abuse can be emotional, financial, sexual or physical and can include threats, isolation and intimidation. Abuse tends to escalate over time. When someone uses abuse and violence against a partner, it is always part of a larger pattern of control.

Source : stoprelationshipabuse.org/educated/what-is-relationship-abuse/

IT IS NOT YOUR FAULT

If you are being abused by your partner, you may feel confused, afraid, angry and/or trapped. All of these emotions are normal responses to abuse. You may also blame yourself for what is happening. But no matter what others might say, you are never responsible for your partner's abusive actions. Dating abuse is not caused by alcohol, drugs, stress, anger management or provocation. It is always a choice to be abusive.

Source : stoprelationshipabuse.org/educated/what-is-relationship-abuse/

Get help and get out!

NATIONAL DOMESTIC ABUSE HOTLINE
TOLL FREE PHONE: 800-799-7233 / 800-799-SAFE
TTY: 800-787-3224
stoprelationshipabuse.org/get-help/

If you live outside of the United States, contact your local domestic abuse hotline.

CHAPTER 14

SEX AFTER MENOPAUSE, MALE ANDROPAUSE PROSTATE PROBLEMS, TOO OLD FOR SEX?

If you think that your grandparents or parents are too old to have sex, think again. In 2007, the New England Journal of Medicine, published the national survey of sexual attitudes, behaviors and problems among older adults in the United States. This study determined that most people ages 57 to 85 engaged in sexual activities and found them an important part of their lives. Furthermore, those who were sexually active said that the frequency of their sexual activities declined only a little from their 50s to the early 70s. The University of Chicago's National Social Life, Health and Aging Project (NSHAP) published data stating that many women and men had sex well into their 70s and 80s. They participated in oral sex, vaginal intercourse and masturbation. Several other studies confirmed these findings.

This chapter also discusses female menopause, male andropause, hormone replacement therapy (HRT) for both men and women and prostate problems in older men.

Did you know that in the U.S. alone, 600,000 hysterectomies (uterus removals) are performed each year? Statistics say that one-third of all American women will have a hysterectomy before they turn 60 and a half during their life time. Is this necessary? Why is this practice different from Europe?

Older people have their specific problems when it comes to sex. Many of them are discussed here.

Menopause – The curse or transit to freedom?

As women age, their reproductive physiology changes as well. Around the age of 40, the ovaries begin to shrink, thus, slowing down estrogen production. This period can last up to 10 years and is called perimenopause. Menopause can start at any time between the ages of 45 and 55, the average age being 51 according to the U.S. statistics. In 1% of women, this happens before the age of 40 and is called premature menopause. Alternatively, some women menstruate until they are in their 60s. It doesn't mean that they can still get pregnant though, as the eggs are too old by this age.

Debra (53) says:
> *Sex has never been better. No worries about bleeding, menstruation cramps and pains, or getting pregnant. I finally feel free. I have a younger lover who knows how to give me pleasure. For the first time in my life, I am experiencing multiple orgasms.*

The ovaries gradually shrink in size, producing less estrogen and progesterone. Usually the time between periods get shorter at first (than the regular 28 days), then become longer and finally the bleedings will stop. Some women experience irregular menstruations; some may have exceptionally heavy bleeding (often a reason for hysterectomy – removal of the uterus). A woman is officially in menopause one year after her periods cease.

Heidi (49) says:
> *Night sweats are the worst. I wake up at night and find myself soaked in perspiration. My nightgown, my hair, my bedsheets, everything is wet. I also get them during the day. They usually last a couple of minutes, but I feel very embarrassed when this happens.*

Hot flashes are the most common symptom around the time of menopause. Other frequent signs and symptoms include mood changes, perspiration, sleep disturbances, depression, anxiety, fatigue, urinary tract infections, palpitations, loss of libido, vaginal dryness, thinning and bleeding. Though some women might not feel any significant changes, the majority of women do have menopausal symptoms, and in 25% of those women, the symptoms last longer than five years.

Joan (55) says:

> *I don't feel for sex anymore. We tried once, but it didn't feel right. It was painful. I guess that we have to live without it now.*

Despite the controversy about the risks and benefits of hormone replacement therapy (HRT), many women and their healthcare providers choose to treat low levels of estrogen in menopause. A recent study conducted at Harvard concluded that the risk of breast cancer increases only by 1.28% in the women on HRT (Manson, 2013). The treatment should stop after seven years though because of higher risk of cardiovascular diseases including heart and head strokes. Previous research from 2002 made by Women's Health Care Initiative (WHI), which was funded by the National Institutes of Health (NIH), showed that women on HRT had a higher risk of breast cancer, heart attack, blood clot and stroke compared to women on placebo. Shortly after the study was published, the majority of women stopped taking hormones and sales of Premarin (an estrogen replacement drug derived from pregnant mares' urine) plunged from $2 billion to $880 million. The problem with this study was that younger women, around 50, and older women past menopause, who were on average 68 years old, were assumed to have the same risk factor, though the younger woman's cardiovascular tissue is different from an older woman's, especially when she starts HRT several years after menopause (Grodstein, Manson, & Stampfer, 2006).

Joan (55) says:

> *My doctor put me on estrogel and progestogel. What a difference it made! I feel so much better now. And I want to have sex again.*

Women who begin HRT at menopause, the combined estrogen and progesterone therapy, do not have a higher risk of breast cancer, at least for the first seven years (Pines, Sturdee, & Birkhauser, 2007). When taking estrogen only, there is no increase of breast cancer for fifteen years (Chen et al., 2006; Pines, Sturdee, & Birkhauser, 2006). After discontinuing the hormone therapy, the higher risk of breast cancer goes away after two years (Chlebowski et al., 2009). When it comes to heart disease, taking estrogen lowers the risk of cardiovascular problems as well as osteoporosis (Speroff & Fritz, 2005).

To HRT or not

There are several risks or benefits to hormonal therapy during menopause. Each woman is different, and the decision should be her own. If you decide to give it a try, there are a few options available. The estrogen can be administered by a skin patch, topic gel or vaginal suppositories. It is often combined with a natural progesterone cream. Some women prefer the vaginal estrogen because it helps the vaginal wall to stay moisturized, preventing it from drying out, which is a common problem in older women. However, the most popular though seems to be Estrogel, a clear gel that can easily be applied directly to the skin on arms, legs or the stomach.

Heidi (49) says:
> *I am scared to take hormones. My mother had breast cancer and my aunt ovarian cancer, so HRT is not an option for me, but I am willing to try homeopathic alternatives to HRT.*

If the woman still has her uterus, it is important to combine the therapy with progesterone because taking estrogen alone may cause endometrial cancer. The reason for this is that the lining of the uterus (endometrium) is usually shed during menstruation. In menopause, there is no menstruation so the estrogen may cause the lining to overgrow and lead to cancer. Progesterone thins the endometrium and, as a result, reduces the risk of cancer. Progestogel is very popular in Europe. Just like Estrogel, it is a clear gel that easily absorbs into the skin and leaves no traces or smell. Hot flashes and similar symptoms usually disappear within the first cycle of HRT treatment. Treatment is started at a low dose that is increased gradually until symptoms improve.

MISTAKE # 146
Hysterectomy

After cesarean sections, hysterectomies (removal of the uterus) are the most common female surgical procedures (Office on Women's Health and Human Services, 2013). In the United States alone, 600,000 hysterectomies are performed each year. There are many reasons for this surgery. In women age 55 and older, uterine prolapse and cancer are the most frequent reasons. In younger women hysterectomies are performed for endometriosis (endometrial tissue outside of the uterus), fibroids (benign tumors growing in the wall of the uterus), pelvic pain and heavy bleeding, only 10% due to cancer. Statistics say that one-third of all American women will have a hysterectomy before they turn 60 and a half during their life time. The U.S. numbers are much higher than statistics in Europe. This sounds rather scary to me, so I wonder if all these operations are justified. After all, most hysterectomies (90%) are performed for benign conditions (Wu, Wechter, Geller, Nguyen, & Visco, 2007). Women should have more information about alternative treatments before succumbing to "hyster-happy" male surgeons. Always ask for a second opinion before making such an important decision because alternative treatments are possible and often available.

Sex after hysterectomy

There are several types of hysterectomy:

- Partial or supracervical or subtotal hysterectomy - cervix remains in place.
- Total hysterectomy – removes the whole uterus and cervix.
- Radical hysterectomy – the whole uterus, the cervix and the top part of the vagina are removed. This is done when cancer is present.
- Sometimes the ovaries will be removed as well – this is called oophorectomy.

What the doctors will rarely tell you is that your sex life will change after a hysterectomy. Here are some points of concern published by the HERS Foundation:

Of the 1,000 women who participated in a HERS Foundation study of the consequences of hysterectomy:

- 75% reported experiencing diminished or absent sexual desire following the surgery.
- 66% experienced diminished or absent pleasure with intercourse.

- 66% diminished or absent sexuality.
- 65% diminished frequency of intercourse.
- 63% diminished or absent sensuality.
- 62% diminished or absent pleasure with foreplay.
- 60% reported experiencing diminished or absent orgasm.

The HERS Foundation is a 501(c)3 non-profit international women's health education organization. HERS provides information about alternatives to hysterectomy and the aftereffects of the surgery (HERS, 2016).

There are several reasons for the above high numbers:

- Uterine orgasm will no longer be possible. The uterus contracts during orgasm thus the feeling for the woman intensifies. Not all women have uterine orgasms before hysterectomy.
- Weight gain, average 25 pounds or 12 kilograms in the first year after surgery.
- Loss of physical sexual sensation.
- Loss of vitality.
- Joint pain.
- Back pain.
- Profound fatigue.
- Depression.
- Personality change.
- Shortened vagina pocket makes intercourse painful.
- Loss of natural elasticity in the vagina.
- Scar tissue in the vagina.

The problem with hysterectomies is that everything inside the female body is interconnected. To remove the uterus, the surgeon must cut through nerves, arteries, veins, muscles and ligaments. This upsets the blood flow to the pelvis including the clitoris, labia and vagina, thus, lowering sexual sensation. Loss of libido, fatigue, irritability and depression are common after hysterectomy. If the ovaries were removed as well, there would be no production of hormones so the woman will find herself in "surgical menopause" (if she was not already menopausal). Removal of ovaries is usually done due to cancer, abnormal growths, tumors (fibromas) or cysts.

Nancy (44) says:

> *After my hysterectomy last year, I fell into depression. I felt empty*
> *inside. A part of my body was missing. I gained weight. My sex*
> *drive diminished. I still feel miserable most of the time. I miss my*
> *uterus.*

Though hysterectomy might be a bad experience for many women, some women report enhanced sexual enjoyment. If they were in pain before or had heavy bleedings, a hysterectomy might come as a blessing. The lack of menstruation and freedom from pregnancy can feel liberating to the woman.

The internal healing process after a hysterectomy may take several years, so be patient and do not give up on your sex life. The sensation in the clitoris might change at first but keep an active mind. With time, the nerves in the pelvis will reconnect again.

If you are not on HRT, then you might need extra lubrication for intercourse. A good lube will solve that problem. If you are single, do not give up on your sexual enjoyment. Use a vibrator, dildo, rabbit or whatever you fancy to bring yourself to climax. Your partner can also help using a vibrator on you, as many women report a need for stronger clitoral stimulation past hysterectomy. It is important to communicate with your partner so that he understands what you went through and how you feel.

MISTAKE # 147
Giving up on your orgasms

The fact is that sex gets better when we grow older so don't give up on your orgasms. A study conducted by researchers from the University of California concluded that sexual satisfaction increased with age (Trompeter, Bettencourt, & Barrett-Connor, 2012). They questioned 806 postmenopausal women about their recent sexual activity. Their median age was 67 years and mean years past menopause was 25. Half of the women reported having sex within the previous month and 67% of those achieving an orgasm. The study concluded that women over 80 years old had a higher frequency of orgasm satisfaction.

Why orgasm is beneficial to your health:

- Releases feeling good hormones oxytocin and vasopressin.
- Eases stress and relaxes you.
- Boosts your immune system.
- Exercises pelvic muscles.
- Improves bladder control.

More about orgasms in Chapter 5.

Incontinence

Urinary incontinence, or loss of bladder control, is the most common problem in older women. About half of older women over 60 may have some form of incontinence. Multiple pregnancies increase the risk of incontinence and pelvic floor prolapses regardless of whether the woman delivered vaginally or through cesarean section. Kegel exercises may help if done correctly (see page 219 for further explanation). According to "AGS Foundation for Health in Aging" (FHA), a national non-profit organization established in 1999 by The American Geriatrics Society, there are four types of incontinence in older people: stress, urge, overflow and functional incontinence.

Stress incontinence (not to be confused with emotional stress) is when urine leaks due to pressure on the bladder. This is most common in women. This pressure, or stress, happens during coughing, sneezing, laughing, exercising or other activities. Common causes are weakened pelvic floor muscles around the bladder and urethra, often a result of childbirth, and lack of estrogen after menopause or surgery.

Urge incontinence is the strong, sudden urge to urinate but not having enough time to go to the bathroom. Usually, the cause is an overactive bladder muscle, bladder spasms or contractions. This can happen during the night as well, and it is called nocturia. Urge incontinence can be caused by Parkinson's disease, stroke, bladder infection and spinal cord disorders. Bladder retraining treatment can help the problem.

Overflow incontinence is when urine leaks from a full bladder. The bladder cannot empty completely, and this leads to overflow.

The leakage may cause discomfort, embarrassment, and even urinary tract infections, as bacteria breeds in the urine left in the bladder. The cause of this condition could be damage to the bladder's nerves, a common condition in diabetes mellitus or injury to the spinal cord. In men, an enlarged prostate can block the urethra and make the bladder weak, and unable to empty.

Finally, there is functional incontinence that occurs when the person cannot physically get to the toilet. The bladder and urethra are working normally, but the person may not move quickly enough, transfer from a wheelchair to a toilet, or have musculoskeletal problems or neurological problems such as multiple sclerosis (MS), Parkinson's disease, Alzheimer's or other types of dementia.

According to APA (2013), the number one reason for admitting an elderly family member to a nursing home is incontinence.

Psychological issues with incontinence

Urinary incontinence is associated with considerable personal stress, loss of self-esteem, social stigma, shame, guilt, anxiety and depression. It restricts the amount of physical activity and can lead to social isolation and poor health. Many women are too embarrassed to discuss this problem with their doctor. They rely on self-management with pads, frequent trips to the toilet, and less fluid intake. If you suffer from incontinence, regardless of your age, don't be afraid to discuss the issue with your gynecologist, as he or she might be able to help you. There are several surgical options for incontinence. The most common procedure is inserting a support sling, a kind of mesh made of synthetic material, to create a pelvic sling around the bladder neck and urethra. The sling provides support and keeps the urethra closed, especially when coughing or sneezing. Over 80% of women with stress incontinence are cured or have considerably improved at a five-year follow-up.

Pelvic floor prolapse

Pelvic support or pelvic floor disorders involve a dropping or prolapse of the uterus, vagina, bladder, urethra, rectum or small intestine. The cause is often a weakness of or injury to the muscles, connective tissue and ligaments of the pelvis. About 60% of women over 75 years old will have some kind of a pelvic floor prolapse. Women who have children are at higher risk for prolapse regardless of whether the woman delivered vaginally or through cesarean section. There is a slight difference between these women, but after the age of 55, the risk is the same.

The sling surgery mentioned earlier for incontinence but adapted specially for the uterus, can be used for pelvic floor prolapses as well. Many women here in Europe prefer this procedure to the more invasive hysterectomy.

Pap smear – When to stop?

If a woman is 70 years old, and the previous two to three Pap smears were normal, there is no need to continue the tests. In the United States, the Institute for Clinical Systems Improvement (ICSI) recommends women between 65 and 70 to stop screening if their last three tests were negative, and they had no abnormal tests results in the past ten years (Wilkinson et al., 2013). However, many women past 70 want to continue testing and should be able to do so. The Pap smear can only show abnormal cell changes in the cervix. On the other hand, uterine cancer can only be confirmed by endometrial biopsy. When a woman starts bleeding after menopause, there is a higher risk of cancer and a biopsy should be done for evaluation.

The most difficult form of cancer is ovarian cancer in women. There are usually no symptoms. Therefore, it is difficult to detect early. When symptoms do occur, they tend to be vague. Detection of ovarian cancer, often called the "silent killer" because many women died of this disease in the past, involves physical examination, pelvic exam, X-ray, MRI, ultrasound, CA-125 blood test and finally biopsy of the ovary. Women aged 55-64 have the highest risk of ovarian cancer. Statistics made in U.S. between 2008-2012 reported 12.1 new cases per 100,000 women (National Cancer Institute, 2016).

Breast cancer

Approximately 13% of women in the United States have or will have breast cancer during their lifetime (Howlader et al., 2012). Approximately 10% of women have a genetic predisposition to breast cancer. Half of breast cancers are detected in women between 50 and 70 years old. Self-examination is helpful, but this method rarely detects any tumors below one centimeter in size. Therefore, breast cancer screening by mammography should be performed every two years. If detected early, the prognosis for recovery is quite good as 80% of women live at least five years after cancer treatment.

MISTAKE # 148
Vitamin D and calcium deficiency in older women

Both men and women need calcium. We store calcium in our bones and teeth, but we also need it for our muscles, brain and blood vessels. People over 50 need supplements of calcium and vitamin D to strengthen the bones and avoid early osteoporosis. Vitamin D is necessary for the body to absorb calcium from the intestines so taking calcium alone is useless. Most people living in northern latitudes are vitamin D deficient, especially during the winter months (Ginde, Liu, & Camargo, 2009). Even during the summer, we don't get enough vitamin D because we are scared of the UV rays causing us skin cancer and premature aging. Though too much sun can be damaging to the skin, 20 to 30 minutes daily of direct sun exposure is needed for good health.

Daily requirement of calcium:

Adult men	51-70 years	1,000 mg
Adult women	51-70 years	1,200 mg
Adults	71 years and older	1,200 mg

Daily requirement of vitamin D:

800 IU daily for men and women ages 71 years and older.

Source: The National Institutes of Health (NIH), a part of the U.S. Department of Health and Human Services.

MISTAKE # 149
Lack of education regarding older women

Because both the number and the proportion of people aged 60 and over are growing in all countries, women comprise the majority of elderly persons because they usually live longer than men do. All health care providers, including gerontologists and counselors, should be educated in topics related to the distinctive problems faced by older women. Physicians, therapists and counselors should have an understanding of the psychological and physiological changes that older women may face. They should use adequate strategies and be able to assist these women to deal with adjustments and changes in their lives.

Male andropause

Male menopause, also called andropause, is caused by decreasing testosterone (androgen) levels. From the age of 30 in men, the levels of testosterone decline by 1% yearly. This happens gradually during many years and is not as abrupt as the menopause for women. The importance of testosterone in men's health is clearly explained in Chapter 4. By the age of 80, the levels of testosterone in men are half to what they used to be (Borst & Mulligan, 2007).

The best way to check your testosterone levels and to confirm testosterone deficiency is by a blood test. Just like for women, hormone replacement therapy is available for men. Testosterone replacement therapy (TRT) can improve bone density, strength, muscle mass and overall well-being (Bhasin et al., 2010). Testosterone can be administered by injection, orally, by skin patches or gel/cream. You will need a proper check-up by a doctor and a prescription. Follow-up screening is necessary to assure appropriate treatment. Just as for women, TRT for men is highly controversial both in Europe and in the U.S. Some clinicians oppose the concept of male menopause stating that low testosterone levels are a sign of hypogonadism – the failure of the gonads, testes in men and ovaries in women, to function properly.

The most common signs of testosterone deficiency in both men and women are:

- Decrease in one's usual customary level of sexual desire.
- Reduced sensitivity of the genitals and the nipples to sexual stimulation.
- Overall reduction in general levels of sexual arousability, possibly accompanied by decreased orgasmic capacity and/or less intense orgasms.
- Diminished energy levels and possibly depressed mood.
- Increased fat mass.
- Decreased bone mineral density, which can result in osteoporosis in both sexes.
- Reduced body hair.
- Decreased muscle mass and strength.

Source: Crooks and Baur (2011).

Prostate problems in older men

The prostate is a walnut-sized gland that sits just under the bladder. The urethra (the tube that carries urine) and ejaculatory ducts pass through the prostate. About 30% of the seminal ejaculatory fluid is made by the prostate. Men over 50 start having problems with the prostate – inflammation (prostatitis), enlargement (benign prostatic hyperplasia, or BPH) and cancer are the most common. If you notice anything unusual such as trouble with urinating or pain, contact your doctor immediately; most of the time these problems are not cancer. Therefore, they can be treated successfully with antibiotics.

Prostatitis

Prostatitis refers to an infection or inflammation of the prostate. It can occur at any age, though men over 65 are at highest risk. Prostatitis is often caused by bacteria that leaks from the urine into the prostate. It is estimated that 50% of men will have prostatitis in their lifetime. Prostatitis can be successfully treated with antibiotics, alpha-blockers and anti-inflammatory agents.

The symptoms of prostatitis include:

- Pain or burning sensation when urinating (dysuria)
- Difficulty urinating, such as dribbling or hesitant urination
- Frequent urination, particularly at night (nocturia)
- Urgent need to urinate
- Pain in the abdomen, groin or lower back
- Pain in the area between the scrotum and rectum (perineum)
- Pain or discomfort in the penis or testicles
- Painful orgasms (ejaculations)
- Flu-like symptoms (with bacterial prostatitis)

Source: Mayo Clinic (2016).

Benign prostatic hyperplasia (BPH)

Benign prostatic hyperplasia (BPH) or enlarged prostate, affects half of men between ages 51 to 60 and 90% of men over 90. The cause of BPH is not clear, but the decrease in the male hormones as men age might be one of the reasons.

The symptoms of BPH include:

- Frequent or urgent need to urinate
- Increased frequency of urination at night (nocturia)
- Difficulty starting urination
- Weak urine stream or a stream that stops and starts
- Dribbling at the end of urination
- Straining while urinating
- Inability to completely empty the bladder

Less common signs and symptoms include:

- Urinary tract infection
- Inability to urinate
- Blood in the urine

Source: Mayo Clinic (2016).

Prostate Cancer

Prostate cancer is one of the most common cancers in men. Statistics between 2010 and 2012 state that approximately 14% of U.S. men will have prostate cancer during their lifetime, and that 21.4 per 100,000 men per year die of the disease based on the statistics between 2008 and 2012 (National Cancer Institute, 2016b). Prostate cancer might not cause any symptoms in the early stages.

The symptoms of more advanced prostate cancer include:

- Trouble urinating
- Decreased force in the stream of urine
- Blood in the semen
- Discomfort in the pelvic area
- Bone pain
- Erectile dysfunction

Source: Mayo Clinic (2016).

The two most common screenings for prostate cancer are a digital rectal exam (DRE) and prostate-specific antigen (PSA) blood test. Your doctor can perform the DRE in his office by inserting his gloved finger into the rectum. Usually, he can feel any abnormal changes to the prostate and if found, refer you for more tests (biopsy). The PSA blood test screens for higher than normal levels of prostate-specific antigen in the bloodstream, which is produced by the prostate gland. If found, it doesn't mean automatically that cancer is present because it can also indicate an enlargement, inflammation or infection of the prostate. Many men will have prostate cancer with no symptoms and die of other causes without knowing about the cancer.

The survival rates are high for prostate cancer:

- The relative 5-year survival rate is almost 100%
- The relative 10-year survival rate is 99%
- The 15-year relative survival rate is 94%

Source: American Cancer Society (2016).

Prostate cancer can be challenging to a couple's sex life. Many people assume that the treatment will automatically lead to erectile dysfunction and lack of orgasms. Impotence is common after prostate surgery, but it is often temporary. In the meantime, Viagra and Cialis can help. Many men do enjoy sex after prostate surgery. Though ejaculation is no longer possible due to the removal of the prostate gland and the seminal vesicles, a man doesn't need ejaculation or even an erection to achieve an orgasm. The feeling of orgasm may not be as intense as before; nevertheless, it is a pleasurable experience. Keep in mind that good sex is not only limited to penetration. There are many other ways to enjoy sexual intimacy in the relationship.

Aspirin

Aspirin or acetylsalicylic acid (ASA), is a medication used for pain, fever or inflammation. Many people take it in low daily doses to prevent heart disease. A new study from Italy has shown that taking low-dose aspirin (LDA) for longer than five years can lower the risk of prostate cancer by 57% (Lapi et al., 2016). The study included 13,453 men with ischemic cardio (heart) or cerebrovascular (stroke) disease. Other studies have shown that aspirin may prevent colorectal cancer as well. LDA comes in 75 mg, 81 mg (baby aspirin in U.S.) and 100 mg here in Switzerland (Aspirin Cardio 100). The regular dose of aspirin is 300 mg, 325 mg or 500 mg depending on where you live. Before taking any medication, please contact your physician. Screening for prostate and colon cancer is important if you are over 50 years old.

MISTAKE # 150
Prostate milking

Massaging the prostate or prostate milking can be done for medical benefits or for sexual pleasure. It's usually performed by fingers or special tools and can cause intense orgasms. The problem is that the massage should be carried out by a health professional because there are many risks involved with this procedure. If done incorrectly, the prostate gland can be damaged or cause hemorrhoid problems in the rectum. If the man is suffering from acute prostatis, then the massage can lead to blood poisoning. And finally, if the prostate is cancerous then this procedure can spread the cancer to other parts of the body. You should always consult your doctor before engaging in prostate massage.

MISTAKE # 151
Not ejaculating frequently

Research shows that frequent ejaculations in men lower the risk of prostate cancer by 22% (Rider et al., 2015). Those men who ejaculated 21 or more times per month had the lowest risk of developing prostate cancer compared to those who ejaculated 4-7 times per month (Rider et al., 2015). The reason for this is not clear. However, the researchers speculated that frequent ejaculations might flush out, or stop, the build-up of toxins in the prostate. This is the largest study to date that includes 32,000 men and 18 years of follow-up. Of these men 3,839 were diagnosed with prostate cancer.

MISTAKE # 152
Too old for sex

In August 2007, the New England Journal of Medicine published the national survey of sexual attitudes, behaviors and problems among older adults in the United States (Lindau et al., 2007). This survey found that most people ages 57 to 85 engaged in sexual activities and found them an important part of their lives. Furthermore, those who were sexually active said that the frequency of their sexual activities declined only slightly from their 50s to the early 70s. The University of Chicago's National Social Life, Health and Aging Project (NSHAP) published data stating that many women and men had sex well into their 70s and 80s. They participated in oral sex, vaginal intercourse and masturbation.

Another survey conducted in Sweden that was published in 2008, states that 70-year-olds have sex far more often than we might think. Among those who were sexually active, more than one in four reported having sex once or more per week (Beckman, Waern, Gustafson, & Skoog, 2008). Lately, a heated debate has been going on in Sweden about sex in nursing homes. There have been complaints that the medical staff is not fully educated on the topic.

Some nursing homes lack the privacy for sexual activities among married couples as the doors must stay open most of the time. The couples that are not married are not allowed to stay in the same room during the night, so one can only imagine what is going on through the day. Several "privacy rooms" have been installed in the nursing homes to accommodate the high demand of Swedish seniors.

Joan Collins on aging

The Hollywood star Dame Joan Collins, who will be 83 years old in May 2016, and who is married to Percy Gibson, 32 years her junior, recently said: "Age is just a number. It's totally irrelevant unless you happen to be a bottle of wine."

Suzanne Somers' sex life

In October 2013, Suzanne Somers revealed on national television, that she has sex with her husband twice a day. Suzanne is 66 and her husband of 37 years, Alan Hamel, is 77. They are both on hormones and apparently still enjoying a very active sex life. This topic came up on the morning show "Today" because 20-year-old Miley Cyrus mentioned that people over 40 do not have sex anymore. Somers revealed more intimate details when she suggested that they make love first at four in the morning and then again at eight o'clock. There was no mention of Viagra. Miley Cyrus is not alone, as many people believe that sex is only practiced in the younger population. The research mentioned earlier contradicts this belief completely.

When a spouse dies

Can you die of a broken heart? Yes, you can. According to a recent study conducted in the UK that investigated 30,447 individuals aged 60 to 89 who lost a partner, the occurrences of fatal or nonfatal heart attacks (myocardial infarction) and strokes were double to the control group in the first 30 days after the death of the spouse (Carey et al., 2014). The study concluded that a death of a partner is connected to a higher risk of heart attack in the first weeks and months of bereavement.

As women live longer than men do, naturally, there are more

senior women, as high as four to every widower. Men seem to remarry faster than women do, often within a year from the death of a spouse. Why? Because they like to be married, to have someone who takes care of them. They are creatures of habit. Only 25% of widows remarry compared to 50% of widowers.

CHAPTER 15

WHEN LOVE ENDS
DYING OF A BROKEN HEART
MOVING ON

When love ends, remember the good moments, the love you had for each other, the laughs, the happiness, the magic that happened. Have fond memories of each other and no regrets because very rarely will you find romantic love that lasts forever. For sure, you can love your parents, your siblings and your children all your life until the day you die, but romantic love is different. Romantic love can come and go few times in your life. Cherish each time it happens but know it's fleeting. This too shall pass. Be in the moment. Appreciate the here and now.

Jennifer says:

> *We were together seven years. He was never ready to settle down. Then he met her and proposed within six months. They are getting married this summer. My heart is broken.*

Ryan says:

> *I will never fall in love again. What's the point? I did everything for her; I quit my job, and I moved across the country to be with her. She left me for her boss - her married boss.*

Where do broken hearts go?

Many songs have been written about broken hearts. The most known must be by Whitney Houston – "Where Do Broken Hearts Go." Then by Toni Braxton – "Un-Break My Heart." Justin Timberlake's – "Cry Me a River." Adele's – "Someone Like You." And how about the iconic Sinéad O'Connor - "Nothing Compares 2 U" originally written by Prince? What is your favorite breakup song? How does it make you feel?

MISTAKE # 153
Holding onto grudges

Cherish each time you were lucky to encounter true love and hold no grudges for the lovers who came into your life. Some people might have hurt you badly by withdrawing their love for you and moving on to someone else. Some might have said hurtful things and some might have done bad things to you. Life is never perfect. "Shit happens" as they say. Try to forgive these people, if only in your heart. You don't need to say it to them. You don't need to contact them. No such thing is necessary. Forgive them in your heart and let the negative feelings go because holding on to the pain and the hate is not good for you. You are poisoning your mind with negative feelings. This is not healthy so set yourself free and move on.

MISTAKE # 154
Dying of a broken heart

Regardless of what you are going through at this moment, the worst time or the best time of your life, remember that nothing stays the same forever. This too shall pass. The only constant in life is change. The first month after a breakup is the worst. Once you endure that, things will get better. On top of the pain that you are feeling you may feel ashamed or humiliated. You may have low self-esteem because you are blaming yourself for the breakup. Negative thoughts may occupy your brain most of the time.

The problem is that we get addicted to love, just in the same way we get addicted to drugs. Dopamine and oxytocin levels peak when we are in love. The intense feelings of love can be seen in brain scans in the same brain regions that are affected when we are high on drugs. When love ends, we get withdrawal symptoms that are hard to cope with. People go to rehab for drug or alcohol addiction, but there should also be rehab for broken hearts.

In the movie *Dangerous Liaisons*, Michelle Pfeiffer's character, Madame Marie de Tourvel, dies of a broken heart. Unfortunately, this happens in real life as well. If you are one of these people who are going through a painful breakup, don't hesitate to talk to a professional mental health practitioner. A good therapist can help you to ease your pain and to move on with your life.

MISTAKE # 155
Fear of rejection

Why is rejection so painful to us? Or unrequited love? Why do we suffer so much when love ends? There are several reasons for this. Going back thousands of years when our ancestors still lived in caves and life outside the cave was dangerous, being rejected from the social group meant death. You needed the support of the group to survive. The fear of death equals fear of rejection. Does it make sense? We are programmed this way. Scientists can prove this by MRI scans of the brain. So, next time you feel rejected by someone, remember the cave. Remember that your brain is coded to feel the pain of rejection to survive. And survival always comes first to us (see the reptilian brain in Chapter 12).

MISTAKE # 156
Ruminating about past lovers

Some people spend years ruminating about past lovers or potential past lovers. They think, "I should have married Johnny or Bob and not my current husband." You may be daydreaming about that person or regretting the past. The thing is that if you would have married Johnny or Bob, there is a high probability that the problems that you are having in your current marriage would have surfaced in those marriages as well. At the beginning of a relationship, we tend to idealize the person but soon enough something will happen that will make you feeling disappointed or hurt. Nobody is perfect. At some point in the relationship, you will discover that your lover has flaws and weaknesses, just like you. It needs to be clarified that the phrase "flaws and weaknesses" does not include disrespectful and violent behavior from your spouse, as emotional or physical abuse should never be tolerated (see Mistake # 145 on page 186). So stop checking the Internet, searching for Johnny and Bob's whereabouts, their Facebook pages or whatever you can find. Stop obsessing about past lovers and live in the here-and-now. Life is too short for that.

> "After another moment's silence, she mumbled that I was peculiar, that that was probably why she loved me but that one day I might disgust her for the very same reason."
> ~ *Albert Camus*

MISTAKE # 157
Regretting the past

Don't regret anything. Learn from your past experiences and see them as feedback for your future. Regretting the past will not get you anywhere. One of my favorite songs is "Non, Je Ne Regrette Rien" (No, I regret nothing) by Edith Piaf.

How to mend a broken heart

The first step to recovery from a breakup is acknowledging the pain. You are not alone though it feels like that. Many people are going through the same painful breakup feelings right now. Allow yourself to grieve but make a deadline, let's say a week or a month (depends on how long you were in the relationship) and then decide to move on. See your friends, exercise, take that yoga class you always wanted to and keep yourself busy. Tell your friends that you are single again and ready to mingle. Dwelling on the past or wallowing in misery are counterproductive and a waste of time.

My grandmother used to say that men are like busses. If you missed one another one would come along soon. And never run after a bus, especially when wearing high heels. Half the world is full of men so why to cry over one? What you are missing is not him but the feeling you had when you were in love. This is what you are craving, and you fear that you will never have that feeling again. But you will. Don't be afraid to love again because sometimes the best is yet to come. Or as Gloria Gaynor sings: "I will survive!" You will too.

MISTAKE # 158
Not loving yourself

The most important relationship is the one that you have with yourself. Before you can love someone else, you need to fill up the love tank within you. Or as they show you on the plane, first you give the oxygen mask to yourself and then to your child. The same goes for love. So many people are searching for someone else to fulfill them, their soul mate, their other half.

MISTAKE # 159
"You complete me"

The statement Tom Cruise made to Renée Zellweger in *Jerry Maguire* (1996) will always be remembered as one of the most romantic love declarations in cinematic history - "You complete me." The reality is that no other person can complete you but yourself. It's practically impossible for someone else to be there for you all the time, to fulfill all your needs and to make you continually happy. To rely on another person for your happiness is wrong; yet, so many people think that if he/she only did this and that, it would make me happy. Don't spend a lifetime waiting for another person to complete you because you will end up disappointed or even worse, bitter. The unrealistic Hollywood fairytale is just that – a fairytale. It's only entertainment.

"Happiness depends upon ourselves."
~ *Aristotle*

Annex

G-spot stimulation exercise

The objective of this exercise is to have a mind-blowing orgasm, a single one to start with, and then to expand this technique to have multiple orgasms that can last for 20-30 minutes or even longer.

The simultaneous G-spot and clitoral stimulation together with optional anal stimulation – not all women like to be touched there so ask her first before starting the exercise – will cause the most powerful and deep orgasm that a woman can experience. Starting at the clitoris, expanding toward the G-spot and finally reaching the uterus with full force will give her a volcanic orgasmic experience she will never forget (or the guy who gave it to her).

Step-by-step procedure:

1. The setup – make sure that you will have at least one hour of uninterrupted time together. Switch off the TV, radio, music, phones, computers and anything that makes a noise; close the windows to shut out the outside noises as well. Why no music? After all, many couples make love to music. Because music is distracting and this exercise needs concentration and subtle communication between the partners, so it's better done in complete silence. Once you master the technique, music can be added at your convenience. If you live with other people or have kids, lock the bedroom door so no one can walk in on you. This will make you feel more relaxed as well.

2. Take a shower or a bath together. Wash each other's body parts, especially the genital area, so it's clean. Groom the pubic hair, either by waxing in advance, trimming (beard trimmers are great for this purpose) or shaving. This will make it easier for him to first find the clitoris and second to give you oral sex without losing track in the jungle. Too much hair down there might put him off though many men

don't mind the hair at all. Communicate and experiment together.

3. Once clean and fresh, lie on a bed and make yourself comfortable.

4. Hugs, kisses and caressing her breasts are a good start to get things going. Once she is aroused, her partner moves down to perform oral sex.

5. The woman lies on her back with her legs slightly bent and open. Her partner should find a comfortable position either between her legs or by her side. This is important because he may stay there for a long time. Some men knee down on the floor when the bed is too small to accommodate both of them. In this case, put a couple of pillows on the floor in order not to strain your knees.

6. Start kissing her on her thighs slowly moving toward her labia and the clitoris. Never go straight to the clitoris, as the key here is to build up the tension slowly. Her clitoris is the most sensitive body organ with more nerve endings than the male glans. It is covered by the clitoral hood (or prepuce), a piece of skin that can be pulled back by your fingers, in the direction of her stomach.

7. Once exposed, start caressing the clitoris with your tongue. This is by far the most pleasurable option compared to a finger or vibrator. If the woman prefers the latter, at least try to convince her that your tongue is softer/warmer and better suited for the job.

8. Start stimulating the clitoris by writing the alphabet with your tongue, starting with capital letter A. If she likes the feeling,

she should communicate it to you by saying "yes." If the feeling is not what she wants then move on to the next letter. She can also suggest which letter you should try. For example capital letter "I" could be long vertical strokes and a small "i" – short strokes. Her feedback is important as it gives her control over your tongue. This is teamwork at its best.

9. Once she is properly aroused with her juices flowing, lick your index finger to make it wet and slowly insert it into her vagina, palm up. Start moving your finger in a circular motion to stimulate her G-spot that is located on her anterior (up toward the clitoris) vagina wall, approximately 5 cm or 2 inches in. When a woman is sexually aroused the G-spot swells in size and feels like a spongy ball. Don't press too hard because just above the G-spot is the urethra. Pressing on it might cause the bladder to release some urine, and this is not what you want at this moment. Emptying the bladder before the exercise will help to avoid accidents.

10. At this point, you are stimulating the G-spot and tongue stroking the clitoris simultaneously. One hand is pulling back the clitoral hood, and the other is stimulating the G-spot. Some men wish that they had three hands because they also want to circle the anal opening. If you hands are big, you can do that with your pinky. However, ask if she likes it first. For some women, anal stimulation takes away the pleasure from the clitoris and the G-spot. It is always better to focus on these first before going farther back.

11. Once she almost reaches a climax stop stroking her clitoris and move down to her labia. Give her a few moments to calm down and then go back to the clitoris. At this point, you can insert a second finger or use a G-spot vibrator. You

can tease her by going up and down from the clitoris to labia a few times but at some point the excitement will be unbearable, and she will explode in an earth-shattering orgasm.

12. You can stop the exercise here and move on to intercourse so you can have your orgasm as well, or continue to give her multiple orgasms. At this point, her clitoris might be too sensitive to continue but if you insist on doing the same as in points 10-11 she should be able to climax a few times more. Some women can climax continuously for one hour or longer if the guy has stamina enough to keep it up for that long. The point is not giving up too soon, as it takes a lot of practice and persistence to become a "multi O" champion. Most importantly – have fun while practicing.

Pelvic Floor or Kegel Exercises

The pelvic floor muscles squeeze involuntarily at orgasm; they can also be trained to contract voluntarily through a series of exercises known as Kegel exercises. These exercises were developed by Arnold Kegel in 1952 to help women regain urinary control after childbirth. (Because of excessive stretching and tearing of perineal muscles during childbirth, women who have recently given birth commonly lose urine when they cough or sneeze.) Kegel exercises have been shown to have other effects besides restoring muscle tone. After about six weeks of regular exercise, many women report increased sensation during intercourse and a general increase in genital sensitivity. This seems to be associated with their increased awareness of their sex organs and their improved muscle tone (Crooks & Baur, 2011, p. 59).

The steps for the Kegel exercises are as follows:

1.   Locate the muscles surrounding the vagina. This can be done by stopping the flow of urine to feel which muscles contract. An even more effective way of contracting the pelvic floor muscles is to contract the anal sphincter as if to hold back gas.

2.   Insert a finger into the opening of your vagina and contract the muscles you located in Step 1. Feel the muscles squeeze your finger.

3.   Squeeze the same muscles for 10 seconds. Relax. Repeat 10 times.

4.   Squeeze and release as rapidly as possible, 10 to 25 times. Repeat.

5.   Imagine trying to suck something into your vagina. Hold for 3 seconds.

6.   This exercise series should be done three times a day.

Adapted from Crooks and Baur (2011).

Sensate Focus
(from counselling-matters.org.uk)

Introduction

The aim of Sensate Focus is to build trust and intimacy within your relationship, helping you to give and receive pleasure. It emphasizes positive emotions, physical feelings and responses while reducing any negative reactions.

The program can help overcome any fear of failure that may have existed previously, building a more satisfying sexual relationship in which both partners feel able to ask for what they want and are able to give and receive pleasure.

Sensate Focus is not a race to an end. Continuous reinforcement is needed to overcome negative reactions to intimacy. How long you spend on the program is up to you. Typically, sessions last twenty to sixty minutes, two to three times a week, spread over six or more weeks.

Ground Rules

- Choose a time and place acceptable for both of you, where you won't be disturbed.
- Make the surroundings as pleasant as possible, choosing music, lighting and aromas to suit you.
- Turn off the phone and, if necessary, lock the door.
- Take turns giving and receiving touch, allowing equal time for each of you.
- The goal is enjoyment and pleasure. Enjoy the journey rather aiming towards any specific destination.
- Take as long as you want over each phase. Often, the slower you take it, the more you will get out of it.
- Only move from one stage to the next when both partners agree.

Instructions

- When it is your turn to touch, take plenty of time to explore the other person's body.
- Experiment with different sensations and types of touch. Take pleasure in experiencing the texture, form and temperature of the other person's body.
- Try to discover the degrees of pressure and types of touch your partner finds most appealing by encouraging feedback or by placing your hand under their hand so they can show you what they want.
- When it is your turn to be touched, make sure you let the other person know what you like and what you don't. You can tell your partner how you feel, make appreciative noises, or move their hand to where you want to be touched.
- Avoid saying, "don't …" as it can be discouraging. It's more encouraging to say things like "it feels better when you…."
- You might find it useful to talk about your experiences afterwards, e.g. "I really liked it when you…"
- If there is something you would like to try, don't be afraid to suggest it.

Phase 1: Non-genital Sensate Focus

Ground Rules

- You can be naked, or wear underwear or relaxed clothing if that feels more comfortable.
- You may find a book or DVD about massage useful, if you want to learn different techniques.
- At this stage, avoid touching the obvious erogenous zones: breasts, nipples, vulva, clitoris or vagina, penis or testicles.
- Only move from one state to the next when you both feel you are ready.
- Sexual intercourse and orgasm are not permitted during this phase.

Instructions

- During first sessions concentrate on touching the parts of the body normally visible: the hands, arms, feet, scalp and face.
- When you are ready, include the back, neck, arms, buttocks and legs, not neglecting the hands, feet and face.
- Finally bring in the chest, stomach, shoulders and thighs, but avoid the breasts, tops of legs and the groin area.

Phase 2: Genital Sensate Focus

Ground Rules:

- Having spent some time on non-genital sensate focus you can bring in touching of the breast and genital areas. You might want to spend some time at this stage before moving on to the next.
- Continue to pay attention to the parts of the body that you explored in the previous sessions, as well as the new areas that you are incorporating.
- The main aim of these stages is to increase each person's pleasure and awareness of each other's responses to different types of stimulation. If one or both of you become aroused this is fine but it is not the aim of the exercise.
- During genital stimulation it is often useful to use a water-based lubricant. Oil-based products should not be used near condoms.
- Sexual intercourse and penetration is not permitted during this phase.

Instructions:

- First incorporate touching of breasts and nipples. Remember, men have nipples too.
- Next include the areas around the genitals, including the testicles of a man.
- Then introduce touching of the genitals themselves (the labia, clitoris and entrance to the vagina on a woman; the penis, shaft and glans on a man).
- After a while you may also want to incorporate oral as well as manual touching (kissing, licking and sucking) into both non-genital and genital touching.
- You may want to try the 'teasing technique'. Manually stimulate the other person's genitals, gently at first then increase the speed of stimulation. Take a rest for a few minutes and then begin again.
- If orgasm occurs at this or later stages, that is fine, but that is not the aim of the process.

Phase 3: Penetrative Sensate Focus

Ground Rules:

- Having spent some time on non-genital and genital sensate focus you can begin to include penetration, using fingers, toys and the penis.
- Continue to pay attention to the other parts of the body that you explored in the previous sessions.
- The person being penetrated should be in control of the depth of penetration and the amount of time spent on it.
- While orgasm and intercourse is permitted in this phase, this is not the goal: the aim remains to enjoy the growing intimacy between you.

Instructions:

- First begin to incorporate forms of gentle penetration, initially try this with little or no thrusting, just enjoying the sensation of containment.
- Try it first with one person on top and then the other.
- Later you can incorporate more thrusting, again with the person being penetrated in control.
- You might find some books of sexual positions useful at this point so you can find out which positions are most comfortable and pleasurable for you, according to the part of the body being caressed.

(counselling-matters.org.uk)

Sensate Focus examples in the movies:

If you want to see what Sensate Focus looks like in practice, watch the movie *Hope Springs* from 2012 with Meryl Streep and Tommy Lee Jones. This movie is about a middle aged couple who have been married for a long time and unfortunately lost the passion (including sex life) in their marriage. They sleep in separate bedrooms because the husband snores loudly at night. He also has a back problem. The wife (Meryl Streep) finds a renowned therapist (Steve Carell) in Great Hope Springs. She persuades her unwilling husband (Tommy Lee Jones) to go with her to therapy. They struggle at first but finally reignite the spark in their marriage. The movie is warm and funny. It won People's Choice Award and was nominated for a Golden Globe.

Index of Sexual Satisfaction – Partner 1

Adapted from Crooks and Baur (2011).

This questionnaire is designed to measure the degree of satisfaction you have in the sexual relationship with your partner. It is not a test, so there are no right or wrong answers. Answer each item as carefully and accurately as you can by placing a number beside each one according to the following scale:

1. Rarely or none of the time
2. A little of the time
3. Some of the time
4. A good part of the time
5. Most or all of the time

1. I feel that my partner enjoys our sex life. _____
2. My sex life is very exciting. _____
3. Sex is fun for my partner and me. _____
4. I feel that my partner sees little in me except for the sex I can give. _____
5. I feel that sex is dirty and disgusting. _____
6. My sex life is monotonous. _____
7. When we have sex, it is too rushed and hurriedly completed. _____
8. I feel that my sex life is lacking in quality. _____
9. My partner is sexually very exciting. _____
10. I enjoy the sex techniques that my partner likes or uses. _____
11. I feel that my partner wants too much sex from me. _____
12. I think sex is wonderful. _____
13. My partner dwells on sex too much. _____
14. I try to avoid sexual contact with my partner. _____
15. My partner is too rough or brutal when we have sex. _____
16. My partner is a wonderful sex mate. _____
17. I feel that sex is a normal function of our relationship. _____
18. My partner does not want sex when I do. _____
19. I feel that our sex life really adds a lot to our relationship. _____
20. My partner seems to avoid sexual contact with me. _____

21. It is easy for me to get sexually excited by my partner. _____
22. I feel that my partner is sexually pleased with me. _____
23. My partner is very sensitive to my sexual needs and desires. _____
24. My partner does not satisfy me sexually. _____
25. I feel that my sex life is boring. _____

Scoring

Items 1, 2, 3, 9, 10, 12, 16, 17, 19, 21, 22, and 23 must be reverse-scored. (For example, if you answered 5 on one of these items, you would change that score to 1.) After these positively worded items have been reverse-scored, if there are no omitted items, the score is computed by summing the individual item scores and subtracting 25. This assessment has been shown to be valid and reliable.

Interpretation

Scores can range from 0 to 100, with a high score indicative of sexual dissatisfaction. A score of 30 or above is indicative of dissatisfaction in one's sexual relationship.

Index of Sexual Satisfaction – Partner 2
Adapted from Crooks and Baur (2011).

This questionnaire is designed to measure the degree of satisfaction you have in the sexual relationship with your partner. It is not a test, so there are no right or wrong answers. Answer each item as carefully and accurately as you can by placing a number beside each one according to the following scale:

1. Rarely or none of the time
2. A little of the time
3. Some of the time
4. A good part of the time
5. Most or all of the time

1. I feel that my partner enjoys our sex life. _____
2. My sex life is very exciting. _____
3. Sex is fun for my partner and me. _____
4. I feel that my partner sees little in me except for the sex I can give. _____
5. I feel that sex is dirty and disgusting. _____
6. My sex life is monotonous. _____
7. When we have sex, it is too rushed and hurriedly completed. _____
8. I feel that my sex life is lacking in quality. _____
9. My partner is sexually very exciting. _____
10. I enjoy the sex techniques that my partner likes or uses. _____
11. I feel that my partner wants too much sex from me. _____
12. I think sex is wonderful. _____
13. My partner dwells on sex too much. _____
14. I try to avoid sexual contact with my partner. _____
15. My partner is too rough or brutal when we have sex. _____
16. My partner is a wonderful sex mate. _____
17. I feel that sex is a normal function of our relationship. _____
18. My partner does not want sex when I do. _____
19. I feel that our sex life really adds a lot to our relationship. _____
20. My partner seems to avoid sexual contact with me. _____

21. It is easy for me to get sexually excited by my partner. _____
22. I feel that my partner is sexually pleased with me. _____
23. My partner is very sensitive to my sexual needs and desires. _____
24. My partner does not satisfy me sexually. _____
25. I feel that my sex life is boring. _____

Scoring

Items 1, 2, 3, 9, 10, 12, 16, 17, 19, 21, 22, and 23 must be reverse-scored. (For example, if you answered 5 on one of these items, you would change that score to 1.) After these positively worded items have been reverse-scored, if there are no omitted items, the score is computed by summing the individual item scores and subtracting 25. This assessment has been shown to be valid and reliable.

Interpretation

Scores can range from 0 to 100, with a high score indicative of sexual dissatisfaction. A score of 30 or above is indicative of dissatisfaction in one's sexual relationship.

Know Your Partner – Partner 1

Adapted from Crooks and Baur (2011).

Test the strength of your relationship in this quiz prepared by John Gottman.

True or False

1. I can name my partner's best friends.
2. I can tell you what stresses my partner is currently facing.
3. I know the names of some of the people who have been irritating my partner lately.
4. I can tell you some of my partner's life dreams.
5. I can tell you about my partner's basic philosophy of life.
6. I can list the relatives my partner likes the least.
7. I feel that my partner knows me pretty well.
8. When we are apart, I often think fondly of my partner.
9. I often touch or kiss my partner affectionately.
10. My partner really respects me.
11. There is fire and passion in this relationship.
12. Romance is definitely still a part of our relationship.
13. My partner appreciates the things I do in this relationship.
14. My partner generally likes my personality.
15. Our sex life is mostly satisfying.
16. At the end of the day, my partner is glad to see me.
17. My partner is one of my best friends.
18. We just love talking to each other.
19. There is lots of give-and-take in our discussions (both partners have influence).
20. My partner listens respectfully, even when we disagree.
21. My partner is usually a great help as a problem solver.
22. We generally mesh well on basic values and goals in life.

Scoring

Give yourself **1** point for each true answer.

Above **12**: You have a lot of strength in your relationship. Congratulations.

Below **12**: Your relationship could stand some improvement and could probably benefit from some work on the basics, such as improving communication.

Know Your Partner – Partner 2
Adapted from Crooks and Baur (2011).

Test the strength of your relationship in this quiz prepared by John Gottman.

True or False

1. I can name my partner's best friends.
2. I can tell you what stresses my partner is currently facing.
3. I know the names of some of the people who have been irritating my partner lately.
4. I can tell you some of my partner's life dreams.
5. I can tell you about my partner's basic philosophy of life.
6. I can list the relatives my partner likes the least.
7. I feel that my partner knows me pretty well.
8. When we are apart, I often think fondly of my partner.
9. I often touch or kiss my partner affectionately.
10. My partner really respects me.
11. There is fire and passion in this relationship.
12. Romance is definitely still a part of our relationship.
13. My partner appreciates the things I do in this relationship.
14. My partner generally likes my personality.
15. Our sex life is mostly satisfying.
16. At the end of the day, my partner is glad to see me.
17. My partner is one of my best friends.
18. We just love talking to each other.
19. There is lots of give-and-take in our discussions (both partners have influence).
20. My partner listens respectfully, even when we disagree.
21. My partner is usually a great help as a problem solver.
22. We generally mesh well on basic values and goals in life.

Scoring

Give yourself **1** point for each true answer.

Above **12**: You have a lot of strength in your relationship. Congratulations.

Below **12**: Your relationship could stand some improvement and could probably benefit from some work on the basics, such as improving communication.

THE POWER OF POSITIVE THINKING

I want to share with you a joke that has been circulating on the Internet for some time. I find it very funny. The setting is at the IRS (Internal Revenue Service) office. IRS is a United States government agency that is responsible for the collection and enforcement of taxes.

The IRS decides to audit Grandpa, and summons him to the IRS office. The auditor was not surprised when Grandpa showed up with his attorney.

The auditor says, "Well, sir, you have an extravagant lifestyle and no full-time employment, which you explain by saying that you win money gambling. I am not sure the IRS finds that believable."

"I am a great gambler, and I can prove it," says Grandpa. "How about a demonstration?"

The auditor thinks for a moment and says, "Okay. Go ahead."

Grandpa says, "I'll bet you a thousand dollars that I can bite my own eye."

The auditor thinks a moment and says, "It's a bet."

Grandpa removes his glass eye and bites it. The auditor's jaw drops.

Grandpa says, "Now, I'll bet you two thousand dollars that I can bite my other eye."

Now the auditor can tell Grandpa isn't blind, so he takes the bet. Grandpa removes his dentures and bites his good eye.

The stunned auditor now realizes he has wagered and lost three grand, with Grandpa's attorney as a witness. He starts to get nervous.

"Want to go double or nothing?" Grandpa asks. "I'll bet you six thousand dollars that I can stand on one side of your desk, and pee into that wastebasket on the other side, and never get a drop anywhere in between."

The auditor, twice burned, is cautious now, but he looks carefully and decides there's no way this old guy could possibly manage that stunt, so he agrees again.

Grandpa stands beside the desk and unzips his pants, but although he strains mightily, he can't make the stream reach the wastebasket on the other side, so he ends up urinating all over the auditor's desk.

The auditor leaps with joy, realizing that he has just turned a major loss into a huge win. But Grandpa's own attorney moans and puts his head in his hands.

"Are you okay?" the auditor asks.

"Not really," says the attorney. "This morning, when Grandpa told me he had been summoned for an audit, he bet me twenty-five thousand dollars that he could come in here and pee all over your desk and that you would be happy about it!"

(AUTHOR UNKNOWN)

Have a nice day ☺

References

Acevedo, B. P., Aron, A., Fisher, H. E., & Brown, L. L. (2011). Neural correlates of long-term intense romantic love. *Social Cognitive and Affective Neuroscience, 7* (2), 145-159. doi:10.1093/scan/nsq092

Ainsworth, M., & Bowlby, J. (1965). *Child Care and the Growth of Love.* London: Penguin Books.

Akmal, M., Qadri, J. Q., Al-Waili, N. S., Thangal, S., Haq, A., & Saloom, K. Y. (2006). Improvement in Human Semen Quality After Oral Supplementation of Vitamin C. Journal of Medicinal Food, 9(3), 440–442. doi:10.1089/jmf.2006.9.440

Albom, M. (1997). *Tuesdays with Morrie: An old man, a young man, and life's greatest lesson.* New York: Doubleday.

Al-Krenawi, A., & Slonim-Nevo, V. (2008). The psychosocial profile of Bedouin Arab women in polygamous and monogamous marriages. *Families in Society, 89*, 139-149. doi:10.1606/1044-3894.3718

American Cancer Society (2016). *Survival rates for prostate cancer.* Retrieved from: http://www.cancer.org/cancer/prostatecancer/detailedguide/prostate-cancer-survival-rates

American Psychiatric Association. (2000). *Diagnostic and statistical manual of mental disorders* (4th ed., text revision). Washington, DC: Author.

American Psychiatric Association. (2013). *Diagnostic and statistical manual of mental disorders: DSM-5* (5th ed.). Arlington, VA: Author.

American Psychiatric Association. (2013). *Psychology and aging – addressing mental health needs of older adults.* Retrieved from http://www.apa.org/pi/aging/resources/guides/aging.pdf

Anderson, K. D., Borisoff, J. F., Johnson, R. D., Stiens, S. A., & Elliott, S. L. (2006). The impact of spinal cord injury on sexual function: Concerns of the general population. *Spinal Cord, 45*, (5):328-37. doi:10.1038/sj.sc.3101977

Apt, C., & Hurlbert, D. F. (1995). Sexual Narcissism: Addiction or Anachronism? *The Family Journal, 3*(2), 103–107. doi:10.1177/1066480795032003

Arntz, A., & Genderen, H. (2009). *Schema therapy for borderline personality disorder.* Chichester, West Sussex, England: Wiley-Blackwell.

Bateman, A.W., & Fonagy, P. (2004). Psychotherapy for Borderline Personality Disorder: Mentalization based treatment. Oxford: Oxford University Press.

Baumeister, R., Catanese, K., & Wallace, H. (2002). Conquest by force: A narcissistic reactance theory of rape and sexual coercion. *Review of General Psychology, 6*, 92-135. doi:10.1037/1089-2680.6.1.92

Beckman, N., Waern, M., Gustafson, D., & Skoog, I. (2008). Secular trends in self reported sexual activity and satisfaction in Swedish 70 year olds: Cross sectional survey of four populations, 1971-2001. *British Medical Journal, 337*, 3, a279-a279. doi:10.1136/bmj.a279

Behary, W. T. & Dieckmann, E. (2011). Schema therapy for narcissism: The art of empathic confrontation, limit-setting, and leverage. In W. K. Campbell & J. Miller (Eds.), *The handbook of narcissism and narcissistic personality disorder*, pp.445-457. New York: John Wiley & Sons. doi:10.1002/9781118093108.ch40

Behary, W. T., & Dieckmann, E. (2013). *Schema therapy for pathological narcissism: The art of adaptive reparenting. Understanding and treating pathological narcissism.*

Washington, DC, US, American Psychological Association, Washington, DC: 285-300. doi:10.1037/14041-017

Bering, J. (2013). *Perv: The sexual deviant in all of us*. Scientific American / Farrar, Straus and Giroux. New York, NY.

Berman, J., & Berman, L. (2001). *For women only: A revolutionary guide to overcoming sexual dysfunction & reclaiming your sex life*. New York: Henry Holt.

Bhasin, S., Cunningham, G. R., Hayes, F. J., Matsumoto, A. M., Snyder, P. J., Swerdloff, R. S., & Montori, V. M. (2010). Testosterone therapy in men with androgen deficiency syndromes: An Endocrine Society clinical practice guideline. The Journal of Clinical Endocrinology & Metabolism, 95 (6), 2536–2559. doi:10.1210/jc.2009-2354

Binks, C., Fenton, M., McCarthy, L., Lee, T., Adams, C. E., & Duggan, C. (2006). Psychological therapies for people with borderline personality disorder. *Cochrane Database of Systematic Reviews, 1,* CD005652.

Birnbaum, G. E. (2015). On the convergence of sexual urges and emotional bonds: The interplay of the sexual and attachment system during relationship development. In J. A. Simpson & W. S. Rholes (Eds.), *Attachment theory and research: New directions and emerging themes* (pp. 170–194). New York, NY: The Guilford Press.

Borst, S. E., & Mulligan, T. (2007). Testosterone replacement therapy for older men. *Clinical Interventions in Aging, 2* (4), 561-566.

Bos, P. A., Hofman, D., Hermans, E. J., Montoya, E. R., Baron-Cohen, S., & van Honk, J. (2016). Testosterone reduces functional connectivity during the "Reading the Mind in the Eyes" Test. Psychoneuroendocrinology, 68, 194–201. doi:10.1016/j.psyneuen.2016.03.006

Bouchard, S., Godbout, N., & Sabourin, S. (2009). Sexual attitudes and activities in women with Borderline Personality Disorder involved in romantic relationships. *Journal of Sex & Marital Therapy, 35* (2), 106–121. doi:10.1080/00926230802712301

Bouchard, S., Sabourin, S., Lussier, Y., & Villeneuve, E. (2009). Relationship quality and stability in couples when one partner suffers from Borderline Personality Disorder. *Journal of Marital and Family Therapy, 35* (4), 446–455. doi:10.1111/j.1752-0606.2009.00151.x

Brown, T. M. & Fee, E. (2003). Alfred C. Kinsey: A pioneer of sex research. *American Journal of Public Health, 93* (6), 896-897. doi:10.2105/ajph.93.6.896

Bullough, V. L. (1998). Alfred Kinsey and the Kinsey report: Historical overview and lasting contributions. *Journal of Sex Research, 35* (2), 127–131. doi:10.1080/00224499809551925

Burkman, L. J., Bodziak, M. L., Schuel, H., Palaszewski, D., & Gurunatha, R. (2003). Marijuana (MJ) impacts sperm function both in vivo and in vitro: Semen analyses from men smoking marijuana. *Fertility and Sterility, 80,* 231. doi:10.1016/s0015-0282(03)01534-6

Bushman, B., Bonacci, A., Dijk, M., & Baumeister, R. (2003). Narcissism, sexual refusal, and aggression: Testing a narcissistic reactance model of sexual aggression. Journal of Personality and Social Psychology, 84, 1027-1040. doi:10.1037/0022-3514.84.5.1027

Camchong, J., Lim, K. O., & Kumra, S. (2016). Adverse effects of cannabis on adolescent brain development: A longitudinal study. *Cerebral Cortex, bhw015*. doi:10.1093/cercor/bhw015

Carey, I. M., Shah, S. M., DeWilde, S., Harris, T., Victor, C. R., & Cook, D. G. (2014). Increased Risk of Acute Cardiovascular Events After Partner Bereavement. *JAMA Intern Med, 174* (4), 598. doi:10.1001/jamainternmed.2013.14558

Caronia, L. M., Dwyer, A. A., Hayden, D., Amati, F., Pitteloud, N., & Hayes, F. J. (2013). Abrupt decrease in serum testosterone levels after an oral glucose load in men: implications for screening for hypogonadism. *Clinical Endocrinology, 78*(2), 291–296. doi:10.1111/j.1365-2265.2012.04486.x

Chen, W. Y., Manson, J. E., Hankinson, S. E., Rosner, B., Holmes, M. D., Willett, W. C., & Colditz, G. A. (2006). Unopposed Estrogen Therapy and the Risk of Invasive Breast Cancer. *Archives of Internal Medicine, 166* (9), 1027. doi:10.1001/archinte.166.9.1027

Chlebowski, R. T., Kuller, L. H., Prentice, R. L., Stefanick, M. L., Manson, J. E., Gass, M., … Anderson, G. (2009). Breast cancer after use of estrogen plus progestin in postmenopausal women. *New England Journal of Medicine, 360* (6), 573-587. doi:10.1056/nejmoa0807684

Clarkin, J. F, Yeomans, F., & Kernberg, O. (2006). Psychotherapy for Borderline Personality. Washington, DC: American Psychiatric Publishing.

Clarkin, J. F., Levy, K. N., Lenzenweger, M. F., & Kernberg, O. F. (2007). Evaluating three treatments for Borderline Personality Disorder: A multiwave study. *American Journal of Psychiatry, 164* (6), 922-928. doi:10.1176/ajp.2007.164.6.922

Cohler, B. J. & Galatzer-Levy, R. M. (2008). Freud, Anna, and the problem of female sexuality. *Psychoanalytic Inquiry, 28*, 3-26. doi:10.1080/07351690701787085

Coppen, A. (2005). Treatment of depression: time to consider folic acid and vitamin B12. Journal of Psychopharmacology, 19(1), 59–65. doi:10.1177/0269881105048899

Courtois, F. J., Mathieu, C., Charvier, K. F., Leduc, B., & Bélanger, M. (2001). Sexual rehabilitation for men with spinal cord injury: Preliminary report on a behavioral strategy. *Sexuality and Disability, 19*(2), 149-157. doi:10.1023/a:1010629907408

Cowell, D. D. (2009). Autoerotic asphyxiation: Secret pleasure--lethal outcome? *Pediatrics, 124*(5), 1319–1324. doi:10.1542/peds.2009-0730

Crooks, R., & Baur, K. (2011). Our sexuality. (11th ed). Belmont, CA. Wadsworth.

Cukrowicz, K. C., Poindexter, E. K., & Joiner, T. E. (2011). Cognitive Behavioral Approaches to the Treatment of Narcissistic Personality Disorder. The Handbook of Narcissism and Narcissistic Personality Disorder, 457-465. doi:10.1002/9781118093108.ch41

Dake, D. (2015). Autoerotic fatalities – asphyxia. Retrieved from http://coronertalk.com/23

Daling, J. R., Doody, D. R., Sun, X., Trabert, B. L., Weiss, N. S., Chen, C., … Schwartz, S. M. (2009). Association of marijuana use and the incidence of testicular germ cell tumors. *Cancer, 115*(6), 1215–1223. doi:10.1002/cncr.24159

Davidson, K. M., Norrie, J., Tyrer, P., Gumley, A., Tata, P., Murray, H., & Palmer, S. (2006). The effectiveness of Cognitive Behavior Therapy for Borderline Personality Disorder: Results from the Borderline Personality Disorder Study of Cognitive Therapy (BOSCOT) Trial. *Journal of Personality Disorders, 20* (5), 450-465. doi:10.1521/pedi.2006.20.5.450

Davidson, K. M., Tyrer, P., Norrie, J., Palmer, S. J., Tyrer, H. (2010). Cognitive therapy v. usual treatment for borderline personality disorder: prospective 6-year follow-up. *The British Journal of Psychiatry, 197*: 456-462. doi:10.1192/bjp.bp.109.074286

Davidson, K. M., Tyrer, P., Tata, P., Cooke, D., Gumley, A., Ford, I., . . . Crawford, M. J. (2009). Cognitive behavior therapy for violent men with antisocial personality disorder in the community: an exploratory randomized controlled trial. *Psychological Medicine, 39*:569-577. doi:10.1017/s0033291708004066

DiFrancesco, C., Roediger, E., & Stevens, B. (2014). *Schema Therapy for couples: A practitioner's guide to healing relationships.* New York: Wiley.

Ditzen, B., Schaer, M., Gabriel, B., Bodenmann, G., Ehlert, U., & Heinrichs, M. (2009). Intranasal Oxytocin Increases Positive Communication and Reduces Cortisol Levels During Couple Conflict. *Biological Psychiatry, 65* (9), 728-731. doi:10.1016/j.biopsych.2008.10.011

Ellis, H. (1925). *Studies in the psychology of sex.* Philadelphia: F. A. Davis.

Finger, W. W., Lund, M., & Slagle, M. A. (1997). Medications that may contribute to sexual disorders. A guide to assessment and treatment in family practice. *The Journal of family practice, 44* (1), 33-43.

Fischbach, F. T., & Dunning, M. B. III, eds. (2009). *Manual of Laboratory and Diagnostic Tests,* 8th ed. Philadelphia: Lippincott Williams and Wilkins.

Flannery, D., Ellingson, L., Votaw, K., & Schaefer, E. (2003). Anal intercourse and sexual risk factors among college women 1993-2000. *American Journal of Health Behavior, 27,* (3), 228-234. doi:10.5993/ajhb.27.3.4

Francis, A. M., & Mialon, H. M. (2014). A diamond is forever and other fairy tales: The relationship between wedding expenses and marriage duration. *SSRN Journal, 9.* doi:10.2139/ssrn.2501480

Frederick, D., Lever, J., Gillespie, B. J., & Garcia, J. R. (2016). What Keeps Passion Alive? Sexual Satisfaction Is Associated With Sexual Communication, Mood Setting, Sexual Variety, Oral Sex, Orgasm, and Sex Frequency in a National U.S. Study. *The Journal of Sex Research, 1–16.* doi:10.1080/00224499.2015.1137854

Freud, S. (1905). *Three Essays on the Theory of Sexuality.* New York, NY: Basic Books Classics.

Freud, S. (1912). Über die allgemeinste Erniedrigung des Liebeslebens. [The most prevalent form of degradation in erotic life]. *Jahrbuch für psychoanalytische und psychopathologische Forschungen 4:* 40-50.

Freud, S. (1923). *Das Ich und das Es.* Internationaler Psychoanalytischer Verlag, Vienna, W. W. Norton & Company.

Freud, S. (1925), Some psychical consequences of the anatomical distinction between the sexes, in Strachey, J. (Eds), *The Standard Edition of the Complete Psychological Works of Sigmund Freud,* Vol. 19. London: The Hogarth Press, pp. 241-60.

Freud, S. (1933). *New introductory lectures on psychoanalysis*. New York: Norton. (Translated by W.J.H. Sprott)

Freud, S. (1949). *An outline of psychoanalysis*. New York: Norton. (Translated by J. Stratchley; originally published, 1940).

Gebhard, P. H. & Johnson, A. B. (1979). *The Kinsey data: Marginal tabulations of the 1938-1964 interview conducted by the Institute for Sex Research*. Bloomington, IN: Indiana University Press.

Giddens, A. (1991). *Modernity and self-identity*. Cambridge: Polity.

Giddens, A. (1992). *The Transformation of intimacy: Sexuality, love, and eroticism in modern societies*. Stanford, California: Stanford University Press.

Ginde, A. A., Liu, M. C., & Camargo, C. A. (2009). Demographic Differences and Trends of Vitamin D Insufficiency in the US Population, 1988-2004. *Archives of Internal Medicine, 169* (6), 626. doi:10.1001/archinternmed.2008.604

Golomb, B. A., & Evans, M. A. (2008). Statin Adverse Effects. American Journal of Cardiovascular Drugs, 8(6), 373–418. doi:10.2165/0129784-200808060-00004

Goodman, M. P. (2011). Female genital cosmetic and plastic surgery: A review. *The Journal of Sexual Medicine, 8*(6), 1813–1825. doi:10.1111/j.1743-6109.2011.02254.x

Gordon, C. M., & Carey, M. P. (1995). Penile tumescence monitoring during morning naps to assess male erectile functioning: An initial study of healthy men of varied ages. *Archives of Sexual Behavior, 24*(3), 291-307. doi:10.1007/bf01541601

Grant, B. F., Hasin, D. S., Stinson, F. S., Dawson, D. A., Chou, S. P., Ruan, W. J., & Pickering, R. P. (2004). Prevalence, correlates, and disability of Personality Disorders in the United States. *Journal of Clinical Psychiatry, 65*(7), 948–958. doi:10.4088/jcp.v65n0711

Green, R., & Weiner, M. (2003). Cheaters: 180 telltale signs mates are cheating and how to catch them. Far Hills, N.J.: New Horizon Press.

Grodstein, F., Manson, J. E., & Stampfer, M. J. (2006). Hormone therapy and coronary heart disease: The role of time since menopause and age at hormone initiation. *Journal of Women's Health, 15* (1), 35-44. doi:10.1089/jwh.2006.15.35

Haake, P., Exton, M. S., Haverkamp, J., Krämer, M., Leygraf, N., Hartmann, U., … Krueger, T. H. C. (2002). Absence of orgasm-induced prolactin secretion in a healthy multi-orgasmic male subject. *International Journal of Impotence Research, 14*(2), 133–135. doi:10.1038/sj.ijir.3900823

Hallett, G. (2008). *Hitler was a British agent*. London: Progressive Books.

Hartmann, U. (2009). Sigmund Freud and his impact on our understanding of male sexual dysfunction. *Journal of Sexual Medicine, 6* (8), 2332-2339. doi:10.1111/j.1743-6109.2009.01332.x

Hazan, C., & Shaver, P. (1987). Romantic love conceptualized as an attachment process. *Journal of Personality and Social Psychology, 52* (3), 511–524. doi:10.1037/0022-3514.52.3.511

He, J., Reynolds, K., Chen, J., Chen, C.-S., Wu, X., Duan, X., … Gu, D. (2007). Cigarette Smoking and Erectile Dysfunction among Chinese Men without Clinical Vascular Disease. *American Journal of Epidemiology, 166*(7), 803-809. doi:10.1093/aje/kwm154

HERS (2016). *Sexual Loss*. Retrieved from
    http://www.hersfoundation.com/docs/Sexual_Loss.html

Hopwood, C. J., Morey, L. C., Markowitz, J. C., Pinto, A., Skodol, A. E.,
    Gunderson, J. G., … Sanislow, C. A. (2009). The Construct Validity of
    Passive-Aggressive Personality Disorder. *Psychiatry, 72*(3), 256-267.
    http://doi.org/10.1521/psyc.2009.72.3.256

Howlader, N., Noone, A. M., Krapcho, M., Neyman, N., Aminou, R., Waldron, W.,
    … Cronin KA (eds). *SEER Cancer Statistics Review, 1975-2009 (Vintage 2009
    Populations)*. National Cancer Institute. Bethesda, MD. Retrieved from
    http://seer.cancer.gov/csr/1975_2009_pops09/
    based on November 2011 SEER data submission, posted to the SEER web
    site, April 2012.

Hulbert, C. A., Jennings, T. C., Jackson, H. J., & Chanen, A. M. (2011). Attachment
    style and schema as predictors of social functioning in youth with borderline
    features. *Personality and Mental Health, 5*, 209-221. doi:10.1002/pmh.169

Hunt, M. (2007). Borderline Personality Disorder across the life span. *Journal of
    Women & Aging, 19* (1-2), 173-191. doi:10.1300/j074v19n01_11

James, E. L. (2012). *Fifty shades of Grey*. New York: Vintage Books.

Jenkins, A. P. (2000). When self-pleasuring becomes self-destruction: Autoerotic
    asphyxiation paraphilia. *International Electronic Journal of Health Education,
    3(3)*:208-216.

Johnston, C., Dorahy, M. J., Courtney, D., Bayles, T., & O'Kane, M. (2009).
    Dysfunctional schema modes, childhood trauma and dissociation in
    borderline personality disorder. *Journal of Behavior Therapy and Experimental
    Psychiatry, 40*, 248-255. doi:10.1016/j.jbtep.2008.12.002

Jones, E. (1953). *The Life and Work of Sigmund Freud*. New York: Basic Books, Inc.

Jones, J. H. (1997). *Alfred C. Kinsey: A Public/Private Life*. New York:
    Norton.

Joyal, C. C., Cossette, A., & Lapierre, V. (2015). What Exactly Is an Unusual Sexual
    Fantasy? *The Journal of Sexual Medicine, 12*(2), 328–340. doi:10.1111/jsm.12734

Joyal, C. C., & Carpentier, J. (2016). The prevalence of paraphilic interests and
    behaviors in the general population: A provincial survey. *The Journal of Sex
    Research, 1* (11). doi:10.1080/00224499.2016.1139034

Kamp Dush, C. M., & Taylor, M. G. (2012). Trajectories of marital conflict across
    the life course: Predictors and interactions with marital happiness trajectories.
    Journal of Family Issues, 33 (3), 341-368. doi:10.1177/0192513X11409684

Kellogg, S. H., & Young, J. E. (2006). Schema therapy for borderline personality
    disorder. *Journal of Clinical Psychology, 62*, 445-458. doi:10.1002/jclp.20240

Kendler, K. S., Myers, J., & Reichborn-Kjennerud, T. (2010). Borderline personality
    disorder traits and their relationship with dimensions of normative
    personality: a web-based cohort and twin study. *Acta Psychiatrica Scandinavica,
    123* (5), 349-359. doi:10.1111/j.1600-0447.2010.01653.x

Khoo, J., Piantadosi, C., Duncan, R., Worthley, S. G., Jenkins, A., Noakes, M., …
    Wittert, G. A. (2011). Comparing effects of a low-energy diet and a
    high-protein low-fat diet on sexual and endothelial function, urinary tract
    symptoms, and inflammation in obese diabetic men. *The Journal of Sexual
    Medicine, 8*(10), 2868–2875. doi:10.1111/j.1743-6109.2011.02417.x

Kinsey, A., Pomeroy, W., & Martin, C. (1948). Sexual behavior in the human male. Philadelphia: Saunders.

Kinsey, A., Pomeroy, W., Martin, C., & Gebhard, P. (1953). Sexual behavior in the human female. Philadelphia: Saunders.

Kirkpatrick, L. A., & Davis, K. E. (1994). Attachment style, gender, and relationship stability: A longitudinal analysis. *Journal of Personality and Social Psychology, 66 (*3), 502–512. doi:10.1037/0022-3514.66.3.50217:16 2016-02-12

Klusmann, D. (2002). Sexual motivation and the duration of partnership. *Archives of Sexual Behavior, 31,* 275–287. doi:10.1023/a:1015205020769

Kremers, I. P., Giezen, A. E. van, Does, A. J. van der, Dyck, R. van, & Spinhoven, P. (2007). Memory of childhood trauma before and after long-term psychological treatment of borderline personality disorder. *Journal of Behavior Therapy and Experimental Psychiatry, 38,* 1-10. doi:10.1016/j.jbtep.2005.12.003

Kreuter, M., Siösteen, A., & Biering-Sørensen, F. (2008). Sexuality and sexual life in women with spinal cord injury: A controlled study. *Journal of Rehabilitation Medicine, 40* (1), 61-69. doi:10.2340/16501977-0128

Lachkar, J. (1992). *The Narcissistic/borderline couple: Psychoanalytic perspectives on marital treatment.* London: Taylor and Francis.

Lapi, F., Levi, M., Simonetti, M., Cancian, M., Parretti, D., Cricelli, I., … Cricelli, C. (2016). Risk of prostate cancer in low-dose aspirin users: A retrospective cohort study. International Journal of Cancer, 3. doi:10.1002/ijc.30061

Laumann, E. O., Paik, A., & Rosen, R. C. (1999). Sexual Dysfunction in the United States: Prevalence and predictors. *JAMA, 281*(6), 537. doi:10.1001/jama.281.6.537

Lenzenweger, M. F., Lane, M. C., Loranger, A. W., & Kessler, R. C. (2007). DSM-IV Personality Disorders in the National Comorbidity Survey Replication. *Biological Psychiatry, 62*(6), 553–564. doi:10.1016/j.biopsych.2006.09.019

Leproult, R., & Van Cauter, E. (2011). Effect of 1 Week of Sleep Restriction on Testosterone Levels in Young Healthy Men. *JAMA, 305*(21), 2173. doi:10.1001/jama.2011.710

Lever, J. (1994). Sexual revelations. *Advocate*, August 23, 17-24.

Lever, J., Frederick, D. A., & Peplau, L. A. (2006). Does size matter? Men's and women's views on penis size across the lifespan. *Psychology of Men & Masculinity, 7* (3), 129. doi:10.1037/1524-9220.7.3.129

Li, C.-Y., Kayes, O., Kell, P. D., Christopher, N., Minhas, S., & Ralph, D. J. (2006). Penile suspensory ligament division for penile augmentation: Indications and results. *European Urology, 49*(4), 729–733. doi:10.1016/j.eururo.2006.01.020

Lindau, S., Schumm, P., Laumann, E., Levinson, W., O'Muircheartaigh, C., & Waite, L., (2007). A study of sexuality and health among older adults in the United States. *New England Journal of Medicine, 357,* 762-774. doi:10.1056/nejmoa067423

Livesley, W. J. (2001). *Handbook of personality disorders: Theory, research, and treatment.* New York: Guilford Press.

Lobbestael, J., Arntz, A., & Sieswerda, S. (2005). Schema modes and childhood abuse in borderline and antisocial personality disorders. *Journal of Behavior Therapy and Experimental Psychiatry, 36,* 240-253. doi:10.1016/j.jbtep.2005.05.006

Lobbestael, J., & Arntz, A. (2010). Emotional, cognitive and physiological correlates of abuse-related stress in borderline and antisocial personality disorder. *Behavior Research and Therapy, 48*, 116-124. doi:10.1016/j.brat.2009.09.015

Långström, N., & Seto, M. C. (2006). Exhibitionistic and voyeuristic behavior in a Swedish national population survey. *Archives of Sexual Behavior, 35* (4), 427-435. doi:10.1007/s10508-006-9042-6

MacLean, P. D. (1962). New findings relevant to the evolution of psychosexual functions of the brain. *The Journal of Nervous and Mental Disease, 135*(4), 289-301. doi:10.1097/00005053-196210000-00003

Madorsky, J. G. B. & Dixon, T. P. (1983). Rehabilitation aspects of human sexuality. *The Western Journal of Medicine, 139*, 174-176.

Maier, T. (2009). *Masters of sex : The life and times of William Masters and Virginia Johnson, the couple who taught America how to love.* New York: Basic Books.

Manson, J. E. (2013). Menopausal hormone therapy and health outcomes during the intervention and extended poststopping phases of the women's health initiative randomized trials. *Journal of the American Medical Association, 310*, 13, 1353-1368. doi:10.1001/jama.2013.278040.

Martínez-García, M.-A., Campos-Rodríguez, F., Catalán-Serra, P., Soler-Cataluña, J.-J., Almeida-Gonzalez, C., De la Cruz Morón, I., ... Montserrat, J.-M. (2012). Cardiovascular mortality in obstructive sleep apnea in the elderly: Role of long-term continuous positive airway pressure treatment. *American Journal of Respiratory and Critical Care Medicine, 186*(9), 909–916. doi:10.1164/rccm.201203-0448oc

Masters, W. H., Johnson, V. E., & Kolodny, R. C. (1992). *Human sexuality.* New York: Harper Collins Publishers.

McCoy, M. G., Welling, L. L. M., & Shackelford, T. K. (2015). Development and Initial Psychometric Assessment of the Reasons for Pretending Orgasm Inventory. Evolutionary Psychology, 13(1). doi:10.1177/147470491501300108

McNulty, J. K., & Widman, L. (2014). Sexual Narcissism and Infidelity in Early Marriage. *Archives of Sexual Behavior, 43* (7), 1315–1325. doi:10.1007/s10508-014-0282-6

Meston, C. M., & Frohlich, P. F. (2000). The neurobiology of sexual function. *Archives of General Psychiatry, 57* (11), 1012-1030 doi:10.1001/archpsyc.57.11.1012

Meyer, C., Leung, N., Feary, R., & Mann, B. (2001). Core beliefs and bulimic symptomatology in non-eating-disordered women: The mediating role of borderline characteristics. *International Journal of Eating Disorders, 30*, 434-440. doi:10.1002/eat.1104

Moalem, S., & Reidenberg, J. S. (2009). Does female ejaculation serve an antimicrobial purpose? Medical Hypotheses, 73(6), 1069–1071. doi:10.1016/j.mehy.2009.07.024

Murphy, W. D., & Page, I. J. (2008). Psychopathology and Theory. *Sexual deviance: Theory, assessment, and treatment,* p. 61. The Guilford Press, N.Y.

Murray, S. H., & Milhausen, R. R. (2012). Sexual desire and relationship duration in young men and women. *Journal of Sex & Marital Therapy, 38* (1), 28-40.

doi:10.1080/0092623x.2011.569637

Nadort, M., Arntz, A., Smit, J. H., Giesen-Bloo, J., Eikelenboom, M., Spinhoven, P., . . . Dyck, R. van (2009). Implementation of outpatient schema therapy for borderline personality disorder with versus without crisis support by the therapist outside office hours: A randomized trial. *Behavior Research and Therapy, 47*, 961-973. doi:10.1016/j.brat.2009.07.013

National Cancer Institute (U.S.) (2016). SEER Stat Fact Sheets: Ovary Cancer. Retrieved from http://seer.cancer.gov/statfacts/html/ovary.html

National Cancer Institute (U.S.) (2016b). SEER Stat Fact Sheets: Prostate Cancer. Retrieved from http://seer.cancer.gov/statfacts/html/prost.html

National Institute of Clinical Excellence (2009). *CG78 Borderline Personality Disorder (BPD): NICE Guideline.* Retrieved from http://publications.nice.org.uk/borderline-personality-disorder-cg78

National Institute of Mental Health. (2015). *Borderline Personality Disorder.* Retrieved from http://www.nimh.nih.gov/health/topics/borderline-personality-disorder/index.shtml

Neuman, G. (2008). *The truth about cheating. Why men stray and what you can do to prevent it.* John Wiley & Sons, Inc., Hoboken, New Jersey.

Nieto, F. J., Peppard, P. E., Young, T., Finn, L., Hla, K. M., & Farré, R. (2012). Sleep-disordered breathing and cancer mortality. *American Journal of Respiratory and Critical Care Medicine, 186*(2), 190–194. doi:10.1164/rccm.201201-0130oc

O'Connell, H. E., Sanjeevan, K. V., Hutson, J. M. (2005). Anatomy of the clitoris. The Journal of Urology, 174(4), 1189–1195. doi:10.1097/01.ju.0000173639.38898.cd

Office on Women's Health, U.S. Department of Health and Human Services (2013). *Hysterectomy fact sheet.* Retrieved from http://womenshealth.gov/publications/our-publications/fact-sheet/hysterectomy.cfm#d

Ohl, L. E. (2007). Essentials of female sexual dysfunction from a sex therapy perspective. *Urologic Nuring, 27*, 57-63.

Ondaatje, M. (1993). The English Patient. New York: Vintage Books.

Oumaya, M., Friedman, S., Pham, A., Abou Abdallah, T., Guelfi, J.-D., & Rouillon, F. (2008). Personnalité borderline, automutilations et suicide : revue de la littérature. [Borderline personality disorder, self-mutilation and suicide: literature review]. *L'Encéphale, 34* (5), 452–458. doi:10.1016/j.encep.2007.10.007

Oxman, T. (2015). *Personality Disorders.* The American Psychiatric Publishing Textbook of Geriatric Psychiatry. doi:10.1176/appi.books.9781615370054.ds18

Pastor, Z. (2013), Female ejaculation orgasm vs. coital incontinence: A systematic review. *Journal of Sexual Medicine, 10*: 1682–1691. doi: 10.1111/jsm.12166

Perel, E. (2003). *Erotic intelligence: Reconciling sensuality and domesticity.* Networker May/June.

Perel, E. (2006). *Mating in captivity: Reconciling the Erotic and the Domestic.* New York: HarperCollins.

Perel, E. (2013). *Esther's Blog.* Retrieved from http://www.estherperel.com

Piaget, J., & Inhelder, B. (1969). *The psychology of the child.* New York, Basic Books.

Pines, A., Sturdee, D., & Birkhauser, M. (2006). *A response to a recent publication from the Women's Health Initiative: The WHI data revisited.* Press statement issued on behalf of the International Menopause Society, April 11.

Pines, A., Sturdee, D., & Birkhauser, M. (2007). *Hormone therapy and cardiovascular disease in the early postmenopause: The WHI data revisited.* Press statement issued on behalf of the International Menopause Society, April 3.

Prause, N., Park, J., Leung, S., Miller, G. (2015). Women's preferences for penis size: A new research method using selection among 3D models. *PLoS ONE 10*(9): e0133079. doi:10.1371/journal.pone.0133079

Putnam, F. (2003). Ten-year research update review: Child sexual abuse. *Journal of the American Academy of Child and Adolescent Psychiatry, 42*, 269-278. doi:10.1097/00004583-200303000-00006

Ramos, A. S., & Samsó, J. V. (2004). Specific aspects of erectile dysfunction in spinal cord injury. *International Journal of Impotence Research, 16*, Suppl. 2:42-45. doi:10.1038/sj.ijir.3901242

Rapaille, C., & Roemer, A. (2015). *Move UP: Why some cultures advance while others don't.* Penguin UK.

Reitz, A., Tobe, V., Knapp, P. A., & Schurch, B. (2004). Impact of spinal cord injury on sexual health and quality of life. *International Journal of Impotence Research, 16* (2), 167–174. doi:10.1038/sj.ijir.3901193

Richters, J., de Visser, R., Rissel, C., & Smith, A. (2006). Sexual practices at last heterosexual encounter and occurrence of orgasm in a national survey. *Journal of Sex Research, 43* (3), 217-226. doi:10.1080/00224490609552320

Rider, J., Wilson, K., Kelly, R., Ebot, E., Giovannucci, E., & Mucci, L., (2015). Ejaculation frequency and risk of prostate cancer: updated results from the Health Professionals Follow-up Study. American Urological Association Annual Meeting, New Orleans, LA.

Robinson, P. (1976). *The Modernization of Sex.* New York, NY: Harper & Row, Publishers.

Roghmann, F., Becker, A., Sammon, J. D., Ouerghi, M., Sun, M., Sukumar, S., … Trinh, Q.-D. (2013). Incidence of priapism in emergency departments in the United States. *The Journal of Urology, 190*(4), 1275–1280. doi:10.1016/j.juro.2013.03.118

Ronningstam, E. (2013). An update on narcissistic personality disorder. *Current Opinion in Psychiatry, 26* (1), 102-106. doi:10.1097/yco.0b013e328359979c

Rosen, R. C., Goldstein, L., Scoles, V., & Lazarus, C. (1986). Psychophysiologic correlates of nocturnal penile tumescence in normal males. *Psychosomatic Medicine, 48*(6), 423-429. doi:10.1097/00006842-198607000-00004

Rosenberger, J. G., Reece, M., Schick, V., Herbenick, D., Novak, D. S., Van Der Pol, B., & Fortenberry, J. D. (2011). Sexual behaviors and situational characteristics of most recent male-partnered sexual event among gay and bisexually identified men in the United States. *The Journal of Sexual Medicine, 8*(11), 3040–3050. doi:10.1111/j.1743-6109.2011.02438.x

Rosman, J. P., & Resnick, P. J. (1989). Sexual attraction to corpses: A psychiatric review of necrophilia. *Bulletin of the American Academy of Psychiatry and the Law 17* (2): 153-163. PMID 2667656.

Ruppen-Greeff, N. K., Weber, D. M., Gobet, R., & Landolt, M. A. (2015). What is a good looking penis? How women rate the penile appearance of men with surgically corrected hypospadias. *The Journal of Sexual Medicine, 12*(8), 1737–1745. doi:10.1111/jsm.12942

Ryan, K. M., Weikel, K., & Sprechini, G. (2008). Gender Differences in Narcissism and Courtship Violence in Dating Couples. *Sex Roles, 58* (11-12), pp. 802–813. doi:10.1007/s11199-008-9403-9

Sae-Chul, K. (2006). Regaining of morning erection and sexual confidence in patients with erectile dysfunction. *Asian Journal of Andrology, 8*(6), 703-708. doi:10.1111/j.1745-7262.2006.00216.x

Salter, A. (2003). *Predators: pedophiles, rapists & other sex offenders: Who they are, how they operate, and how we can protect ourselves and our children.* New York: Basic Books.

Sansone, R. A., Barnes, J., Muennich, E., & Wiederman, M. W. (2008). Borderline personality symptomatology and sexual impulsivity. *The International Journal of Psychiatry in Medicine, 38* (1), 53–60. doi:10.2190/pm.38.1.e

Sauvageau, A., & Racette, S. (2006). Autoerotic deaths in the literature from 1954 to 2004: A review. *Journal of Forensic Sciences, 51* (1), 140–146. doi:10.1111/j.1556-4029.2005.00032.x

Scheele, D., Wille, A., Kendrick, K. M., Stoffel-Wagner, B., Becker, B., Gunturkun, O., ... Hurlemann, R. (2013). Oxytocin enhances brain reward system responses in men viewing the face of their female partner. *Proceedings of the National Academy of Sciences, 110* (50), 20308–20313. doi:10.1073/pnas.1314190110

Schouten, B. W. V., Bohnen, A. M., Groeneveld, F. P. M. J., Dohle, G. R., Thomas, S., & Ruud Bosch, J. L. H. (2010). Erectile dysfunction in the community: Trends over time in incidence, prevalence, GP consultation and medication use - the Krimpen study: Trends in ED. *The Journal of Sexual Medicine, 7*(7), 2547-2553. doi:10.1111/j.1743-6109.2010.01849.x

Schredl, M., Ciric, P., Götz, S., & Wittmann, L. (2004). Typical dreams: Stability and gender differences. *The Journal of Psychology, 138*(6), 485–494. doi:10.3200/jrlp.138.6.485-494

Schultz, D. P. & Schultz, S. E. (2009). *Theories of personality.* Belmont, CA: Wadsworth.

Sengoopta, C. (2003). "Dr Steinach coming to make old young!": sex glands, vasectomy and the quest for rejuvenation in the roaring twenties. Endeavour, 27(3), 122–126. doi:10.1016/s0160-9327(03)00102-9

Shamloul, R., & Bella, A. J. (2011). Impact of cannabis use on male sexual health. *The Journal of Sexual Medicine, 8*(4), 971–975. doi:10.1111/j.1743-6109.2010.02198.x

Sipski, M. L., Alexander, C. J., & Rosen R. (2001). Sexual arousal and orgasm in women: Effects of spinal cord injury. *Annals of Neurology, 49*, (1):35-44. doi: 10.1002/1531-8249(200101)49:1<35::AID-ANA8>3.0.CO;2-J

Smith, M. J., Cobia, D. J., Wang, L., Alpert, K. I., Cronenwett, W. J., Goldman, M. B., ... Csernansky, J. G. (2013). Cannabis-related working memory deficits and associated subcortical morphological differences in healthy individuals and schizophrenia subjects. *Schizophrenia Bulletin, 40*(2), 287–299. doi:10.1093/schbul/sbt176

Speroff, L., & Fritz, M. (2005). Clinical Gynecologic Endocrinology and Infertility (7th ed.). Philadelphia: Lippincott Williams and Wilkins.

Spinhoven, P., Giesen-Bloo, J., Dyck, R. van, & Arntz, A. (2008). Can assessors and therapists predict the outcome of long-term psychotherapy in borderline personality disorder? *Journal of Clinical Psychology, 64*, 667-686. doi:10.1002/jclp.20466

Sternberg, R. J. (1986). A triangular theory of love. *Psychological Review, 93* (2), 119–135. doi:10.1037/0033-295x.93.2.119

Sternberg, R. J. (1988). *The triangle of love: Intimacy, passion, commitment.* HarperCollins, Canada.

Stoffers, J., Völlm, B. A., Rücker, G., Timmer, A., Huband, N., & Lieb, K. (2012). Psychological therapies for people with borderline personality disorder (Review). *Cochrane Database of Systematic Reviews (8).* New York: John Wiley & Sons. doi:10.1002/14651858.CD005652.pub2

Taylor, B. & Davis, S. (2007). The extended PLISSIT model for addressing the sexual wellbeing of individuals with an acquired disability or chronic illness. *Sexual Disability, 25,* 135-139. doi:10.1007/s11195-007-9044-x

Torgersen, S., Myers, J., Reichborn-Kjennerud, T., Røysamb, E., Kubarych, T. S., & Kendler, K. S. (2012). The heritability of cluster B personality disorders assessed both by personal interview and questionnaire. *Journal of Personality Disorders, 26* (6), 848-866. doi:10.1521/pedi.2012.26.6.848

Travison, T. G., Araujo, A. B., O'Donnell, A. B., Kupelian, V., & McKinlay, J. B. (2007). A population-level decline in serum testosterone levels in American men. *The Journal of Clinical Endocrinology & Metabolism, 92* (1), 196-202. doi:10.1210/jc.2006-1375

Trompeter, S. E., Bettencourt, R., & Barrett-Connor, E. (2012). Sexual Activity and Satisfaction in Healthy Community-dwelling Older Women. *The American Journal of Medicine, 125* (1), 37-43.e1. doi:10.1016/j.amjmed.2011.07.036

Veale, D., Miles, S., Bramley, S., Muir, G., & Hodsoll, J. (2015). Am I normal? A systematic review and construction of nomograms for flaccid and erect penis length and circumference in up to 15 521 men. *BJU International, 115*(6), 978–986. doi:10.1111/bju.13010

Vliet, E. (2001). *Screaming to be heard: Hormonal connections women suspect and doctors still ignore* (Rev. and exp. ed.). New York: M. Evans and Co.

Wallace, M. A. (2008). Assessment of sexual health in older adults. *American Journal of Nursing, 108*, (7), 52-60. doi:10.1097/01.naj.0000325647.63678.b9

Walum, H., Westberg, L., Henningsson, S., Neiderhiser, J. M., Reiss, D., Igl, W., ... Lichtenstein, P. (2008). Genetic variation in the vasopressin receptor 1a gene (AVPR1A) associates with pair-bonding behavior in humans. *Proceedings of the National Academy of Sciences, 105* (37), 14153–14156. doi:10.1073/pnas.0803081105

Weschler, Toni (2002). *Taking Charge of Your Fertility.* (Revised ed.). New York: HarperCollins.

Wilkinson J, Bass C, Diem S, Gravley A, Harvey L, Maciosek M, ...Vincent P. (2013). *Institute for Clinical Systems Improvement.* Preventive Services for Adults.

Wilson, G. (2015). *Your brain on porn: Internet pornography and the emerging science of addiction.* Richmond, VA: Commonwealth Publishing.

Winters, S. (1999). Current status of testosterone replacement therapy in men. *Archives of Family Medicine, 8,* 257–263. doi:10.1001/archfami.8.3.257

Women's Health Initiative (2002). Risks and benefits of estrogen plus progestin in healthy postmenopausal women: Principal results from the Women's Health Initiative randomized controlled trial. *Journal of the American Medical Association, 288,* 321-333. doi:10.1001/jama.288.3.321

World Health Organization. (1992). *The ICD-10 classification of mental and behavioural disorders: Clinical descriptions and diagnostic guidelines.* Geneva: World Health Organization.

World Health Organization (2016). What do we mean by "sex" and "gender"? Retrieved from http://apps.who.int/gender/whatisgender/en/

Worthman, C. (1999). Faster, farther, higher: Biology and the discourses on human sexuality. In D. Suggs & A. Miracle (Eds.), *Culture, Biology, and Sexuality.* Athens: University of Georgia Press.

Wu, J. M., Wechter, M. E., Geller, E. J., Nguyen, T. V., & Visco, A. G. (2007). *Hysterectomy rates in the United States, 2003. American Journal of Obstetrics and Gynecology, 110,* 5, 1091–1095.doi:10.1097/01.aog.0000285997.38553.4b

Yalom, I. (1980). *Existential psychotherapy.* New York: Basic Books.

Yasan, A., & Gürgen, F. (2009). Marital Satisfaction, Sexual Problems, and the Possible Difficulties on Sex Therapy in Traditional Islamic Culture. *Journal of Sex & Marital Therapy, 35*(1), 68–75. doi:10.1080/00926230802525687

Young, J. E., Klosko, J. S., & Weishaar, M. E. (2006). Schema therapy. A practitioner's guide. New York: The Guilford Press.

Zanarini, M. C., Parachini, E. A., Frankenburg, F. R., Holman, J. B., Hennen, J., Reich, D. B., & Silk, K. R. (2003). Sexual relationship difficulties among borderline patients and Axis II comparison subjects. *The Journal of Nervous and Mental Disease, 191* (7), 479-482. doi:10.1097/01.nmd.0000081628.93982.1d

Zukav, G. (2012). *Spiritual partnerships.* Retrieved from http://www.huffingtonpost.com/gary-zukav/spiritual-partnerships_b_1266742.html

Zukav, G. (2014). *The seat of the soul.* Simon & Schuster, New York, NY.

Index

ABOUT THE AUTHOR

Dr. Bea M. Jaffrey is an American-trained clinical psychologist and psychotherapist in Geneva, Switzerland. In her private practice, she counsels couples, families and individuals. She feels passionate about helping people creating the fulfilling relationships that they desire. Using a warm, interactive and practical approach, she has assisted hundreds of couples to form a closer connection, to revitalize their sexual life and to improve their communication skills. Dr. Jaffrey believes that everyone is capable of having a great sex life regardless of how long they have been married (or in a committed relationship). "We need to be proactive and educate ourselves to create happy families," she says.

Dr. Bea Jaffrey is also a wife and a mother of six children and six Chihuahuas. She is a member of the American Psychological Association (APA) and several Swiss associations.

Translations of

159 Mistakes Couples Make In The Bedroom

And How To Avoid Them

French

159 Erreurs Faites Par Les Couples

Dans La Chambre À Coucher

Et Comment Les Éviter

Spanish

159 Errores De Las Parejas En La Cama

Y Cómo Evitarlos

Italian

159 Errori Che Le Coppie Commettono A Letto

E Come Evitarli

German

159 Fehler Die Paare Im Schlafzimmer Machen

Und Wie Man Sie Vermeidet

Made in the USA
Columbia, SC
02 May 2019